The Portable Wedding Consultant

The Portable Wedding Consultant

Invaluable Advice from the Industry's Experts for Saving Your Time, Money, and Sanity

Leah Ingram

CB

CONTEMPORARY BOOKS

Library of Congress Cataloging-in-Publication Data

Ingram, Leah.
    The portable wedding consultant : invaluable advice from the
industry's experts for saving your time, money, and sanity / Leah Ingram.
      p.   cm.
    Includes index.
    ISBN 0-8092-3086-0
    1. Weddings—Planning.   2. Wedding etiquette.   I. Title.
HQ745.I65   1997
395.2′2—dc21
                                        97-18253
                                          CIP

Cover photograph © Chris Cassidy
Cover and interior design by Mary Lockwood

"Bridal Chorus/Wedding March" copyright © Hal Leonard Corporation. Used by
permission of Hal Leonard Corporation.

Published by Contemporary Books
An imprint of NTC/Contemporary Publishing Company
4255 West Touhy Avenue, Lincolnwood (Chicago), Illinois 60646-1975 U.S.A.
Printed in the United States of America
International Standard Book Number: 0-8092-3086-0

18   17   16   15   14   13   12   11   10   9   8   7   6   5   4   3   2

Contents

Acknowledgments

*A*fter putting my first book, *The Bridal Registry Book*, to bed, I doubted I would venture down the wedding-book aisle again. Sure, I expected that I would continue to write magazine articles on the topic, plus make appearances to promote *The Bridal Registry Book*. But I never imagined that a year later I would be writing a comprehensive book on weddings. And it's all thanks to my editor at the time, Alina Cowden.

You see, I had been out of the wedding market (personally) for nearly four years, but Alina was still steeped in it. She had just gotten married, and many of her friends are getting married as well. (Most of my friends are having babies, but that shows you the age gap between Alina and me.) Anyway, after Alina got through her wedding, she realized that there wasn't any book out there that compiled expert opinions on wedding planning—something, it seems, brides-to-be are desperate to have. So, Alina came to me with the idea for *The Portable Wedding Consultant*, and off we went on another wedding-book adventure.

My publishing this book would also not have been possible without the help of my agent Denise Marcil, of the Denise Marcil Literary Agency, who is always looking out for my best interests. In addition, I thank her assistant, Jeff Rutherford.

I also thank all my friends, both old and new, who let me pick their brains for any "wedding wisdom" they might have to share with future brides and grooms. The couples from the newsgroups alt.wedding and soc.couples.wedding were invaluable as well, and I thank them all for their help.

Mostly I would like to thank my husband, Bill, for being a babysitter when I needed him to be, as well as an editor and idea-bouncer-offer. My daughter, Jane, was my inspiration to get this book done fast (so I could take her trick-or-treating), as was her new sibling, who will be born a few months before this book hits bookstores. I guess one could say that I'm having two babies in 1997!

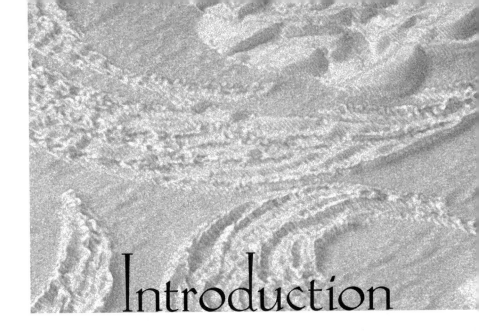

Introduction

I'll never forget what it was like trying to fall asleep the night my husband, Bill, proposed to me. After a romantic dinner at a cozy French restaurant, during which Bill popped the big question, we drove around our hometown, showing off the ring to our families. When we got home I called everyone in my Filofax to let them know I was getting married. Not surprisingly, it was pretty hard to just hop into pajamas, climb into bed, and drift off to sleep that night. Immediately, I started ticking off in my head all the things I needed to do. Bill and I had to settle on a date, find a site where we could get married, and track down an officiant to do it, since we're of different religious backgrounds. We also had to decide on a reception site. I'd always dreamed of having my wedding in my grandfather's backyard, but I didn't know if that was indeed possible. If it was, we'd have to a find a company from which we could rent tables, linens, china, and a tent. Besides interviewing caterers, going to register, and finding a dress, I also had to figure out a way to get my divorced parents to act civilly toward each other on the big day.

Needless to say, I didn't get much sleep that night and was truly wired the next day at work. How could I focus on doing my job, then a copywriter at a nonprofit association, when I had all these plans to make? Truthfully, I couldn't, and for the next few weeks, I spent more time on the phone planning my wedding than at my computer doing my work. After my boss called me into his office and explained that he was paying me to write copy—not my wedding vows—I realized that putting together my big day was turning into a full-time job itself.

With no time during the day to get items on my wedding to-do list done, at night I called all my married friends for advice. I spent hours on the phone hearing wedding horror stories, like the one about the photographer who spent more time on the buffet line than taking pictures, the caterer who charged for Tanqueray and Absolut but instead slipped guests low-end gin and vodka, and the bait-and-switch honeymoon advertisement that was too good to be true. But then Bill and I got our phone bill—this was before E-mail, mind you—and Bill suggested that there must be a way to get advice without going bankrupt.

Starting the next day, during my lunch hour I began haunting local bookstores and libraries. I did the same on weekends. I bought or checked out any title I thought would help me in my quest to plan the perfect wedding. But much to my chagrin, I discovered that there was no book out there that combined my friends' real-life advice with information from expert authorities who live and breathe weddings.

Had I been a professional party planner, I would have had a leg up on planning a wedding. I would have known which vendors to call, what questions to ask, and how to negotiate a contract. But the reality is I do not plan parties for a living and neither do you. Once you become engaged you may find yourself lost in the bridal business world. Yes, you could hire a bridal consultant to do all this research for you, and for some couples, that's an excellent choice. (See the chapter on hiring a bridal consultant.) But maybe you're like me and want to do things yourself. Until now there was no source of information available to help you plan your wedding like a professional. But now there's *The Portable Wedding Consultant*.

What This Book Will Do for You

The Portable Wedding Consultant is a compilation of expert advice that covers every aspect of planning a wedding. This book is chock-full of tips and tidbits of wedding-planning information and helpful hints from those in the know—more than sixty professionals who specialize in travel, catering, photography, flowers, and even dieting and dealing with divorced parents. I've tapped book authors whose work may interest you for additional reading, and I've included advice from real-life brides (called Wedding Wisdom) and fun factoids about weddings and marriage (called Nuptials News) that will make your reading both enjoyable and informative. You'll need a lot of hand-holding through your wedding planning. Not only will *The Portable Wedding Consultant* be able to give you the moral support you need, but it should also make planning your ultimate wedding that much easier.

In addition, I hope this book will make you a smarter consumer when it comes time to hire the various vendors who specialize in weddings. To that end, please read the following section carefully.

Becoming a Smart Shopper

Many couples have no idea how much it costs to throw a wedding these days. While the Association of Bridal Consultants quotes a nationwide average of about $8,000, in reality, weddings in some major metropolitan areas, like New York, Boston, and San Francisco, can cost upward of $20,000. Therefore, in order to spend your dollars wisely, you're going to have to take a crash course in becoming a smart shopper.

Smart shopping has nothing to do with waiting for sales or clipping coupons. Because there are businesses out there that could rip you off, you need to arm yourself with information about vendors before you hire them. "Weddings are a highly emotional time. There are so many things happening all at once that couples oftentimes don't know what they're getting themselves into," says Steve Bernas, director of operations for the Better Business Bureau of Chicago and Northern Illinois.

To avoid getting ripped off, use vendors that friends and family recommend personally or those that have a stellar record with the Better Business Bureau (BBB). Like all BBB offices around the country (there are 106 of them), Bernas's office compiles complaints about unfair business practices and helps mediate disputes between consumers and businesses. Each BBB office issues reliability reports, which can tell you a lot about how a business has treated its customers in the past. You can get one for free by calling your local BBB office. To find the office nearest you, look in the phone book or call the Council of Better Business Bureaus in Arlington, Virginia, at 800-664-4435 for a referral. Besides the BBB, you can also check with a local consumer protection agency or office of consumer affairs—usually part of your state's attorney general's office.

If a company you're interested in doesn't have a reliability report on record, that's probably a good sign. But just to be sure, ask the company owner for the names of three or four couples who've used the company recently for their wedding. Then be sure you call the couples to hear a firsthand account of how everything went. "You want to ask questions like, 'How long ago did you use them?' and 'Were you happy with the services they provided?'" suggests Holly Cherico, a spokesperson for the Council of Better Business Bureaus, an umbrella organization for the nation's Better Business Bureaus.

Don't be bashful about asking for these references. Good companies are more than happy to put you in contact with people who can do nothing but gush about their services. Those that are hesitant to provide references should be crossed off your list. There's probably a reason they don't want you talking to past customers, and it's very possible it's because they didn't serve these customers well.

Bernas suggests calling the BBB and previous clients well before you make an appointment to meet the vendor. That way you won't waste your precious time talking with someone you don't want to work with anyway.

Besides checking out the vendors' reputations, following are tips from the BBB on finding companies that can make your wedding-day dreams come true.

* Always get three or four estimates per specialty—that is, talk to three or four photographers, three or four caterers, and so on. This way you can compare prices and services rendered.

* Review samples of a person's work. For example, when hiring a photographer, make sure you're looking at the original work of the person who would photograph your wedding, not a compilation of the best work the studio has to offer.

* When you meet with a vendor, ask to see a copy of their contract and ask to take a copy home with you. Having a variety of contracts in your files will help you become acquainted with common terms of agreement for wedding vendors, plus help you weed out unfair stipulations.

* If you don't understand what certain contract terms mean, ask for an explanation. Likewise, if you're not comfortable with the way the contract reads, amend it (as long as your changes are reasonable), and make sure the vendor countersigns the changes.

* Put everything in the contract, down to the time the flowers will be delivered and the kind of clothing the band members will wear. And make sure there's a clause in there that talks about the ramifications of a vendor's not delivering as promised. (Bernas says that some companies will put in a contract that they'll refund 100 percent of their fee if they fail to do the job right.)

* In most cases, only hire a business that has been around a while. Unfortunately, many new ventures fail within the first

year of business, and if you happen to hire a start-up company, there is a risk that it could go under before your wedding day rolls around. In addition, with a business that has been around for only a month or two, there hasn't been enough time for disgruntled customers to lodge complaints.

* Pay for everything with a credit card. This is a great safety net for you, thanks to the Fair Credit Billing Act. This act says that within three months of the time of purchase, you can dispute the charges on your credit card. Not only will the credit card company intervene on your behalf in trying to resolve the matter, but also you won't have to pay the balance of the purchase or any interest accrued during this period of investigation.

* Confirm everything with your vendors one to two weeks before your wedding day so you don't end up with any surprises, such as discovering that your catering hall is under construction or the florist has gone out of business.

* Finally, if you're dissatisfied with the service you receive from any firm you hire, write a letter to the company owner and let him or her know. Also let the BBB know. This will help consumers down the line know what to expect from certain vendors and help them greatly in making better buying decisions of their own.

The Portable Wedding Consultant

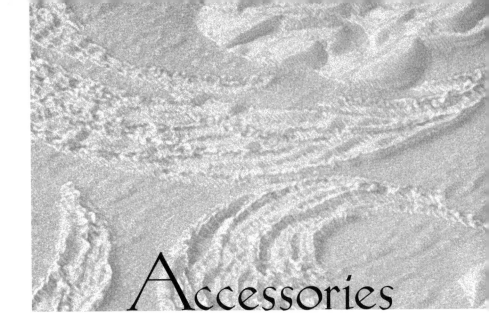

Accessories

The accessories you choose to wear on your wedding day can really make or break the look you want to create. For example, if you're wearing a lavishly decorated wedding gown with an extensive train, you'll probably want to keep your veil and jewelry simple so as not to distract from the dress — and yourself, of course. When I chose my wedding dress, an off-white linen number with pearlescent buttons and intricate detailing down the front, I knew I couldn't go overboard with my headpiece, jewelry, and shoes. So what were my accessories of choice? A simple yet elegant off-white hat, pearl earrings, lace gloves, and off-white T-strap pumps.

When you shop for accessories for you and your attendants, make sure that you will have a chance to see your selections as a finished package. Therefore, when you go to buy shoes or earrings, take the dress with you. Or make sure you have the option of returning items if, when you try everything on at home, they don't look quite right. It is very important that your entire ensemble looks good together.

Jan Larkey is an image consultant who helps women find clothing and accessories that flatter their figures. Her highly popular book is called Flatter Your Figure *(Fireside, 1991), and it includes more than four hundred figure and style illustrations to help women combat nineteen common figure problems. Larkey, who is based in Pittsburgh, recently shared her tips with me on finding the right wedding accessories.*

wedding wisdom

"I got my veil at JCPenney. It cost only $45, and it is what I always wanted."
Allison, married 11/1/96

"As a bride, this is your time to wear formalwear that under any other circumstances would look just too formal or, in some cases, ridiculous. I wore gloves on my wedding day, and it was a lot of fun."

Careen, married 11/26/93

Veils and Headpieces

One of the first things you must take into consideration when choosing your veil is the size and scale of the veil in relation to you and your dress. A veil should complement a bride, not overwhelm her. For example, if you are diminutive, you do not want a huge veil. To your guests you'll look as if you're all veil, and you'll just get lost in it. Likewise, if you're very tall and thin, you may look silly with a small sprig of tulle sticking out of your headpiece.

Considering how much time and thought you will put into selecting your dress, you don't want the veil to cover the dress up. Remember: your back will be to the audience for most of the ceremony. If the back of your dress is wonderful to look at, don't cover it up with a long veil.

Not only will your size and the decoration of your dress determine the veil you choose, but so will your face shape. If you have a narrow face, you may want to add width to the top of your face with a veil that puffs out around your head instead of hanging down around it. Likewise, if you have a round face, you'll want to find a more subdued veil that creates more of a vertical line around your face. It will help slim your face.

If you're unsure of what kind of veil would look good on you, you can always decide to wear a garland of natural flowers in your hair. Keep in mind that the scale of the flowers has to stay in proportion to your size and hairstyle. You don't want to look as if you have an unruly garden sprouting from your head. Nor do you want the delicate rosebuds you choose to get lost in your gigantic French twist.

Hats

I recently attended a wedding where the bride wore what looked like an English riding hat, which was secured on her head at an awkward angle. Even though the hat itself was gorgeous, I found it distracting. Whenever I looked at her, all I saw was hat. Also, because of the angle at which she wore the hat, I kept waiting for it to fall off her head.

You don't want your guests to be like me and focus on one particular element of your ensemble—especially if you choose to wear a hat or have your bridesmaids wear them. A hat should look natural, and it should be comfortable. I can't imagine how many pins were holding that hat on that bride's head.

One way to make sure a hat looks natural is to have it complement your features. A full, round face is never enhanced by a round-looking hat. Anytime you repeat a shape, you emphasize it. Similarly, if you have a long, narrow face, you'll want to avoid a narrow hat and go with one that has a fuller brim.

The same is true of your hat's proportion to your body: a hat should fit your figure as well as your face. If you have bigger hips, a wide-brimmed hat will help balance you out better than a small-brimmed hat or a pillbox. Likewise, just as a petite bride would get lost under a huge veil, she would do the same under a large hat. However, a larger woman can more easily wear a larger hat and have it look natural on her.

Jewelry

In my opinion, simple is always better. Between a gown that has some ornate characteristics to it and something fancy on your head, you'll want to keep your jewelry to a minimum. You definitely don't want to wear a watch. I mean, who cares what time it is? It's your wedding day.

If you wear a lot of rings on your hands, I suggest that for your wedding day you wear only your wedding set. The same goes for your attendants.

Your decision about wearing a necklace depends more on the neckline of your gown. If you're wearing a high-necked gown, it doesn't make any sense for you to hang a necklace over it. For a gown with a lower-cut neckline, stick with a strand of pearls eighteen to twenty inches long. Anything shorter could make your face look fat. What's perfect about a necklace of this length is it won't be so long that the strand of pearls hangs over the neckline of your dress. However, it's just the right length to create a V on your upper chest. This elongates the neck, thins the face, and creates a fabulous frame for the face.

Many brides think a pearl choker is appropriate to wear on their wedding day. If you've got a swanlike neck like actresses Gwynneth Paltrow and the late Audrey Hepburn, then you can probably pull this look off. However, for most women a choker creates a horizontal line across the neck and shortens and widens it. I'd avoid wearing one.

Keep in mind that the necklines of many gowns are beautifully cut and detailed. Therefore, wearing a necklace would just detract from the inherent beauty of the gown.

"I originally selected what I thought was a very 'practical' wedding outfit and planned on having a hat made, but my heart wasn't in it. So I tried on wedding gowns and veils, and my true Cinderella fantasy was revealed. I realized only after I bought the gown and veil that had I not decided to wear them at my wedding, I would have forgone some of the ceremony and magic that a bridal gown and veil can convey."

Nancy, married 11/16/96

Accessories

When it comes to earrings, my general guideline is that the earrings should not be larger than the tip of your thumb. Stick with an earring that is stable, not one that dangles and moves when you walk. This activity around your ears could be distracting to look at.

This rule of thumb, so to speak, applies to your attendants as well. Each woman's face is different, but simple, stable earrings complement a range of face shapes.

The color of the earring you choose should complement your gown or your attendants' dresses as well. Pearls and diamonds are always an excellent choice. Remember: you want the focus to be on the face, not the earrings you choose to wear.

Shoes

Shoes are perhaps one of the most important purchases you will make. You're going to be on your feet practically all day, so invest in a pair of shoes that will be comfortable for hours. A shaped, low or medium heel will provide enough of a lift to create an attractive line yet be low enough so that your feet don't get too tired.

In addition to the comfort factor of the shoe, you'll want to go with a shoe that offers some "toe cleavage," if you will. It looks dressier, and it will make your feet and legs look slimmer.

Usually, leather shoes aren't fancy enough to go with an elaborate wedding gown. So select a shoe that is made of satin or silk shantunglike fabric. However, if your dress is superornate, keep your shoe simple. Conversely, if you're wearing a simpler dress, you can go with a more elaborate shoe. Remind bridesmaids to keep the same advice in mind when selecting their shoes.

Hosiery

Hosiery comes into view, so to speak, if you're going to remove your garter at your reception. That's when all eyes will be on your legs. You'll want to stick with white or off-white hosiery.

A hose with a delicate lace pattern can look very pretty. However, if you've got heavier legs, find a lace pattern that creates a vertical image. It will slim your leg. If you have heavier legs you should also stay away from pantyhose with a sheen to them. Matte hose are more flattering.

No matter how hot it is on your wedding way, do not wear kneehighs. It may be comfortable in the short run, but imagine the horror on your husband and guests' faces if they were to catch a glimpse of your hosiery. In addition, it can look ghastly in wedding photographs.

Gloves

Not many brides and attendants today wear gloves. If you decide you'd like them to be a part of your wedding ensemble, keep in mind that the wrong glove can blow your whole look.

If your dress is short-sleeved, you have two options. You can wear long gloves, which look especially glamorous with a sleeve-less dress. Or, if it's a summer wedding, you can wear wrist-high gloves.

Crocheted gloves are fancier and dressier than gloves made of a solid, simple fabric. Your gloves must complement the fabric of your dress and must not compete with it. For example, if you're wearing a dressy, detailed gown, you'll want to stick with a simple glove.

Finally, not every arm looks good in a pair of gloves. A really heavy arm will not be enhanced by gloves. In fact, if your arms are not your best feature, you should probably stick with a long-sleeved gown. And then you wouldn't wear gloves at all, because gloves do not go with long sleeves; it's too much.

Handkerchiefs

In years past, a bridal handkerchief was passed down through generations and often was made from a family member's wedding gown. Actually, having a hankie at your disposal is a good idea. You can tuck it into the sleeve of your gown, assuming you're wearing long sleeves. Or you can place the hankie in your Bible, if you'll be carrying one during the service.

You can use a hankie to do the following:

* dab your eyes if you get emotional during the service
* wipe lipstick off your and your husband's cheeks if heavily lipsticked guests kiss you
* wipe your brow if you get sweaty dancing at the reception

Bridal Purses

The only bag that you could conceive of carrying on your wedding day is a gift sack. That would be appropriate at your reception only, and then only if you come from a family or an ethnic background

File under The Bride Wore Tennis Shoes. Inspired by the movie *Father of the Bride*, one California bride decided that it would be fun (and comfortable) if she and her attendants wore tennis shoes at her wedding. She purchased her white sneakers and four pairs of pink ones at Payless Shoes, removed the laces, sprayed the shoes with a light coat of spray adhesive, then lightly sprinkled glitter on the shoes. After they dried she replaced the shoelaces with white lace for her shoes and pink lace for her attendants. Finally, she stenciled red hearts on the heel of each shoe. Total cost? About $11 per pair, and there were no sore feet at the end of the evening.

Accessories

Nuptials News

According to Jan Larkey, if you've got an ornate hat, ornate shoes, and an ornate gown, you're too much. Remember KISS, Keep It Simple, Sweetheart.

in which that is acceptable. Otherwise you have no need for a purse. If you will need a makeup touchup, you can ask one of your bridesmaids to hold your lipstick, compact powder, and such. That's one of the ways attendants are there to help you.

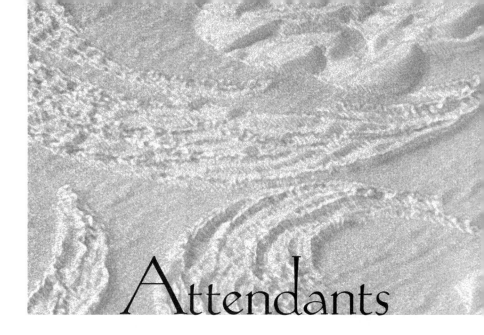

Attendants

When Bill proposed to me, I knew right off the bat that I wouldn't have a wedding with a lot of attendants. I'm an only child, and Bill has one brother. Therefore, it would make sense for us to have a small wedding party, with one attendant each.

While the decision for Bill to ask his brother to be his best man was an easy one, I had a harder time deciding which of my close girlfriends would be my maid of honor. I have a number of childhood friends who I still hold near and dear in my heart, but in the years surrounding my wedding, we'd fallen out of touch. Once-a-year Christmas cards and a phone call here and there sufficed to keep our relationships alive. With that in mind, I couldn't ask one of these women to be in my wedding. I mean, I couldn't even remember the last time I'd seen them face-to-face, let alone talked about such serious a subject as their being my maid of honor.

Once I'd ruled out my childhood friends, I started thinking about my current roster of friends, and the choice for my maid of honor became very easy. My best friend in my current life was a sweet gal named Laura, whom I had met at a company where we both worked in entry-level positions. We supported and cheered each other as we went for promotions and bigger responsibilities, and even though we'd both since moved on to better jobs at different companies, we still saw each other at least once a month and spoke on the phone even more often. She was thrilled to be my maid of honor, and I was equally happy with my decision.

When Bill and I told Laura that we had decided to elope, she still insisted on being my maid of honor. Laura took the day off from work and stood up with us, along with Bill's brother John, as we tied the knot in a five-minute service at the local courthouse. Afterward,

wedding wisdom

"I decided to pick my sister as my maid of honor since we had become close in the couple of years previous to my engagement."

Jacinda, married 7/1/95

7

"We each chose one attendant and involved other friends in other ways (as greeters, candlelighters, readers, and so forth). This allowed us to cut costs on flowers for attendants and attendant wear—and made the planning infinitely easier—while including all our friends in our wedding."

Nancy, married 11/16/96

she joined us for a lunchtime celebration at our favorite restaurant. Asking Laura to be my maid of honor was one of the best wedding-planning decisions I made.

Choosing Attendants

Rita Bigel-Casher, CSW, Ph.D., is the author of Bride's Guide to Emotional Survival *(Prima Publishing, 1996) and an individual, couples, and family therapist in New York City. I spoke with her recently about how brides- and grooms-to-be can choose attendants without hurting anyone's feelings. To contact Bigel-Casher, write her at 274 Madison Avenue, New York, NY 10016; call her at 212-532-0032; or visit her website at http://www.dbsinyc.com/bigel/bridesguide/.*

I think that choosing your attendants is one of the most difficult decisions you'll make when planning your wedding. When you think about it, selecting someone to be your maid of honor or best man is saying to that person, "You are one of the most meaningful people in my life, and it would be an honor for me to have you stand up for me when I get married."

Where you run into problems—and why some bridal parties are so huge—is when you or your fiancé has a hard time determining who the most meaningful people in your life are. You also run into a problem when you don't want to hurt anyone's feelings so you include everyone in the wedding party. In fact, I once heard of a bridal party with twenty-two bridesmaids in it. The bridal party was almost as big as the guest list. Now, that's a little bizarre.

You can solve your problem by not having a bridal party at all, but that's probably not a realistic solution for many brides and grooms. Instead, you've got to put a lot of thought and consideration into whom you choose for your attendants. Keep in mind that you should have one attendant for every fifty or so guests you invite.

One way to avoid many problems is to apply a specific criterion to how you choose an attendant. For example, you could say that you'll consider longevity of friendship only, or that you're going to stick with familial connections when choosing your attendants. That way, if you have to leave someone out of your bridal party, you can explain it by saying, for example, "I've chosen only family members to be in the bridal party."

Unfortunately, many women attach a great amount of significance to being chosen (or not chosen) to be in a friend's wedding.

There are times that the choice a bride makes can cause a shift in her friendship with a woman who is not chosen to be a bridesmaid, and sometimes it can sever a friendship altogether. That's why you have to consider very carefully how you're going to choose your attendants and whom you choose. Women take being asked or not being asked to be a bridesmaid very seriously. They take it as a compliment or an insult.

If you find yourself having to tell a friend that you are unable to include her in your wedding party, have a conversation with her—ideally face-to-face—about your decision. If you live a long distance from her, don't tell her over the telephone. Write a letter instead. That way you can take time to think about what you want to say. Of course, if time is of the essence and there's a chance she'll hear the "bad news" through the grapevine before your letter arrives, then by all means call her.

The best way to break the news to your friend is to present it as a problem. You can say, "I've been struggling with the issue of selecting bridesmaids. I consider you a very important person in my life, but circumstances dictate that I must limit the size of my bridal party." For example, if your fiancé is having only three attendants, explain that you don't want to create a lopsided bridal party by having more than three bridesmaids. Or if family ties affect whom you choose as attendants, say so.

You have to offer your friend a valid point for excluding her from the bridal party, and you should offer her an alternate way to be included in the wedding itself. Tell her it would be an honor for you to have her read a poem or do a religious reading during the ceremony. Offering an alternative like this is a good way to tell this person that she means something to you and that you want to maintain your friendship. However, being honest and forthright is no guarantee that she's going to like what you have to say. Of course, a good friend should understand what a difficult decision it was to approach her on such an honest level. If she doesn't and your friendship fails because of it, then maybe that friendship wasn't as worthwhile as you thought it was.

Another issue that comes up when selecting attendants is the pressure your family puts on you to include certain people in your wedding. For example, your future mother-in-law may insist that you have your future sister-in-law as a bridesmaid, or your mother may want you to have her grandchildren (your niece and nephew) be the flower girl and ring bearer.

As painful as it is true, you have to keep in mind that your wedding isn't just yours and that during the entire wedding-planning pro-

"I went the traditional route and chose friends as bridesmaids and asked my ten-year-old half sister to be a junior bridesmaid. My husband asked his siblings to be his groomsmen and his best friend from the Navy to be his best man. My twelve-year-old half brother was our junior groomsman. All in all, we had eight attendants."
    Julie, married 3/8/97

Attendants

9

cess, you'll have to compromise on certain things. You may be the director of your own wedding and have the last word on all decisions, but you must recognize that a wedding is a family affair. Any decision you and your fiancé make affects your parents, siblings, and extended family. You have to be a benevolent dictator and take into consideration other people's needs.

For every decision you make, you should ask yourself, "Is this really important to me or can I let it go? Is it possible to compromise?" For almost every decision you compromise on, you can stand fast on another. So, if it won't kill you to have your sister-in-law be your bridesmaid or your niece be your flower girl, then go ahead and agree to it. However, if you're certain that you want your bridesmaids to wear blue and your sister-in-law hates blue, you can feel comfortable putting your foot down on this issue. It's OK to make some compromises—just don't make so many that you feel as if your wedding is no longer yours.

Another situation that may make choosing attendants more difficult is if you or your fiancé have been married before and are bringing children into the union. The best way to integrate the two families into one new family is to have all the children be a part of the wedding party.

While you know including such children is in the best interest of your new family, the children may not. If they are rebelling against the idea of their mother or father's getting married, they may refuse to have anything to do with your wedding. Understand their feelings and accept their answers. But leave the invitation to be in the wedding party open so that if they change their minds, they will feel they have the option to participate after all.

Restrictions on Attendants

You may be limited in the number of attendants you choose not because of family alliances but because of restrictions your ceremony site puts on you. "That's why you should do your site selection before choosing your bridal party," says Joyce Scardina Becker, owner of Events of Distinction, a San Francisco company that specializes in corporate events and meetings, private parties, and weddings.

If you choose more than six attendants, you may find it difficult to have all of them standing up front with you at the ceremony—especially if you get married in a small synagogue or church. "Keep in mind that chancel furnishings are often built in and can't simply be moved to accommodate a large bridal party," says Jim Vuocolo, D. Min., the senior minister at Redlands United Church of Christ in Redlands, California. "I once had a wedding with twelve attendants, and the bride and groom were demanding that the pulpit be moved, the communion table be pushed back, and the advent wreath be removed so that the altar could accommodate all the attendants. I was incensed."

A great way to make sure your ceremony site can handle all your attendants is to reserve the front pew or a row of chairs for your bridesmaids and ushers. Then the attendants can sit down during the ceremony so things don't look too crowded. "I would caution against making your bridal party so huge that orchestrating everything gets cumbersome," adds Vuocolo. "You have to think about why you want so many people in your bridal party."

Including Others in Your Wedding

It isn't always possible to include every single friend and family member in your bridal party, but there are other ways to make good friends and loved ones feel special on your big day. You can always list special friends and relatives in your service program, but if you'd like to get them more involved, here are some suggestions for including people in your wedding. Ask a special friend to

* register guests in the guest book. Choose a person with an outgoing personality who you know won't be afraid to approach people as they arrive to sign the guest book.
* read a poem or religious reading during the ceremony.
* hand out flowers to guests as they arrive.
* act as your personal assistant on the day of the wedding.
* help call invited guests who forgot to respond to their invitations on time.
* go with you when you buy your wedding dress.
* sing a song or play a musical selection during the ceremony, if he or she is musically inclined, of course.
* be responsible for taking care of your dress after the wedding.
* hand out birdseed or rose petals for guests to throw as you and your husband exit the church or synagogue.
* work with the photographer to make sure he or she doesn't miss any important shots.

If you do assign a friend or relative one or more of these tasks, have a boutonniere or corsage made for that person to wear on your wed-

According to *Bride's Magazine*, on average, a bridesmaid will spend about $137 on her dress.

Attendants

wedding wisdom

"There are four girls in our family—ready-made bridal attendants. However, in order to avoid choosing one sister over another as the maid of honor, we all agreed that at our wedding we would select a close friend to be the maid of honor and then have the three sisters as bridesmaids."

Kimberly, married 8/25/90

ding day. That way all the guests will know he or she is someone special.

Source: Kathy Moore, bridal consultant and owner of Ambiance Party Services, a full-service wedding and special-event planning company in Garner, North Carolina.

What an Attendant Does

Barbara Hoffman, a certified etiquette expert in Louisville, Kentucky, and president of Manners, Incorporated, has come up with a delightful series of brochures titled "The Wedding Party," which highlight the jobs and responsibilities of each attendant in the wedding party. To order copies of the brochures, write Hoffman & Hoffman, P.O. Box 7411, Louisville, KY 40207 or call 502-458-2300 or fax 502-459-1504. Here are brochure excerpts, printed with permission, highlighting some of the responsibilities of the men in the bridal party.

A Guide for the Best Man

Some of the responsibilities of a best man include

* organizing the bachelor party
* consulting with ushers about a joint gift for the bridegroom, collecting the money, buying the gift, and presenting it to the bridegroom at the bachelor party or rehearsal dinner
* assisting the bride's parents, well in advance of the date, in arranging cars and limousines for the wedding and reception
* seeing that the bridegroom's suitcase is packed for the honeymoon and keeping getaway plans a secret
* carrying the bride's ring for the bridegroom in his own vest pocket and producing it at the proper time

A Guide for Ushers

During a church or synagogue wedding, an usher

* seats all wedding guests where they wish
* seats bride's friends on the left side (facing the altar) and bridegroom's friends on the right side
* politely asks unrecognized guests if they are friends of the bride or bridegroom and seats them accordingly
* if seating becomes one-sided, tries to even it up
* gives right arm to women and escorts them down the aisle

Attire

s Bill and I began planning our wedding, we knew we wanted to have a less-than-formal ceremony and reception. I planned on wearing an off-white linen dress that I'd picked up off the rack at Lord & Taylor, and Bill planned on wearing linen pants and a blue blazer. My only attendant, my good friend Laura, got a great dress at Laura Ashley, and Bill's brother John, his best man, planned on wearing an outfit similar to Bill's.

Of course, our attire was completely appropriate, since we planned a morning ceremony and an early-afternoon brunch to be held outdoors. However, had we decided on a Saturday evening wedding with a sit-down dinner and wanted everyone to be in black-tie, everything we wore would have been affected by that decision.

I have not included specifications on what guests should wear to your wedding (as some etiquette books do), because it doesn't seem right. In fact, one bridal consultant I interviewed for the book said that you can never tell your guests what to wear to your wedding. You may put "black-tie" on the invitation, but guests don't have to honor it if they don't want to.

With that in mind, I've compiled a number of resources to create lists of traditional garb for the bride and groom, their attendants, and their parents for weddings occurring at different times of the day. According to Jack Springer, executive director of the International Formalwear Association, you should use the following rule of thumb when determining whether you need to have daytime or evening attire: if it will be dark when your wedding ceremony is over, then you should follow evening attire guidelines; otherwise, daytime apparel is appropriate.

Nuptials News

Attire accounts for approximately 19 percent of a bridal budget, according to the Association of Bridal Consultants.

According to the Association of Bridal Consultants, June is still the most popular month to have a wedding. However, August and September are nipping at the heels of June's number-one status. Here's a breakdown of percentages of weddings held in each month:

Month	Percent
January	4.3 percent
February	4.9 percent
March	5.7 percent
April	7.5 percent
May	10.1 percent
June	12.6 percent
July	9.5 percent
August	11.2 percent
September	11.8 percent
October	9.2 percent
November	6.8 percent
December	6.4 percent

Formal Daytime Wedding

Bride: Floor-length gown or dress in white or off-white with a train and veil.

Maid of Honor, Bridesmaids, and Flower Girl(s): Floor-length dress in matching colors with matching shoes.

Groom: Gray classic cutaway coat (think Rhett Butler), white shirt with a turn-down collar, gray striped trousers, gray vest with matching four-in-hand tie or ascot, and patent leather shoes. Top hat is optional.

Ushers and Junior Groomsmen: Similar to groom's attire, with possible variation in shirt and tie.

Bride's and Groom's Mothers: Long or short dress and, if they prefer, a hat with a veil. Gloves are optional.

Bride's and Groom's Fathers: Same as groom's attire.

Formal Evening Wedding

Bride: Same as formal daytime attire.

Maid of Honor, Bridesmaids, and Flower Girl(s): Same as formal daytime attire.

Groom: Black full-dress tailcoat with white wing-collar piqué formal shirt, white piqué vest and bow tie, and patent leather shoes. Or black tuxedo with white pleated formal shirt, bow tie, and vest or cummerbund to match tuxedo lapels, and patent leather shoes. In summer or in tropical locales, a white dinner jacket with formal trousers is also acceptable. Groom may take a sprig from the bride's bouquet and wear it as his boutonniere.

Ushers and Junior Groomsmen: Same as groom's attire, but bow tie and vest or cummerbund may match bride's attendants' dresses. Boutonniere will be different from groom's and possibly match flowers carried by bride's attendants or coordinate with wedding colors.

Bride's and Groom's Mothers: More formal-looking dress, possibly a long evening gown. Or a short cocktail dress. Hat and gloves are optional.

Bride's and Groom's Fathers: Identical to groom's attire, including his boutonniere.

Semiformal Daytime Wedding

Bride: Floor-length dress or gown in white or off-white. A shorter veil is more appropriate, and gloves are optional.

Maid of Honor, Bridesmaids, and Flower Girl(s): Same as formal daytime attire.

Groom: Gray stroller jacket, with striped trousers, pearl gray vest, four-in-hand tie with white pleated formal shirt, and black smooth-toed shoes.

Ushers and Junior Groomsmen: Identical to groom's attire but with a different boutonniere.

Bride's and Groom's Mothers: Floor-length or street-length dress. Gloves and hat are optional.

Bride's and Groom's Fathers: Identical to groom's attire, including his boutonniere. Or dark suits.

Semiformal Evening Wedding

Bride: Same as semiformal daytime attire.

Maid of Honor, Bridesmaids, and Flower Girl(s): Same as semiformal daytime attire or in keeping with the length and formality of bride's attire.

Groom: Tuxedo or tailcoat, in range of colors. Dark colors, such as black or navy, for fall and winter weddings; white or pastels for spring or summer weddings. However, white is appropriate for any time of the year. White shirt, which may be pleated or flat, black tie and cummerbund, and black patent leather shoes.

Ushers and Junior Groomsmen: Formalwear similar to groom's attire. However, if the groom chooses a tailcoat, it is appropriate for ushers to wear tuxedos in a similar color. White shirt. Tie and vest or cummerbund match tuxedo or wedding colors.

Bride's and Groom's Mothers: Same as semiformal daytime attire.

Bride's and Groom's Fathers: Similar to ushers' attire, a classic black tuxedo, or a dark suit.

Informal Daytime Wedding

Bride: A suit, cocktail dress, or street-length dress in white or off-white are all appropriate.

Maid of Honor, Bridesmaids, and Flower Girl(s): Dress should be the same tenor of formality (or informality, as the case may be) as the bride's dress.

Groom: Formalwear appropriate to bride's clothing selection. Or dark suit for winter affairs. In spring and summer, light-colored pants and a navy or dark-colored jacket may be worn.

Ushers and Junior Groomsmen: Same as groom's attire.

Nuptials News

Traditional weddings are a growing trend. When *Bride's Magazine* surveyed its readers, it found that 91 percent had had a formal wedding.

Attire

15

Bride's and Groom's Mothers: Afternoon or cocktail dress. Short length is appropriate, and mother's dress should not be more formal than the bride's.

Bride's and Groom's Fathers: Same as groom and ushers' attire.

Informal Evening Wedding

Bride: Same as informal daytime attire, except bride may wear a longer dress.

Maid of Honor, Bridesmaids, and Flower Girl(s): Same as informal daytime attire.

Groom: If bride chooses a longer dress, groom should wear a tuxedo. Otherwise, same as informal daytime attire.

Ushers and Junior Groomsmen: Same as informal daytime attire.

Bride's and Groom's Mothers: Same as informal daytime attire.

Bride's and Groom's Fathers: Same as groom's attire.

Bridal Consultant

When most people hear the term *bridal consultant,* they think of assistants to debutantes and celebrities. Truth is rich people do use bridal consultants. (In fact, a New Jersey bridal consultant planned the wedding of actress Brooke Shields to tennis star Andre Agassi.) However, average folks can benefit from hiring a bridal consultant as well.

For example, one bride I know, who is an attorney, was marrying a Hollywood heavy, and they were planning to tie the knot on Tortola in the British Virgin Islands. Because neither this bride nor her groom-to-be had the time to plan their faraway wedding, they relied on a bridal consultant to do all the legwork for them.

Even brides who are planning weddings closer to home can benefit from the services of a consultant. Not only can a consultant bring his or her expertise to the planning table, but he or she can help things run smoothly on the wedding day, too. One bridal consultant I ran into recently told me she keeps a bag of tricks with her on wedding-day jobs. If the bride tears her pantyhose, the hem of the bride's dress falls down, or the heel on one of the bridesmaids' shoes breaks, the consultant can reach into her bag for a new pair of hose, a stapler to fix the hem, or some glue to secure the heel.

Gerard Monahan is president of the Association of Bridal Consultants (ABC), an organization in New Milford, Connecticut, which he runs with his wife, Eileen Monahan, the organization's vice president. ABC has approximately 1,300 members in forty-six states and twelve countries, and members include not only bridal consultants but also other companies that cater to weddings, such as reception sites, gift shop owners, and invitation suppliers. ABC provides referrals to

Nuptials News

The Association of Bridal Consultants (ABC) has a brochure called "Do I Need a Bridal Consultant?" To receive one, call ABC at 860-355-0464 or send E-mail to BridalAssn@aol.com.

"The advantage of a wedding consultant is that he or she has been doing weddings in your area for a long time and knows all the caterers, deejays, bands, sites, and so on. The consultant can tell you what photographers are in your price range, and depending on how much you pay, he or she can contact everyone and arrange everything for you. That's why I hired a consultant to help me with my wedding."

Nyla, married 8/16/97

brides all over the country free of charge. For a list of association members in your area, call ABC at 860-355-0464 or send E-mail to BridalAssn@aol.com. Here Monahan answers some commonly asked questions about bridal consultants.

LI: *Why does using a bridal consultant make sense in today's world?*

GM: The demographics of today's weddings have changed significantly. Men and women are getting married later in life. Today, the average age for a bride is 24½ and a bridegroom is 26½. Unlike couples of yesteryear that married straight out of college, today's couples have been working for a few years and are probably established in their careers. They don't have a lot of free time, and, frankly, they don't have time to plan a wedding. However, what they do have is more disposable income. These couples are usually willing to spend money to make sure they get what they want, such as the wedding of their dreams.

Another factor affecting the growing need for a consultant is the advent of weekend and destination weddings. Both are a factor of our mobile society and the fact that families are spread out all over the place. For example, if the bride lives in Manhattan, Kansas, the bridegroom lives in Manhattan, New York, the bridegroom's family lives in Salem, Oregon, and the bride's family lives in Winston-Salem, North Carolina, then pulling together a wedding is going to be a bit of a challenge. But if you hire a consultant who has contacts all over the country, he or she can help make planning the wedding easier for all parties involved.

LI: *How exactly can a bridal consultant help with wedding plans?*

GM: When a bridal consultant helps a bride plan her wedding from start to finish, he or she brings a level of expertise and know-how that the bride probably doesn't possess.

Think about it. Any vendor you approach knows that it's a one-time job. For example, if you find a florist that is reputable, chances are that florist will do a great job. But there's no guarantee. However, should a bridal consultant approach a florist that the consultant works with repeatedly, the florist knows that if he or she messes up this order, the shop won't get any more business after that. A consultant is more likely to get you vendors that will do their job and do their job well, and it's even possible that the consultant can get you discounts that the vendor might not offer you as a one-time customer.

Look at it this way. You can change the oil in your car, but you take it to a service station because they are professionals; they change oil for a living. Bridal consultants plan weddings for a living. Isn't your wedding at least as important as having the oil in your car changed?

LI: *OK, so a bridal consultant can help you with a long-distance wedding or get you a discount on a vendor. But is that all a consultant can do?*

GM: No. A good consultant knows how to wear many different hats. A bridal consultant can act as a mediator if members of the family are fighting among themselves. For example, if your stepmother refuses to cooperate on certain wedding plans, you would probably start World War III if you told her how obnoxious she was being. But the consultant is an impartial outsider, and one who'll probably have more luck taking your stepmother aside, telling her what her role in the wedding should be, and leaving it at that.

A bridal consultant can help keep you calm when it seems as if plans are getting out of control. One of our members who does big weddings in New York City often finds that she has to sit her brides down and say, "Look, we're not curing cancer. This is not brain surgery. Yes, it's an important day in your life, but in the grand scheme of things, does it really matter if the flowers aren't the exact shade of pink that you wanted?"

LI: *How much should you expect to pay a consultant?*

GM: Prices vary dramatically all over the country. However, our rule of thumb is this: If a consultant plans a wedding from start to finish, he or she will usually charge 10 percent to 15 percent of the cost of the entire wedding. A consultant who is hired for the day of the wedding, on the other hand, usually charges a flat fee or an hourly rate.

LI: *Don't some consultants make extra money by getting kickbacks from the vendors they use?*

GM: If the consultant is working for you and is being paid by you, then the consultant shouldn't be getting any money from vendors. However, some consultants do not charge you a fee and rely on vendor commissions to earn their living. Make sure you discuss this ahead of time with the consultant you hire. You should feel that the consultant is your advocate and that the consultant's decisions aren't being affected by anything but your wants and desires.

According to *Bride's Magazine*, about 12 percent of the magazine's readers will hire a wedding consultant to oversee their wedding plans. They spend on average about $170 for the consultant's service.

Bridal Consultant

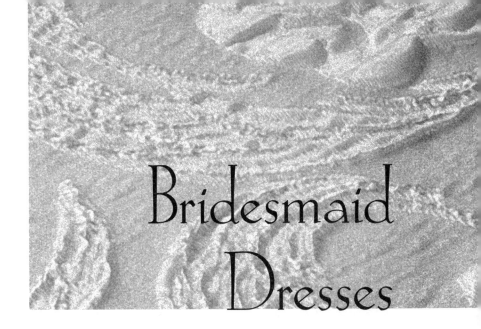

Bridesmaid Dresses

When I made the decision to have one attendant only, I saved myself the headache that shopping for bridesmaid dresses can become. I've talked to numerous brides who discovered that finding a dress to satisfy every woman in her bridal party was next to impossible. But you've got to remember that this is your day and you've got the final say on all decisions. While it is kind of you to take other people's comments into consideration, you should feel free to choose whatever kind of bridesmaid dress you want and expect your attendants to wear it with a smile.

Finding Dresses You and Your Bridesmaids Will Love

Sue Winner is an Atlanta-based representative of Discount Bridal Service, a nationwide network of dealers that buy directly from dress manufacturers and promise to save brides 20 percent to 40 percent on retail price. As long as you can provide the dress manufacturer's name, the dress style and color, and the measurements of the women who are going to wear the dress, Winner can work with you no matter where in the country you live. For more information call Winner at 404-255-3804. Here Winner shares her thoughts on what you should keep in mind when finding a dress that both you and your attendants will love.

You should plan to start shopping for your attendants' dresses as soon as you go for your gown. Like wedding gowns, bridesmaid dresses

"When it comes to the bridesmaids, try to remember that they are people with distinct personalities and styles— they're not Barbie dolls. I let mine choose their own dress; luckily they all agreed on one. Everyone wore whatever shoes, accessories, hairstyles, and makeup that they felt comfortable wearing. The results were great. Our pictures looked just as uniform and beautiful as any wedding I've seen, and my friends felt comfortable all day."
Carreen, married 11/26/93

are made to fit a specific order and aren't just pulled off a hanger in some warehouse somewhere. That's why it's so important to have your attendants' measurements on file when you select a dress. Each bridesmaid's dress will be made to fit her, and a dress manufacturer needs about six to eight months to fill an order.

Even though dress shopping will occur fairly early in the planning time line, you should have a pretty good sense of what your wedding colors are going to be by the time you begin looking at dresses. That way you'll know what color bridesmaid dress is appropriate. Or you can let the color dress you choose lead all your other decorating decisions. For example, if you find a forest green dress that you love and will look great on your bridesmaids, then maybe forest green should be one of your colors—even if you hadn't considered it previously. Then, you can use forest green as a base for such decisions as flowers, tablecloths, and invitations.

Please throw away the notion that you're going to find a dress that your attendants are going to wear again and again. While it's a wonderful idea, it doesn't often happen. But if it does, it's just gravy. Instead of searching for a dress that you believe won't be left hanging in your attendants' closets after your wedding day has come and gone (because it probably will), pick a dress that is in a price range your attendants can afford. If you accept the truth that this dress has one life to live and you make it affordable for your bridesmaids to buy, then there won't be any hard feelings if the dress never gets worn again.

It's impossible to have a bridal party of women with the same body types. Therefore, it's important to find a dress that complements every one involved. A great way to avoid problems down the line is to ask the woman or women with unusual body types or a few extra pounds on her to accompany you when you shop for bridesmaid dresses. By having her try on dresses, you can find one that looks good on her, which in turn will probably look just as good on the women who have bodies that are less difficult to fit. However, if her body is so unusual that it's becoming impossible to find an off-the-rack dress that looks good on her, you'd be wise to select a dress for your other attendants. Then order fabric that matches the dresses you select and help your hard-to-fit bridesmaid hire someone to custom-make a dress to match the others.

To find a designer to make such a dress, don't just pick a name from the yellow pages. Instead, visit fine fabric stores and informally poll the employees there. Ask them who they would go to in order to have a dress made. Anytime a name comes up two or more times, that's who your hard-to-fit bridesmaid should go to. By helping her find a reputable seamstress, you're guaranteeing that her custom-made dress will look as good as the off-the-rack dress your other bridesmaids will be wearing.

While having a dress made may seem an unreasonable expense for your bridesmaid to incur, it may be a price worth paying to keep the peace long after you've exchanged your wedding vows. For example, if it's the groom's sister who has a large body and she's very self-conscious about it, you'd be wise to find a dress that complements her—even if it means having one custom-made. This woman is going to be your sister-in-law for the rest of your life. The more considerate you are of her feelings, the more loving she will be toward you in the future.

Of course, you'll want to do some preliminary research before you hit the stores. That's why having tear sheets from bridal magazines of bridesmaid dresses you like can be helpful when you start shopping for dresses. Don't worry if a store you visit—be it a department store or a boutique—doesn't have the exact dress in the advertisement or fashion feature that you've torn out of the magazine. By showing salespeople styles you like, you're giving them a head start, so they'll know what kinds of dresses to show you.

You may find it easiest to do your bridesmaid dress shopping solo, unless you have a hard-to-fit bridesmaid as mentioned before. In my experience, I've found that you're never going to please all your bridesmaids. If you choose an identical style for them, they'll probably complain about how they hate scoop-necked dresses or below-the-knee skirts. On the other hand, if you give them a little freedom and tell them that the only requirement is that they have a dress made or find a dress made of the same color and fabric, they'll probably complain about the color. So find the dress that you like and let that be the end of the discussion. Personally, I like bridesmaids to look like bridesmaids and wear matching dresses.

The one decision that you cannot or should not make for your bridesmaids is what kind of shoes they should wear. Feet are a hard thing to fit, and not every woman feels comfortable in the same style shoe. Remember: a bridesmaid cannot smile when her feet hurt her. Each bridesmaid should buy shoes that fit her taste, are the heel height of her choice, and, ideally, are something she will wear again.

Dyeable shoes aren't the only option for bridesmaids. For example, if you've chosen a black velvet bridesmaid dress, then your bridesmaids can get away with black suede shoes. However, if you do decide to have your bridesmaids dye their shoes to match their dresses, specify what fabric shoe your attendants should buy. Different fabrics take dye differently, so you have to keep that in mind.

Bridesmaid Dresses

Personally, I like satin, which is shiny, or *peau de soie*, which is more like a silk shantung.

When your bridesmaids have their shoes dyed, make sure they don't have it done separately. Dye lots change from day to day. All the bridesmaids should ship their shoes to one bridesmaid whose responsibility it will be to have the shoes dyed together. This way they'll match. To ensure that each bridesmaid has her respective pair of shoes returned to her, have each bridesmaid write her name on the soles of the shoes.

Besides giving your bridesmaids the freedom to pick their own shoes, you should also allow each to have any alterations done in her hometown—especially if she's going to be traveling a great distance to your wedding. Not only will she be able to find a seamstress she likes and trusts, but also she can have the alterations completed with plenty of time to spare. I think it just adds stress to the days before the wedding if your bridesmaids are waiting around for their dresses to be altered. Instead, I would rather see a bridesmaid be able to walk off the plane and be ready to walk down the aisle.

Sue Winner's Advice for Making Sure Your Measurements and Any Alterations Measure Up

Many bridal shops make their money on alterations. That's why it's so important for you and each of your bridesmaids to know how to take your own measurements so that the numbers you get match what the bridal shop gets. You don't want to incur any unnecessary—and costly—alterations.

I suggest that you each get a good vinyl measuring tape (as opposed to cotton, which can stretch) and take your measurements the morning before you go dress shopping. Measure your bust (over the nipple, not under the breast), waist, and hips (at the widest part); write the numbers down; and take that information with you. Then don't be afraid to ask the bridal shop clerk what she got for each measurement. If she got a 40 for your bust and you got a 38 this morning, have her measure it again. If you know what you're doing when you walk in there, then you'll probably be able to cut down on the number of alterations you'll need when your dress finally arrives.

When it comes to alterations, keep the following in mind: With a floor-length bridesmaid dress, make sure the hem is about 1½ inches off the ground with shoes on. That way the dresses will look as if they touch the floor when photographs are taken, but your bridesmaids won't be tripping over the dresses throughout the affair.

Bridesmaid Dresses

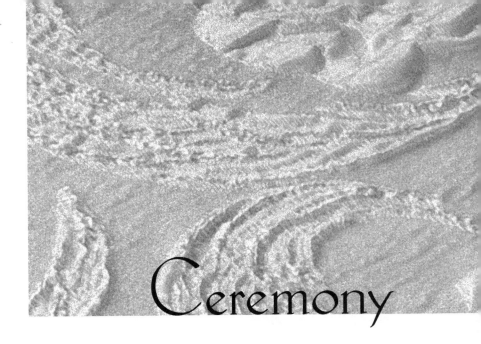

Ceremony

Although most couples end up spending an inordinate amount of time finding wedding attire, hiring a photographer, and deciding where to go on their honeymoon, by and large the most important part of the wedding day is the ceremony itself. Therefore, determining where you're going to get married and who is going to officiate at the wedding are both important decisions that, like marriage, should not be entered into lightly.

Originally Bill and I had planned to have two Episcopal priests, a husband and wife, marry us at a nondenominational university chapel near where we grew up. We chose these officiants and the setting because I was raised Jewish and Bill was raised Roman Catholic. As many men and women of differing faiths soon discover when planning their wedding, it isn't always easy to find someone to officiate at a wedding of two people of disparate religions. The rabbi at the temple where I used to attend services would rather suffer mutilation than preside at my wedding to a non-Jew, and Bill had no desire to have a Roman Catholic mass during our wedding ceremony—not that we would have been able to anyway, what with my being Jewish and all. These Episcopal priests were close friends of ours who we knew would help us create a ceremony that would be uniquely ours.

In the end, we were married by a justice of the peace in a five-minute ceremony that had us saying "I do" so fast that I didn't even have time to start crying tears of happiness. But it ended up being the perfect ceremony for us, because it was simple, to the point, and exactly what we wanted.

Nuptials News

Clergy/church fees are 1.2 percent of the total wedding budget, according to the Association of Bridal Consultants.

Officiants, Ceremony Sites, and Vows

Years ago, when people got married, they usually wed someone from their hometown who belonged to the same church or synagogue as they did. Arranging for their wedding ceremony was a snap, because all it required was contacting their priest, minister, or rabbi; expressing their desire to get married in their house of worship; and booking a date on the calendar. Now things aren't as simple.

Today finding a place to get married and a person to preside over it can be quite complicated. Men and women don't always attend the same church or temple, if they go at all, and sometimes they don't even share the same religious background. If they desire a religious setting for their ceremony, they may discover that getting a priest or rabbi to consent isn't as easy as they might think.

Some priests and ministers take offense when the only reason you want to get married in their church is that it's convenient for some logistical reason. "If a couple isn't in the same place in terms of their faith position, and the only reason they're approaching a religious official is to gain access to a religious architectural setting that will look nice in photographs," says Jim Vuocolo, D. Min., senior minister at Redlands United Church of Christ in Redlands, California, "then I politely suggest that they find a justice of the peace or someplace else to have their ceremony.

"I think that a couple needs to understand that when a pastor or rabbi is approached simply to perform a ceremony," Vuocolo continues, "he often feels rightly or wrongly used."

While Vuocolo may not agree with couples approaching him on a one-time basis for a wedding and not expressing any desire to become members of his congregation either before the wedding or after, that doesn't mean that there aren't religious officials who will consent to such a job. For example, religious officials at university chapels are more likely to agree to officiate at a wedding where neither the bride nor groom is a member of the congregation.

In addition, when an interfaith (Jewish/Christian) ceremony is involved, it may take a bit of researching, but it is possible to find a rabbi to officiate. "Most Jewish people who are marrying someone of a different religion are turned down by their childhood rabbis, who see the intermarriage as an affront to their religion," says Joan Hawxhurst, editor of "Dovetail," a newsletter by and for Jewish/Christian families, and author of *Interfaith Wedding Ceremonies: Samples and Sources* (Dovetail Publishing, 1996). "This has spawned a cottage industry on the fringes of organized Judaism of rabbis and cantors who make it their profession to perform interfaith weddings."

The same phenomenon has occurred in the Christian churches as well. "Some churches and pastors are not exactly immune from social pressures," says Vuocolo. "These churches utilize their wedding facilities as a money-making facility."

If you are a member of a congregation, you shouldn't expect to pay a fee. If not, you can expect to pay a nominal fee for the services of an officiant and his or her church. For example, Vuocolo charges $100.

The best way to find someone to perform your ceremony, especially if you don't belong to a church or you're marrying someone of a different religion, is to talk to other couples you know who have had similar weddings. Many Reform temples in America share quarters with Protestant churches, and it's likely that the pastors and rabbis there are more open to marrying people of differing religions. Hawxhurst's *Interfaith Wedding Ceremonies* is also a great resource for finding officiants, such as those affiliated with the Unitarian Universalist Church or Ethical Culture. "Many interfaith couples choose to get married on neutral ground," says Hawxhurst, "and oftentimes that ends up being at a Unitarian Universalist church." Her book also includes interfaith support groups.

If you decide to approach someone affiliated with a religious setting, be it a Reform temple or a Roman Catholic church, understand that "the services of a religious official come with religious baggage, and I mean that in a good way," says Vuocolo. This baggage usually takes the form of premarital counseling and possibly the request that the couple join the congregation in the months preceding the wedding. "A benefit of joining a congregation is you can befriend the pastor ahead of time. And if he gets to know you ahead of time, he can make personal remarks during your wedding, which will make it more meaningful," adds Vuocolo.

If you decide that a religious setting is not the right place for you to exchange vows, there are a number of places where you can hold a ceremony. "You can start with the chamber of commerce. They may know of historical buildings or public places that rent space for weddings," says Teddy Lenderman, owner of Bearable Weddings by Teddy in West Terre Haute, Indiana, and author of *The Complete Idiot's Guide to the Perfect Wedding* (Macmillan, 1995). It's not unheard of for weddings to take place in public parks, in museums, or at bed-and-breakfasts. Lenderman says a great resource for offbeat places to have weddings is a book called *Places: A Directory of Public Places for Private Events and Private Places for Public Events* by Hannelore Hahn and Tatiana Stoumen (Tenth House Enterprises, 1989).

About forty thousand Jewish/Christian weddings happen each year, according to Dovetail Publishing.

Ceremony

29

Nuptials News

According to *Bride's Magazine*, the average fee for the clergy/church/chapel/synagogue is $113.

"A lot of interfaith couples do their wedding outdoors or in a hotel," adds Hawxhurst. In fact, a couple's decision to have the ceremony and reception take place in the same location, be it in a hotel ballroom or on a sailboat, often stems from their need to find a non-religious site where they can be married.

Most couples find that it's easiest to have a justice of the peace perform their wedding ceremony. Word of mouth is a great way to find such an officiant.

However, just because you have your wedding ceremony outside of a house of worship doesn't mean you can't have a minister or rabbi presiding at it. In addition, "just because you go a route that doesn't feel as religious or as spiritual as a church or temple wedding doesn't mean that your wedding can't be spiritual," says Hawxhurst. "In my experience, most couples find ways to incorporate their religion into the ceremony somehow." For example, if the groom is Jewish, he may choose to break a glass at the end of the ceremony or be married underneath a *huppah*. On the other hand, his Christian bride may decide to have them light a unity candle during the ceremony. Adds Hawxhurst, "Those little pieces of traditions that the couple find a way to bring into their ceremonies are what bring together the two families."

Just as couples of differing faiths may include certain traditions from their religions in the ceremony service, couples should feel free to adjust beforehand the vows they're going to take. Vuocolo says that there are standard vows in each religion, but you should feel free to put those vows into a language that you both feel comfortable with. However, in some religions you don't have any leeway on vow writing, so it's a question you'll want to ask your officiant before hiring him or her to do the ceremony.

If you do opt to adjust the vows to your liking, "keep it as succinct as possible while still expressing the sentiment you wish to convey," adds Vuocolo. You don't want to bore your guests, and you don't want to stretch the service out unnecessarily.

Once you've settled on what you want to say at your ceremony, practice it. "Under no circumstances should you try to memorize your vows," warns Vuocolo, who has seen the anxiety of the wedding day cause the ideal orator to stumble on his or her words. Instead, you should rehearse them at home simply so that you get comfortable saying them. Expect your officiant to go over his or her part in the wedding, too. "I tell them where I'm going to pause," Vuocolo says, "but always with the caveat that I may pause more often if it seems more appropriate." For example, if the officiant determines that the bride and groom are too nervous to say more than four words at a time, he or she may pause often while reciting the vows so that the couple won't have too much information to process at once.

Finally, make sure you settle on vows you can live with. "Remember, you're making a vow to God and to your spouse, so you have to be careful about what you assent to," say Vuocolo, who once heard of a couple who had no problem saying "I do" to the fidelity part of the vows, even though they were each having an affair at the time—hard to believe, but true.

Premarital Counseling

Many religious officials expect an engaged couple to go through some sort of premarital counseling. Here, Jim Vuocolo goes over some of the issues that might come up in premarital counseling.

Communication. You need to learn to argue in a way that isn't demeaning.

Financial Pressures. You may be a spender while your fiancé is a saver. You need to figure out a way you'll make money decisions that make you both feel comfortable.

Having Children. Birth control methods need to be determined ahead of time, and you need to clarify when you each see children coming into your lives. In addition, you need to know how you will deal with an unplanned pregnancy.

Extended Family and Friends. This topic includes the relationship you currently have with your parents and friends and how that may change after you get married.

Sexual Relations. Some people are raised to think that sex is not a healthy thing, so they won't communicate with their spouse about what is fulfilling for them. A healthy sex life affects the well-being of your marriage.

Philosophy of Life and Religion. For example, if one of you is a practicing Jew and the other a practicing Christian, you are going to have to figure out how you will accommodate religion in your life.

Butterflies Are Free

Now that throwing rice at the happy couple as they leave their wedding is pretty much forbidden at most ceremony sites and reception halls across the country, couples are forced to come up with a

Ceremony

31

creative way to replace that symbolic gesture. Some people throw rose petals instead; others ring in their new life together with bells; still others set butterflies free.

This last option is the brainchild of Rick Mikula, owner of Hole-in-Hand, a Hazleton, Pennsylvania, business that breeds butterflies. It was back in 1980 that Mikula first conceived of the idea of releasing butterflies at the end of a wedding ceremony. "I was lecturing at a garden club meeting, and I mentioned the idea," Mikula recalls. "There was a minister there whose niece was getting married soon and he said, 'Let's try it.'" At that wedding, he released two dozen orange-and-black monarch butterflies, and "it worked out beautifully."

Word of mouth has helped grow Mikula's business. Today, he no longer raises and ships all the butterflies that are used at weddings nationwide. Instead, he relies on local breeders. "You see, each butterfly population has its own diseases," says Mikula, and in order to not upset the balance of nature, "I have breeders stationed all over the country who can supply butterflies that are indigenous to their area."

What makes releasing butterflies such a wonderful part of a wedding ceremony is the unique beauty of it. For example, Mikula supplied butterflies for a New Jersey wedding where the bride wore flowers in her hair. When the butterflies were released by her guests, the butterflies flew toward the bride and landed in her hair.

At another wedding, the bride was of Eastern Indian descent. Mikula says that in different parts of an Indian ceremony, the officiant refers repeatedly to the butterfly. Then the groom's family is supposed to present the bride with a gift. "In this case, we supplied them with a huge pipevine swallowtail butterfly," Mikula recalls. (Swallowtails have metallic blue wings and a silver, red, and orange underside.) "When they released the butterfly, it circled the couple throughout the remainder of the ceremony."

Mikula offers his butterfly supply at $100 per dozen. The most popular varieties are the monarch, pipevine swallowtail, and painted lady, whose wings are orange and black on top and gray, white, and pink below. All three varieties are available in most areas of the United States.

Butterflies are shipped in a triangle-shaped envelope that protects their wings and is easy to open. When guests lift the envelope flap, out fly the butterflies. Each shipment of butterflies comes with a Native American legend that tells of the butterfly as the best message carrier for making a wish come true. "Because butterflies make no sound, they can tell no one but the Great Spirit the wish," explains Mikula. "They can take the wish to heaven, where it will be granted." He finds that many couples will read this myth out loud before asking their guests to release the butterflies.

For information on ordering butterflies from Hole-in-Hand, call Rick Mikula at 717-459-1327.

Huppah Artist

Traditionally a Jewish wedding ceremony is performed under a *huppah*, a piece of cloth stretched between four poles. This tentlike structure is supposed to represent the first home of biblical characters Abraham and Sarah.

Some *huppahs* are simply religious shawls; others are rose trellises; still others are bona fide works of art.

Corinne Soikin Strauss has made a name for herself by creating handpainted silk *huppahs* that are commissioned by engaged couples. She asks each couple what some of the more meaningful symbols in their lives are so she can integrate these themes into their *huppah*. One interfaith couple had a *huppah* that featured stained glass windows like the ones the Christian bride loved to stare at as a child while sitting in church. For another couple, from Trinidad, she made a *huppah* with palm trees and water painted on it.

Her work is so breathtaking that it's been displayed in New York City's Jewish Museum and the Skirball Museum in Cincinnati. She suggests that after their wedding, a couple display the *huppah* in their home as they would any other piece of art.

For more information about Corinne Soikin Strauss's Artist's Wedding Studio, located in Croton-on-Hudson, New York, call 914-271-8807.

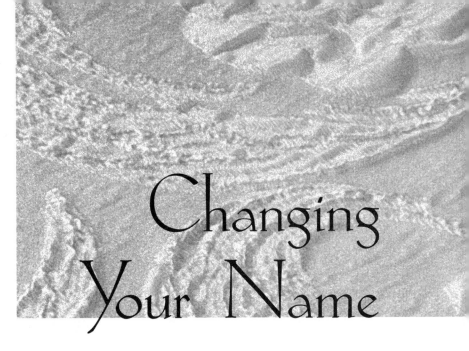

Changing Your Name

*I*f you are like me, you are guilty of trying on your boyfriends' last names—even the names of guys you had no intention of marrying. When you met and fell in love with your fiancé, you probably did the same thing. I know I did, and because I wasn't thrilled with the way Bill's name sounded with mine, I figured I'd be a three-named person—Leah Ingram Behre—after I got married. That is, I would use my first name as my first name, my maiden name as my middle name, and my married name as my last name. However, that idea lasted about six months after we got married.

People had such a hard time pronouncing my married name, which is not said as it's spelled, that I was forever correcting them. Plus, I never introduced myself as the three-named person; I used only my maiden name. Finally, frustrated by my confused identity, I decided to revert to my maiden name. Since I'd never changed my name on things like my Social Security card and my passport, my decision wasn't such a big deal.

Then my daughter, Jane, came into the picture, and suddenly I wanted to have the same last name as she and my husband. But Bill, being the feminist-minded guy that he is, insisted that I continue as Leah Ingram. Then he made the greatest suggestion: so that our daughter feels connected to me, even though I have a different last name, why don't we give her my maiden name as her middle name? We did, and that's what we plan to do with all of our children.

Time for a Change

Most women do not have a terribly hard time changing their names. It's what they expect to do from childhood, and when the time

"I realized that I wanted to change my name but only if I could pick a new name to go along with it. I liked the idea of being able to assume a new identity, and I wanted to choose part of it. I decided to drop my current middle name and surname, take my husband's name, and then take my mother's maiden name as my new middle name. It made me feel like I was thoughtfully entering my new life."

Nancy, married 11/16/96

comes to change their names at marriage, women happily take their husbands' names. However, a growing number of women are finding it difficult to change their names.

"There is an identity wrapped around our names," says Rita Bigel-Casher, a therapist in New York City. "Plus, the women's movement made us more sensitive to the inequity of the husband's not having to give up his name."

If a woman has a professional identity associated with her name, she's more likely to keep it. What many women are doing is assuming two identities. They might be Mary Smith professionally and then become Mary Jones, her husband's last name, personally. "I hyphenated my name so I could use both names or just one at a time" she says, "and sometimes it can be confusing as to who I am."

One of the reasons that a woman may choose to go by more than one name is so name-related decisions in the future are easier to make, such as when she has children. "The decisions you make now about your name will come up again when you have children," says Bigel-Casher. For example, if a woman keeps her name, she may need to figure out a way to stay connected to her children, possibly by giving them her last name as a middle name. On the other hand, if a woman decides to hyphenate her name, she'll need to decide if her children will have hyphenated names, too. "Keep in mind that a hyphenated name can be a big name," she adds.

Broaching the issue of not changing your name is not easy. Since it is still considered going against the norm, the very topic itself can cause conflict in your relationship with your fiancé. "A lot of women reason with their future husbands, saying, 'You want me to take your name. Why don't you take mine?' A great majority of men aren't keen on that idea, but you know what? Some actually do take their wives' names," says Bigel-Casher.

Here are seven steps for bringing up the subject without picking a fight.

1. If you want to keep your own name, think it through clearly. Make sure that you're arriving at this decision from a position of being true to yourself as opposed to being contrary to tradition for the sake of being contrary. The bottom line is be clear about your motivation.

2. Present the issue to your fiancé in a conversation that is free of interruption. Make sure you do it on neutral territory where you

can feel comfortable raising your voices if you need to. The key is to present the topic as a problem you're having. For example, you can say, "I'm having a problem giving up my name and taking on a new identity."

3. Make sure you take the feelings of your fiancé into consideration and word what you're going to say accordingly. Try saying "I'm worried about how you might feel about this, and I would be very upset if I hurt your feelings." Be clear that you're considering rejecting his name—not him.

4. Stop talking, be quiet, and give him the chance to express his feelings—even if his response is negative. However, there is a chance that his response will be positive, and then you'll have the satisfaction of knowing that you solved the problem without having a fight. If his response isn't positive, move on to the fifth step.

5. Ask your fiancé who he thinks would be the most upset if you keep your name. If it's not himself but his parents he's worried about, then it's a conversation you need to have with your future in-laws.

6. If you can't find common ground, shelve the issue for a little while. Tell your future spouse, "Why don't we take some time to think about this? We're getting very upset." You don't want to get into a fight about this, which is why it's so important to keep your tone of voice moderated, respectful, and loving.

7. End the conversation by saying, "Let's set a time and date when we can sit down and talk about it again."

If you find the name-changing discussion has you at such an impasse that you're considering calling off the engagement, then it's time to see a marriage therapist. "You're going to have to deal with conflict, and you're going to have to learn to negotiate," says Bigel-Casher. "The engagement period is a time when many couples set the rules for the rest of their relationship," which is why premarital counseling may be a very viable option for you at this point.

Source: Rita Bigel-Casher, csw, Ph.D., the author of Bride's Guide to Emotional Survival *(Prima Publishing, 1996) and an individual, couples, and family therapist in New York City.*

"We compromised. I hyphenated my name legally so I could use both names. I use my maiden name at work, and my married name socially."
Carreen, married 11/26/93

Changing Your Name

The Process of Changing Your Name

Mike McCurley is a senior partner at the Dallas law firm McCurley, Kinser, McCurley & Nelson and the president of the American Academy of Matrimonial Lawyers. Here he explains the process of changing your name.

Your legal name is the one that appears on the most recent formal document of maximum authority in your life. Those documents are your birth certificate, marriage license, passport, and divorce decree. As a woman who is getting married, the legal document that will affect you most is your marriage certificate. Therefore, whatever name you choose on your marriage certificate becomes your legal name.

Ideally all other legal documentation in your life, such as your passport, should then reflect this name change. But, for example, if your passport doesn't need to be renewed around the time of your marriage, it really isn't going to matter that it still has your maiden name on it. You haven't defrauded anyone by not changing your name, but you might run into trouble if you try to travel to a different country. I suggest traveling with a copy of your marriage certificate, so that if the name on your plane ticket is different from the one on your passport, you can explain the discrepancy.

If you decide to keep your maiden name professionally or keep using your maiden name because you like it better than your married name, you need to understand that your maiden name is still not your legal name. However, if you don't get around to changing your credit cards or driver's license, you won't get into any legal trouble. That is, you won't unless you're assuming a different name to defraud people. Then not changing your name could be seen as a fraudulent act, which could cause legal problems down the line.

If you do decide to change your name, then you'll probably want to make a list of all the documents you'll need to update. Start with the most formal documents in your life, such as your marriage license, passport, and perhaps the deed to your house, if you own one. Then add other everyday items like your credit cards, Social Security card, driver's license, bank statement, personal checks, investment accounts, and insurance policies. Also, don't forget to notify the post office.

While the regulations for supporting a name change request may differ from credit card company to bank, all you'll probably need to complete the transaction is a copy of your marriage certificate. That means that if you'd like to get all this paperwork out of the way before you get married, you can't. Just be prepared to do it all when you get back from your honeymoon.

Who Changes Her Name?

David R. Johnson, a professor of sociology at the University of Nebraska-Lincoln, and his wife, Laurie K. Scheuble, a professor of sociology at Doane College in Crete, Nebraska, recently studied the phenomenon of women's retaining their maiden names after marriage. They discovered that in a university setting, women were more likely to make nontraditional name choices when compared with a national sample. For example, 32.1 percent of women in a university setting kept their birth name. On a national scale, only .5 percent of women made the same choice. In addition, 9.5 percent of these women chose a hyphenated name, whereas only .1 percent of women across the country took a hyphenated name.

Based on their studies, Professors Johnson and Scheuble have come up with a list of characteristics and demographics that best describe the woman who is probably going to keep her maiden name. She will

* have cohabited
* be in her first marriage
* have lived in the Northeast
* have a higher level of education
* have a lower level of religiosity
* hold nontraditional gender role attitudes

Source: "Women's Marital Name Choice: Determinants and Effects"
by David R. Johnson and Laurie K. Scheuble.

Dieting and Losing Weight

Many brides have an image of themselves on their wedding day. While it includes a to-die-for dress and gorgeous makeup, this image may also include a skinny body. If you've got some weight to lose, it is admirable to want to shed it before your wedding, but it shouldn't become an obsession.

You should ask yourself why you want to lose the weight. Is it because you're afraid the camera will add ten pounds to you in your wedding pictures? Is it because you want your husband to love you more? According to most registered dietitians, those are both the wrong reasons to lose weight. If you're wearing a dress that complements your body, you're going to end up looking gorgeous in your pictures no matter what. Plus, your husband-to-be already loves you. In fact, he loves you for who you are right now. Otherwise, he wouldn't have asked you to marry him.

One of the right reasons to embark on a weight-loss plan is that you want to do it for yourself—not for your photographer. If so, then you should start thinking about a sensible eating plan and exercise regimen that starts around the time your wedding planning does. This way you'll be able to give yourself enough time to take off the weight in a healthy manner.

Painless Ways to Lose Weight Before Your Wedding

* For three or four days before you start to change your eating habits, write down what you typically eat and at what time of the day. You needn't be concerned with keeping track of

"Eight months before the wedding, I went on NutriSystem to lose weight. My dress had been ordered over a year before, when I was a size 16. They ordered my dress in a size 20 in case I gained—not lost—weight. By the time I was fitted for my dress, I was a size 12. The seamstress did an excellent job at taking it in."

Kimberly, married 8/25/90

calories; you're keeping this record to uncover any glaring dieting faux pas in your diet.

* When you go over your food journal, look for any sources of extra sugar or fat. Do you eat a lot of fast food? Do you drink too much cola?

* Start cutting out these sources of extra calories, but do it in a way that you don't feel deprived. For example, if you drink a couple of cans of cola during the day, switch to diet cola. Or if you do a drive-through lunch a couple of times a week, switch to a grilled chicken sandwich instead of a greasy hamburger.

* Keep portions under control. Think about a portion of meat (be it chicken, beef, or pork) being no bigger than a deck of cards, which is approximately the size of three ounces of meat. You should have no more than three three-ounce servings of meat in a day.

* Increase your exercise. Research has shown that doing thirty cumulative minutes of exercise each day is a great way to shed unwanted pounds. So if you walk ten minutes to the bus stop, ten minutes to the office, and ten minutes during your lunch break, you've gotten all thirty minutes of your exercise for one day done without breaking a sweat, so to speak.

* If you need help with portion control and meal planning, join a program like Weight Watchers. What's great about Weight Watchers is they don't make you buy special foods, as some other weight-control programs do, so you'll have the chance to learn about better eating with "real" food. In addition, Weight Watchers has an excellent program to help you maintain your goal weight once you've reached it.

Source: Franca Alphin, R.D., nutrition director at Duke University Diet and Fitness Center in Durham, North Carolina.

Registered Dietitian Franca Alphin's Honeymoon Eating Tips

If you've managed to lose weight before your wedding, the last thing you want to do is gain it all back on your honeymoon. While you should enjoy yourself on your first trip together with your groom as husband and wife, you will still want to be able to button your pants at the end of your honeymoon. Here are a few tips to make sure you can.

- If you're going to a tropical locale where there is an abundance of fresh fruits, enjoy the local specialties for dessert instead of cake or pie.

- When in doubt, choose chicken or seafood (especially if it was caught fresh that day) over red meat.

- Limit your alcohol intake to one drink per day. Choose champagne or wine, which have fewer calories per serving than mixed drinks.

- Enjoy some physical activity. If your hotel is on a beach, go for a romantic stroll on the beach each day before breakfast or after dinner.

- Drink plenty of water, especially if you are honeymooning in a warm climate. Also, be sure to drink bottled water to avoid any illness.

Wedding-Day Eating Ideas

Many brides are so nervous on the day of their wedding that they can't eat anything. Or they're so busy with last-minute tasks that they forget to have a meal. Unfortunately, not eating will lead to your being a crabby and shaky bride. Add to this the possible tendency to load up on caffeine as an energy source, and soon you will have all the symptoms of low blood sugar—headache, sweating, irritability, and the shakes.

Not eating good food can also wreak havoc on your face. If you don't eat anything on your wedding day, you could end up with sallow-looking skin, circles under your eyes, and even cold sores on your mouth.

The best plan of action on your wedding day is to eat foods with carbohydrates and protein in them. The combination of the two will raise your blood sugar level and give you the energy you need to make it through the ceremony. Excellent carbohydrate and protein snacks include a bowl of cereal, cheese and crackers, and a cold-cut sandwich.

Source: Tammy Vitale, R.D., M.S., a lecturer in nutrition and food science at Utah State University in Logan, Utah.

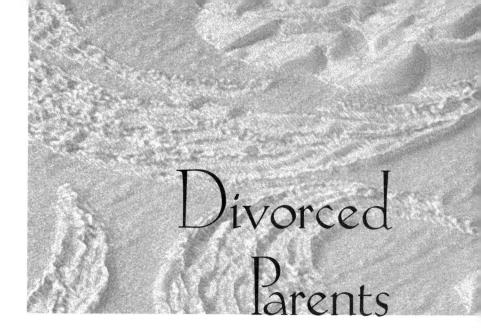

Divorced Parents

With the divorce rate somewhere around 50 percent of all marriages, chances are that you will probably have to deal with at least one set of divorced parents. Bill and I have two sets of divorced parents and a few stepparents to boot. Needless to say, pulling everything together for our wedding day was quite a challenge. One of the reasons we eloped was we found it too difficult to deal with parents who don't get along, parents who wouldn't work with other parents, and various other wrenches that having divorced parents helped throw into the works.

I'm not saying that if you're a child of divorce you must elope. In hindsight I realize that perhaps we were asking too much of our parents. For example, my mother and father, while cordial to each other, have not been the best of friends since they divorced. My dad has remarried and has children of his own, so it was probably unreasonable for me to expect my dad, his new wife, and my mother to all sit together at the wedding ceremony. The problem is that planning a wedding is a high-pressure endeavor, and that pressure may cause you and your fiancé (and even your parents) to make foolish requests or unfair decisions, as I did. But if you act sensibly throughout the wedding-planning process and keep everyone's feelings in mind, you'll probably be able to pull off a great event—even with divorced parents—without shedding any tears.

Nuptials News

Of children living in a single-parent situation, 18.4 percent live with a separated parent and 37 percent live with a divorced parent, according to *Marital Status and Living Arrangements*, a March 1994 study from the Bureau of the Census.

Wedding Planning with a Complicated Family

Margorie Engel is a writer and speaker who specializes in families that are complicated by divorce. Here, Margorie talks about what you and your fiancé need to keep in mind when planning a wedding with divorced parents.

The first piece of advice I can offer to you is this: Planning a wedding is stressful without the divorce in the picture. Please don't think that the problems you run into or the disagreements you have are being caused by the divorce. Even couples with happily married parents find that their mothers and fathers argue over certain wedding-planning details. So it isn't just divorced parents that fight.

With that said, you've got to approach your wedding plans in one of two ways. If your parents get along well and will cooperate as you see fit, then you can forge ahead with your wedding plans as any other bride or groom would. However, if your parents tend to fight, don't get along, or aren't on speaking terms, then you'll need to keep them separate and figure out a way to have them both be involved with the wedding without causing any conflict.

Assuming that just your parents are going to be involved in planning because they'll be footing the bill, here's a way to do it. Have your father handle the reception and your mother deal with the ceremony. That means your father will be involved with helping to select a reception site, the meal, the flowers for the table, and the entertainment. Your mother will work with the church or ceremony site coordinator, book a musician for the ceremony, and handle flowers for the wedding.

Because proper etiquette says that the person giving a party is supposed to issue an invitation, a wedding of this caliber will require two invitations. Your mother will issue the wedding invitation and include a response card of her own or an RSVP phone number on the invitation. Your father, on the other hand, will issue a similar invitation and response card, but to the reception only. Each invitation will follow proper etiquette and include the name(s) of the people paying for that portion of the celebration.

I suggest that these two separate invitations be mailed as one to cut down on confusion. They should also be printed on the same paper stock and with the same typeface to establish continuity. It is your job to coordinate the printing and assembly of the invitations. It shouldn't be too hard a task to accomplish because technically you don't have to act as a go-between. Because your parents are approaching the wedding as if they're two separate parties, they never have to talk to each other or compare notes.

By following this line of thinking, you also create the need for separate seating and receiving lines.

The people who are sponsoring the ceremony are usually the ones who sit farthest forward in the church, synagogue, or ceremony site. If your mother is paying for the wedding ceremony, then she would sit in the first pew. Your father would sit in the second pew. However, if their sitting near to one another would cause problems, you can create a buffer pew in between the parents and perhaps seat siblings or relatives there.

If your mother and her new spouse sponsor the ceremony portion of the wedding, then they are the ones to stand in the receiving line with you and your attendants after the ceremony. If your father and his new spouse are funding the reception, then they are the ones to greet guests as they arrive for the reception.

How to Keep Your Divorced Parents from Making You Want to Call Off the Wedding

* As soon as you get engaged, sit all the parents down—separately if they don't get along. Make it clear what you do (and don't) expect from them in regard to the wedding. Let them know if you're looking for financial support or simply emotional assistance.

* Be prepared for your parents to say "no." You may ask your parents to both walk you down the aisle, but if they're not comfortable with the request, they have the right to refuse.

* Throughout the wedding-planning process, keep everyone updated on what's going on. That may mean having a conference call once a month or sending E-mail on a regular basis. You'll avoid conflicts down the line if all the parents are aware of how the site selection process is going or any ceremony changes you've decided to make.

* Be willing to compromise. You have to keep reminding yourself that, yes, this is your wedding, but you're part of a family unit. You have to decide if an issue like hot pink bridesmaid dresses or tofu for a main course is worth fighting over. You have to prioritize which decisions are worth the trouble. Many aren't, but a good many are.

* If you decide to have a receiving line with all the parents (including the divorced ones) in it, be prepared to separate the parties that don't get along. And if a parent has remarried and his or her spouse would feel slighted by not being included in the receiving line, then by all means, include that person.

* Don't seat divorced parents near each other at the reception. This is an excellent reason to work out a seating plan ahead of time.

* Finally, try to anticipate all the possible situations that may cause hostility and antagonism between divorced parents, and then avoid them like the plague. On the day of the wedding, all you and your groom should have to think about is enjoying yourselves—not about keeping the peace between divorced parents. If you anticipate all the problem scenarios ahead of time, you should have a marvelously peaceful day.

Source: Carroll Stoner, author of Weddings for Grownups: Everything You Need to Know to Plan Your Wedding Your Way *(Chronicle Books, 1993).*

Including Stepsiblings and Half Siblings

The end result of so many divorces and remarriages is that you may have to include stepsiblings and half siblings as well as natural siblings in the wedding. While it's always nice to ask a stepsister or half brother to be in your wedding, that's not always feasible. Margorie Engel offers these tips for including stepsiblings and half siblings in the wedding festivities. Such siblings might

* man the guest book
* greet people at the church or synagogue
* read a poem during the service
* give a special toast at the reception

Invitations from Divorced Parents

If your divorced parents decide to issue separate invitations to the wedding and reception, they would use the following wording on the invitations:

Ceremony

Mrs. Judith Smith
requests the honour of your presence
at the marriage of her daughter
Jane Marie
and
John William Doe
Saturday, the twenty-fourth of October
nineteen hundred and ninety-eight
at five o'clock
St. Thomas Roman Catholic Church
Ann Arbor, Michigan

Reception

Mr. John Smith
requests the pleasure of your company
at the marriage reception
of his daughter
Jane Marie
and
John William Doe
Saturday, the twenty-fourth of October
nineteen hundred and ninety-eight
at seven o-clock
The Michigan League
Ann Arbor, Michigan

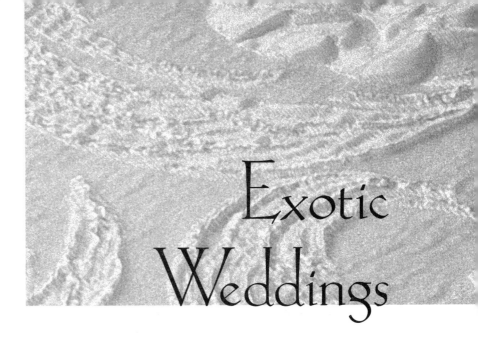

Exotic Weddings

I recently wrote a story for *Islands* magazine about getting married on an exotic island, and I had to research weddings on more than thirty different islands around the world. In the process I interviewed a handful of couples who escaped to a tropical beach or an island resort to tie the knot, and I was jealous of every one of them. Having a wedding in an exotic locale seems about as close to heaven as you can get. Most of these couples didn't have to deal with the same kinds of pressures that having a wedding locally would cause. They got to go barefoot to their wedding ceremony, if they chose to do so, and they had the satisfaction of knowing that they had the kind of wedding that you just don't have every day.

In researching that article and this chapter in the book, I came to realize that you don't have to be superrich or extra resourceful to pull off an exotic wedding. You just have to want to do something a little different. Best part of all? After your wedding is over, you don't have to worry about getting up at 5 A.M. to catch a flight to Miami, because you're already at your honeymoon destination.

Traveling Man ... and Wife

Beatrice York-Blitzer and Myrna Ingram, co-owners of Empress Travel in West Hills–Huntington, New York, have noticed an increasing trend in couples traveling to exotic destinations to marry. Here they share their thoughts on this new wedding phenomenon. To book an exotic wedding or honeymoon with Empress Travel, call 800-291-3313.

Nuptials News

According to the Gatlinburg Visitors and Convention Bureau, in 1995, more than sixteen thousand couples were married in Gatlinburg, Tennessee. That statistic puts the Smoky Mountains town ahead of Las Vegas in the number of weddings performed.

Nuptials News

The Caribbean Tourism Organization has information on the cost of a marriage license, waiting periods, documentation required, and whether you need a blood test or not to get married on the following islands: Anguilla, Antigua and Barbuda, Aruba, Barbados, Belize, Bonaire, British Virgin Islands, Cayman Islands, Curaçao, Dominica, Dominican Republic, French West Indies (Guadeloupe, St. Barthélemy, and Martinique), Grenada, the Islands of the Bahamas, Jamaica, Mexico, Montserrat, Puerto Rico, Saba, St. Eustatius, St. Kitts and Nevis, St. Lucia, St. Martin, St. Vincent and the Grenadines, Trinidad and Tobago, Turks and Caicos, and U.S. Virgin Islands.

For more information, contact the Caribbean Tourism Organization at 20 E. Forty-Sixth Street, New York, NY 10017, 212-682-0435.

Most men and women who are traveling to an exotic location to tie the knot are heading to the Caribbean. With literally hundreds of islands to choose from, this part of the world, with its turquoise blue waters and gentle sea breezes, is a part of paradise that happens to be just a few hours from the U.S. mainland.

One of the primary reasons that you may choose to get married in the Caribbean is financial. It's actually cheaper to go away to get married—especially if you don't invite a large number of family and friends to accompany you. You won't be faced with the same costs you would for a hometown wedding, such as renting a limousine or paying for a ten-piece band. Instead of spending $16,000 for a wedding, you may spend only $5,000, and that might include a week at a resort for your honeymoon.

Other reasons you might slip away for an island wedding are it's a second wedding for one or both of you, there are divorced parents involved and this is an easy way to avoid conflict, or you're untraditional people and having a nontraditional wedding seems the perfect thing for you to do.

Just because you decide to get married in The Bahamas or on Barbados doesn't mean you have to forgo a religious ceremony. There are certainly Roman Catholic and other Christian pastors on most of the islands. Some island nations are just discovering their Jewish roots, and local consultants can help arrange for a rabbi to preside over a Jewish wedding.

Many resorts are recognizing that island weddings could become big business and help boost tourism. Therefore, most major resorts now offer a wedding coordinator on staff to plan your nuptials. This person can do everything from finding a rabbi for a Jewish wedding to hiring a photographer to document the event. If you've invited family and friends to join you in the celebration, don't be shy about asking for a discount on room rates. In addition, it's probably a good idea to make everyone's travel plans through a travel agent. A travel agent will have more leverage with an airline or a resort about getting a volume discount than if you call an 800 number.

If you decide that an exotic wedding is right for you, you need to plan as far in advance as you would any other kind of wedding. For example, high season in the Caribbean runs from December until mid-April, so it may be hard to find a block of rooms to accommodate all your guests at that time of the year. In addition, resorts don't take a mass-production approach to wedding planning and will often book only one wedding per day—if not per weekend. Therefore, if someone else has already booked the day you're interested in, you're going to have to be flexible about your wedding date.

High season is also the most popular time for families to vacation together. So if you happen to plan a wedding during Christmas vacation or February break, you may want to switch dates. Otherwise you may find yourself in a resort that is overrun by children.

The other time of year that you need to keep in mind is hurricane season, which lasts from August to November. Granted, the Windward islands in the Caribbean (St. Lucia and south) are less likely to be hit by hurricanes. However, you wouldn't want to have a wedding the one year the hurricane path switched direction.

Tips for Getting Married in the Tropics

* Plan in advance, especially if you want to get married during high season (December until mid-April).

* Do some research before you choose an island. People choose to get married in Nevis or Grenada, for example, because they want a quiet, less-commercialized island. If you're looking for lively nightlife and gambling, you will want to focus on islands like Puerto Rico or the Cayman Islands.

* Find out if the resort offers any kind of wedding package. At The Calabash Hotel in Grenada, a wedding package costs $750, and it includes room upgrade, if available; two witnesses for the ceremony, if necessary; wedding cake; bottle of champagne and fruit juice; bridal bouquet of tropical flowers; celebration bottle of wine with wedding-night dinner; photographer to take twenty-four prints; minister's fees; marriage license; marriage certificate; and ceremony.

* Fax all your documentation ahead of time so that the wedding coordinator can get started on the paperwork for your marriage license. This way, if any additional information is needed, you can deliver it before you arrive.

* Take into consideration that many islands have residency requirements for nonresidents marrying there. So you may have to arrive as much as ten days before your wedding in order to qualify for a marriage license.

Exotic Weddings

wedding wisdom

"Weddings I've been to are all alike. It seems like they all have the same bands and the same food. Frankly, many of them are quite boring."
Mike, married 4/27/96 on Nassau Beach, the Islands of the Bahamas

wedding wisdom

"We got married at sunrise, barefoot and in the sand, with our children at our side."
Judy, married 5/8/95 in the Florida Keys

* If you want a religious officiant at your wedding, find out ahead of time if that's possible and, if so, what sort of restrictions that person may have. Some Roman Catholic priests, for example, will still want you to go through premarital counseling, even if it's done by mail.

* Ask to see photographs of other weddings that have been held on the island or resort so you can get a good idea of where you'll want your ceremony to take place.

* Plan for a morning wedding. While a sunset ceremony may seem romantic, you'll lose light fast, which will sabotage your pictures. Plus, you'll be getting ready for your wedding during the hottest part of the day. If you plan a wedding for mid-morning, it will be cooler, there will be abundant shade, and best of all, you'll have the rest of the day to celebrate your marriage.

Source: Noreen deGale, wedding coordinator at The Calabash Hotel in Grenada, 800-528-5835.

Going to the Chapel of Love

For some couples, the definition of an exotic wedding is one in an offbeat place, such as the Mall of America in Minneapolis. Nestled between the department stores and the coffee bars in America's largest mall is the Chapel of Love. The front half of the Chapel of Love is a bridal and gift boutique, where you can find invitations, unity candles, garters, cake toppers, and even bride-and-groom bubblegum. Behind the store is a seventy-five-seat wedding chapel. More than two hundred ceremonies have been performed here since the Chapel of Love opened its doors to the public in April 1994.

Just because the Chapel of Love is situated in a mall doesn't mean you can just walk in and get hitched. (This is Minneapolis, remember, not Las Vegas.) Your wedding must be planned three to six months in advance, although the chapel has been known to perform a ceremony with only twenty-four hours notice.

"Ninety-five percent of our couples want a traditional church service but don't belong to a church or can't get married in their church because one of them is divorced," says Mary Anne London Gears, owner of the Chapel of Love, who performs nondenominational ceremonies.

Your wedding must occur during mall hours. Receptions often occur at one of the mall restaurants, such as Planet Hollywood or Twin City Grill. Many brides like to take pictures at Camp Snoopy, the amusement park inside the Mall of America.

Wedding packages start at $195 and go as high as $3,095. The latter package, called the Mega Wedding, includes photography, the Mega floral package (cascading bouquet of seasonal flowers, bouquets for the bridal party, corsages for mothers and grandmothers, boutonnieres for fathers and grandfathers, and a throwaway bouquet or floral cake topper), invitations, guest book, vocalist/musician, limousine service, wedding cake, hotel accommodations for the wedding night, and videography.

It isn't just local brides and grooms who head to the Chapel of Love to tie the knot. Gears says she's had couples come from forty different states and as far away as Great Britain, Denmark, and Japan. Even though the state of Minnesota usually requires a five-day waiting period for a marriage license, the Chapel of Love staff can help you have that waiting period waived if you're from out of town. Or you can fax the necessary documentation to them ahead of time, and they can get the paperwork started long before you arrive.

The Chapel of Love is open Monday through Saturday 10:00 A.M. *to* 9:30 P.M. *and Sunday* 11:00 A.M. *to* 7:00 P.M., *although hours may vary during the holiday season. To request a brochure and information on getting married at the Chapel of Love, call* 800-299-LOVE *or* 612-854-4656 *or fax* 612-854-4642.

wedding wisdom

"I was born in the tropics, and I love the tropics. Plus, my parents are divorced, and I wanted to find a neutral place where everyone could gather to celebrate my wedding."
Suzanne, married 8/17/96 in the Florida Keys

Exotic Weddings

Finances

Even though Bill and I eloped, we decided to have a full-blown wedding reception on our previously set wedding date and then take a traditional honeymoon as originally planned. What that meant for us, as it does for most couples planning a wedding, was we had to save a good chunk of cash and do it in a short period of time. (We eloped seven months before our previously set wedding date.)

Since Bill used to work as a financial writer, we probably had a leg up on putting down on paper a plan to save what amounted to $12,000 in less than a year. However, cutting down on expenses and getting in the habit of putting away money each week wasn't easy. But I'm proud to say that after seven months of brown bagging it for lunch and forgoing cab rides (we lived in New York City at the time), we met our goal. The greatest feeling ever is having your wedding day over and knowing that you don't owe anyone money. And being able to do that isn't as hard as you think as long as you plan ahead and stick to your money-saving strategy. You, too, can start your new life together debt free.

Saving for the Big Day

Nancy Gorski is a certified financial planner in St. Petersburg, Florida, and author of My Own Money Planner, *a personal diary of financial and legal affairs. Call 941-643-6800 to order it. Gorski understands the challenges many couples face when saving for a wedding and offers advice on how you can successfully save for the big day.*

Nuptials News

The marriage market generates $32 billion in retail sales, according to *Bride's Magazine.*

Anytime you have to do major financial planning, be it saving for a wedding or your first house, you might want to contact a certified financial planner. What he or she can do for you that you might not be able to do for yourself is tell you how much you have to save each month and suggest a program under which you can earn an optimal interest rate for your needs. Work with a certified financial planner only. Anyone can call himself or herself a financial planner, but a certified financial planner is board-certified, just as a doctor is.

For example, if you need to save $15,000 for a wedding but need to do so in a year, you have to choose your options carefully. A mutual fund may have a 10 percent return, on average, but if you start saving in January and there's a market blip in October, you'll lose a portion of the money you've saved. In this situation, it might be wise to use a traditional savings account to hold your money.

A great way to save money painlessly is to have a forced savings plan. Ask your employer to do an automatic payroll deduction and deposit into a savings account. This way each time you get paid, money is being put into your savings account without your having to think about it.

Beyond saving dollars, another great way to meet your financial goal is to pay down your credit card debt. You'd be surprised at how much money people spend trying to pay off their credit cards and how it can drain their ability to save. In fact, if you were to pay the minimum amount due each time you got a credit card statement, it would take you years to pay off your credit card. And you would be incurring interest at a very high rate. Instead, it might be wise to plan ahead and get a debt consolidation loan (if you can't figure out a way to pay off your debt on your own). This way you'll have lower monthly payments and a lower interest rate.

If you find that the time frame you've set for yourself to save for your wedding isn't realistic, then ask your parents or grandparents to loan you money for your wedding. Or put your wedding off so you'll have more time to save.

Using Gift Money Wisely

If you live in a region where wedding guests traditionally give cash or checks instead of china and crystal, here are some ideas from Nancy Gorski on how to use your gift money wisely:

* Put it in an investment program that you can eventually tap into when you buy a house. Remember: a house is one of your biggest assets.

* It's never too early to start planning for retirement. So ear-mark some of the cash for a retirement savings program.

* You should always have enough cash in savings to cover three to four months' worth of expenses. If you haven't already done so, put some of the money in a cash investment program, like a money-market fund, treasury bills, or CDs, so that if you need to access it in an emergency, you can.

A Financial To-Do List for After the Wedding

* Do a spreadsheet that compares each person's medical insurance coverage to see which one fits your needs better.

* Make sure you add your spouse's name to your medical and life insurance policies as soon as you're married.

* If your betrothed isn't already listed as a beneficiary on your life insurance policy, change it now.

* Get a will drawn up.

* Keep credit cards and, if you want, bank accounts in separate names. This way you'll be able to establish or continue having separate lines of credit.

* Figure out how much each of you will contribute to a joint savings account. Don't split the contributions 50/50, but rather take into consideration how much each of you earns.

Sources: Nancy Gorski; David Neikrug, president, The Hakol Benefits Group, an employee-benefits firm in Chicago.

Ways to Save Money on Wedding Planning

Sharon Naylor is author of 1,001 Ways to Save Money and Still Have a Dazzling Wedding *(Contemporary Books, 1993), a book that is chock-full of creative advice on how you can cut your total wedding bill but still have the day of your dreams. Here she shares some of her money-saving tips:*

* Think about altering the size of the wedding and its formality. If you have a less formal luncheon wedding with just your

According to *Bride's Magazine*, the average couple will spend more than $22,000 at retail during their engagement and first year of marriage.

"We are paying for the hotel rooms for our attendants only. We made arrangements with the hotel so that they know that Friday night and Saturday night will be billed to our credit card. If any of the attendants decide to stay longer, he or she will have to pay for the additional night."

Gesa, married 8/30/97

closest friends (versus a full-blown black-tie event on a Saturday night), you probably won't have to do a nine-course meal or feed as many people, and you won't have to worry about tuxedos and other kinds of formalwear.

* The time of year can affect wedding costs. Not surprisingly, weddings in June can be the most expensive. So why not have an October wedding instead?

* Allow yourself plenty of time to plan. That way you can comparison shop and bargain prices down. However, if you give yourself only two or three months to pull together the whole wedding, you won't have enough time to explore all your price options.

* You can save a lot of money by having people in your family do the jobs of professionals—as long as they're very good, of course. For example, if your cousin is a music major in college and has experience performing, you can ask him to play at your ceremony and reception. I had my cousin videotape my wedding, and we had very good results.

* You can get great buys in places where you wouldn't normally think of shopping for wedding attire. I went to a formal-dress shop and found a Jessica McClintock dress that I loved. It looked just like a wedding dress, and best of all, it was marked down to $300 from $1,500. You can also check out sale racks at department stores for great deals.

* Limit the menu at your reception. Instead of having a seafood bar or a Viennese table, which can really run up your bill, opt for a variety of passed-around hors d'oeuvres. Appetizers will cost a lot less if you stick to less expensive varieties. For example, stuffed mushrooms are cheaper than lobster tail.

* Buy your own liquor. You'll avoid any markup from the caterer or reception hall. In addition, don't have an open bar. Limit what's available for people to drink. For example, you can offer wine, champagne, and basic mixed drinks, such as vodka, rum, and fruit juices.

* Don't have children at the reception. There are caterers who will charge you a full per-head fee, even if a three-year-old only took two bites of his roast beef. Make it clear to your guests that you're having an adults-only reception.

* Take advantage of local craft shops to make accessories for your wedding. My aunt made my sister's wedding veil for less than $50. If you have the time, sign up for a craft-making class at one of the stores. You can learn things like how to make your centerpieces, and it can be fun.

* Don't be afraid to ask for volume discounts. When you buy a number of bridesmaid dresses or rent a large amount of tuxedos, see if you can talk the shop owner into giving you 15 percent or 20 percent off the total price. Most business owners are willing to negotiate because they know you can walk out the door and go somewhere else to buy a bridesmaid dress or rent a tuxedo.

Real-Life Money-Saving Tips

One of the first things Rosemary Wyckoff discovered while planning her May 19, 1995, wedding to husband Charlie was that neither her parents nor her future husband's folks were going to pick up the tab for the wedding. Based on that experience, she put together a list of ten wedding-planning rules, which she has given me permission to share with you here.

Rule 1: **This is the nineties.** The first thing you should do upon learning that the majority of your wedding expenses are coming out of your pocket is go immediately to buy a wedding magazine, find the page that says who pays for what, rip it out, and destroy it. While your soon-to-be mother-in-law will say, "I thought your side was supposed to pay for the band," she'll conveniently ignore those same ancient rules that say she should pay for the honeymoon when you ask her to do so.

Rule 2: **Plan ahead.** Simply put, the more time you have to plan, the more time you have to collect some cash. A part-time job stuffing envelopes and automatic payroll deductions into my savings account helped my husband and me finance our wedding.

Rule 3: **Be honest.** Once you've decided how much your dream day will cost, talk to your parents and find out how they might be willing to help. Rather than asking them for a sum of money, suggest they pay for a particular expense. For some reason, asking for $500 to pay for the cake is better than just asking for $500 (they don't know; you might go out and buy yourself a new accordion or something). And if you just ask them to pay for the cake, they'll think you're going to find a six-foot Trump

"Buy a separate date book just to keep track of wedding-related appointments. As you approach the big day, your schedule will get very chaotic, and it helps to have a designated appointment book to refer to."
Wendy, married 11/19/95

Finances

special and spend thousands. Proceed with caution on this one: make sure they understand that agreeing to pay for the cake doesn't mean they get to pick it out.

Rule 4: Be shrewd, not cheap. Don't scrimp on this special event. A little creativity and good advice can save you a fortune. I remember slicing more than $2,000 off my catering budget by having a buffet rather than a sit-down dinner of chicken cordon bleu. My catering cost less than $20 a plate, but many of our guests told me that it was the best food they've had at a wedding. If you can't come up with a creative way to save money, spend it. If you're anything like me, you'll remember how you really wanted roses, not carnations, in your bouquet, even twenty-five years after your wedding day.

Rule 5: Ask around. Talk to everyone you know who has been married in the last couple of years. Look at their pictures, find out who their photographer was, and if you are really good friends, ask how much they paid for their band. The best events are often filled with ideas or variations of ideas borrowed from several different weddings. Don't be afraid to "borrow" ideas, but do try to personalize them (especially if many of the same people will attend your wedding).

Rule 6: Pick a number. Sit down with your future husband and decide (based on your catering options) how many people you can afford to invite to your wedding. Make up the list and stick to it. Don't let anyone tell you that you need to invite someone you've never met. And, more important, don't fall into the "But they'll buy you nice gifts" trap. You'll spend $50 a head for a couple who brings you one of sixteen clocks you'll receive that day. You won't know where to return it because they bought it from a factory outlet store while they were vacationing in North Carolina. Invite people because you want them to witness this special occasion, not because of the gifts they'll bring. This is not a political campaign we're talking about; it's your wedding. If your parents want to play politics (and you don't mind the extra people), they should fork over the funds to invite the extra people.

Rule 7: Be organized. Create an itinerary for the day of your rehearsal and the day of the wedding, literally minute by minute. Give one to everyone you are depending on that day: the photographer, the florist, the baker, the videographer, your families, the bridal party, the caterer, your band or deejay—aw, heck, give one to Aunt Pearl, who is supposed to hand out the programs (she's always late on Easter; why should this day be any different?). It's not that you will remember that you were supposed to have your first dance between 4:07 and 4:12 P.M., but that's the point. Your band will remember and so will your caterer. This way, you won't end up tossing the bouquet while the deejay plays "Daddy's Little Girl."

Rule 8: Love your photographer. Believe it or not, this can make or break the entire day. Tell your photographer exactly what you want and when you want it. There's nothing like being pulled away with a mouthful of imported cheese to be told it's time to pose for a photo with Grandma Simmons. I've seen one too many bridal couples show up forty-five minutes late to the reception because the photographer took too long taking photos at the gazebo. If the photographer is not crystal clear on what your expectations are, it will throw off the entire day. I know getting the best shots for the album is important, but it's certainly not worth ruining the event.

Rule 9: Have fun. Don't let last-minute details throw you off. Just try to enjoy your day. If you start to feel stressed, think honeymoon.

Rule 10: What are you doing? In all the chaos, it is easy to lose sight of the day's purpose. You and your fiancé are pulling together the people you love to witness this important occasion—the day you commit to spend the rest of your lives together. You are starting a new life together, a life filled with love, fun, and happiness. Whatever you do, don't let the details allow you to forget about the partnership you are about to enter. That's more important than any wedding-planning decision or detail you'll encounter.

Flowers

*A*fter I got engaged and started buying bridal magazines religiously, I found myself being mesmerized by all the pages of gorgeously photographed flowers. Forget dresses—I found myself daydreaming of cascading bouquets of white roses and calla lily centerpieces. There truly is nothing prettier than a bunch of beautifully arranged flowers.

Finding a florist who can make your dreams a reality is a huge task, so it's important to know what kinds of questions to ask, what to look for in a well-run business, and how to understand the nature of flowers. Do your research ahead of time, and I'm sure you'll end up with gorgeous flowers.

Finding a Fabulous Florist

As with any other vendor you hire for your wedding day, you'll want to use recommendations from friends and family when finding a florist. If you attend a wedding or an event and see flowers that you think are out of this world, don't be afraid to ask the hosts who they used.

One of the first things you need to talk to a potential florist about is your budget. This way the florist can direct you to the kinds of flowers that would fit your spending goals. "Daisies and carnations are in a whole different price range than roses and lilies," says Maryetta Bartlett, a third-generation owner of Bartlett Florist in Clifton, New Jersey. "I'm flexible enough to work within anyone's budget." Make sure the florist you hire is, too.

A good florist should have a separate area in his or her shop where the two of you can sit and discuss your specific wants and

Nuptials News

Flowers constitute nearly 5 percent of the average wedding budget, says the Association of Bridal Consultants.

desires. You shouldn't have to talk over a busy store counter or be distracted by ringing phones. "I usually make my appointments with brides in the evening when the shop is closed, so I can give them lots of attention," adds Bartlett. If a shop owner can't fit you in during business hours, don't be shy about asking to meet with him or her after hours. However, visiting the store during the day is important. You want to get a sense of how smoothly things run and how the shop treats customers.

When you sit down with a florist, right off-the-bat the florist should ask you about the dress you're wearing and the color of your bridesmaid dresses. It's a good idea to take along a photograph if you have one or a swatch of fabric. A florist who has experience doing weddings may even ask about your wedding colors during your initial phone conversation. Then when you come into the shop, he or she may have a couple of floral arrangements made to give you an idea of what he or she might make for your wedding. "These samples are made even before the bride puts any money down," says Bartlett. A reputable florist won't make you pay a special fee for any samples made for you. If the florist doesn't make a sample, he or she should at least show you photographs of the flowers from weddings the shop has handled previously.

During this initial meeting, you should take a walk around the store. Take notice of the quality of blooms in the refrigerators (are they all dying or do they look vibrant?) and how organized and neat the shop looks. In addition, tune in to your gut feelings about this person. Ask yourself, "Is the florist listening to me when I talk?" and "Does the florist understand the look I want?"

A good florist not only will take your preferences into consideration but also guide you to the best flower choices for the season. "Certain types of flowers are more readily available—and therefore more affordable—at certain times of the year," Bartlett says. "The seasonal flowers will have a higher lasting quality and a better color intensity due to the weather." Many brides make the mistake of taking tear sheets from magazines with them to their meeting with the florist. This approach may work when buying a dress, but it isn't appropriate when shopping for flowers. These pictures can give the florist a good idea of the style of bouquet or centerpiece you want, but they don't help with actual flower selection. "Brides forget that these pictures were shot months before the magazine was published," says Bartlett. "They often ask me about flowers that won't be in season when they're getting married."

Besides finding flowers to fit the season, a florist should help you find a bouquet that's perfect for you. This is where the photograph of your dress and swatch of fabric come into play. "If a dress has a full skirt that's very decorative, you don't want to cover it up with a cascading bouquet," she says. Ideally, the florist should also take into consideration your veil or headpiece when creating a bouquet. In addition, if you're very short, you may look overwhelmed with a huge cascading bouquet, so the florist should design an arrangement that's more in scale with your size.

A florist should also talk to you about your bridesmaid bouquets, any boutonnieres or corsages you want, centerpieces for the reception, and how you want to decorate the ceremony site. Adds Bartlett, "We do everything from aisle runners to bows on the pews at the church."

Before you sign on the dotted line with a florist, ask how many other events the florist is doing on the day of your wedding. "Florists can handle only so many weddings per day," Bartlett says. "I will service only one wedding per day, but that's how I run my shop. Other florists may be different." You may want to steer clear of a florist who you think is juggling too many jobs at once. Such a florist may let something slip through the cracks, and it could be something for your wedding.

Have all of the details of your agreement spelled out in a contract, including what time the flowers will be delivered to the church and, in the event that your first-choice flowers aren't available, what kind of flowers the florist will substitute.

Once you've hired the florist, expect to have two or three more in-person consultations. Then expect to speak with the florist over the telephone to discuss when to deliver the flowers and how many centerpieces you'll need (once all your response cards are returned, of course) and to deliver swatches of fabric from the mothers' dresses so the florist can make corsages that match.

Maryetta Bartlett holds a bachelor of science degree in ornamental horticulture, and she studied floral design in The Netherlands. You can reach her at 201-471-6480.

Important Questions to Ask a Florist

Do you specialize in weddings? Florists who do weddings know that it's better to buy fresh blooms for an arrangement and are less likely to use a flower that's been sitting in the shop for days.

Are you licensed? Not all states have licensed florists, but if yours does, make sure an up-to-date license is displayed in any flower shop you visit.

Flowers

"We used a friend as a florist, who did a great job at a cheap price. I had silk roses and ivy in bright colors in a large cascading bouquet. The bridesmaids' bouquets were smaller versions of mine. Everyone loved the flowers."

Jacinda, married 7/1/95

Do you have proper cooling devices? You'll know the answer to this by the kinds of walk-in refrigeration rooms the shop has. If the flowers in it look alive and healthy, then the shop's cooling devices are probably OK. Avoid someone who works out of the house. Such a florist may keep flowers cool by closing off a room and air-conditioning it, but that's not a sufficient cooling system to keep flowers looking good.

Do you have references I can call? You can hear firsthand from another bride how well this florist delivered.

Do you have pictures of work you've done for other weddings? This will help give you a sense of the different kinds of arrangements this florist has done in the past. It may also help you decide what you like—and don't like—about this person's work.

Are you familiar with the location where I'm having my ceremony and reception? If not, will you go visit it? It's not too much to ask a florist to visit a place where he or she has never worked before. If the florist refuses to go without any money down, find someone else.

Source: Karen Brown, wedding designer and owner of Memories in Bloom, Houston, 713-556-5200.

Flowers of the Month

Certain flowers are more readily available at certain times of the year than others. Knowing this ahead of time will help you choose flowers that will be fresher and more affordable for your wedding.

Here are the flowers of the month, according to 1-800-FLOWERS.

January	carnation
February	tulip
March	iris
April	liatris
May	hybrid lily
June	rose
July	larkspur
August	gladiola
September	snapdragon
October	gerbera daisy
November	mum
December	dendrobium orchid

Do-It-Yourself Floral Centerpieces

There's no hard-and-fast rule that says you have to hire a florist to make your centerpieces for you. If you or someone you know is a gardener, a great way to have a hands-on involvement in your floral centerpieces is to make them yourself. For example, having a cluster of potted flowers can be a gorgeous way to decorate your reception tables. Even better, the plants themselves make a great take-home gift that your guests can plant in their own backyards.

Your best resource for flowers, potting soil, and pots is a home-improvement store like Home Depot, which has more than five hundred stores in thirty-seven states. Before you decide which flowers you want in your centerpieces, find out what varieties are viable at the time of your wedding. "You can't get annuals in the fall, but you can find lovely chrysanthemums and azaleas," says Diane Schanck, a sales associate in the garden department at Home Depot in Taylor, Michigan. For a Christmas wedding, you could get miniature Norfolk pines or baskets of Christmas cactus. In the summer, your options include petunias and impatiens.

Schanck says she can special-order flowers so that they arrive fresh in the store for you. If you don't feel like getting your fingers dirty and you give her enough time, she can do all the potting for you. "If you buy the plants, pots, and soil, we'll do it for you at no extra cost," she says.

For those who like to dig in the dirt, Schanck suggests ordering the flowers at least four days before you'll be doing the transplanting. Then transplant the flowers a day or so before your wedding and store them in a cool place until the big day. "The less you mess with them the day before," adds Schanck, "the better the flowers will look for the wedding."

Guest List

*D*etermining who Bill and I were going to invite to our wedding became a much harder task than we ever expected. Etiquette says that because we were planning on paying for the whole thing, we should have had final say as to who was or was not to be invited. But in the real world, that line of thinking does not fly—mostly because parents have very definite opinions about the friends they want to invite to their children's wedding.

In our case, our parents expected that they would be able to invite whichever friends and business associates they chose. Not long after we announced our engagement, each of them handed us a list of people he or she wanted to invite. In addition, Bill and I originally wanted to keep the guest list limited to immediate family, but soon we realized that by inviting one cousin, you had to invite them all. Add to that the fact that since we eventually decided to have the party in my grandfather's backyard, he added his two cents as to who he thought should be invited. Before long, our guest list was approaching three hundred people.

Finally Bill and I realized that our wedding would be a once-in-a-lifetime event. We threw caution to the wind and invited everyone we were told to invite but with this caveat for our parents: if the person you've asked to invite attends, you need to pay for him or her. That seemed fair all around, and our guest list was written without a major fight ensuing. On the day of our wedding celebration, about 150 people showed up. And as a gift to our parents, we ended up picking up the tab for all of their friends who attended.

wedding wisdom

"The original idea was to have about one hundred people. Then the list went up to two hundred. By the time the invitations were mailed, the guest list was over three hundred! We should have put our foot down at 175 and been done with it!"

Amy, married 8/3/96

Putting Together the Guest List

Recently, I spoke with Joyce Scardina Becker, president of Events of Distinction, a San Francisco event-planning company, about how to put a wedding guest list together. Becker is an expert in this area. She has planned weddings and other special events where guest lists have ranged from a few dozen to a few thousand people.

LI: *What do you need to keep in mind when putting together your wedding guest list?*

JSB: First of all, you need to remember that the size of your guest list and who you invite will greatly affect what site you choose for your ceremony and reception. That's why it's so important to have a good sense ahead of time who your guests will be. For example, if you'll be inviting a lot of elderly people, you would never choose a Victorian mansion without an elevator for your wedding.

Very often your budget and the kind of affair you want to have will affect your guest list as well. Here in San Francisco, wedding receptions can easily cost $150 a head and up. If you want a lavish event with a full bar and a four-course dinner, you might need to keep your guest list limited, especially if you're going to be paying those kinds of prices. Or you could figure out a way to reduce your per-head costs so you can double the number of your guests.

LI: *How can you determine whom you should invite to your wedding?*

JSB: Besides close relatives, you should invite close friends with whom you've had a substantial relationship. If you have a new roommate or recent friend from work whom you've only known a short time, then I wouldn't feel obligated to invite him or her—unless you can afford to do so.

LI: *What about friends from college?*

JSB: If you are a younger couple who have recently graduated from college, you may find that all your fraternity buddies and sorority sisters start lobbying to be invited to the wedding. For them, it's a social event, and if they're not married or dating anyone, it becomes a great place to meet other single people. You have to figure out which of these college friends is most important to you and invite them only.

LI: *How can you make your parents happy with your guest list?*

JSB: If you are paying for the wedding yourselves, you might not include your parents' friends on the guest list. Instead, you might just invite your own friends and close relatives. However, you should keep in mind that a wedding is a tremendous celebration in the lives of both families, and there is a very valid reason that your parents may want their friends to join in the celebration.

The best way to avoid any problems with the guest list is to be generous. Sit down with both sets of parents and let them know that you would like to include their friends at your wedding. Ask them to ask themselves this question: Who are the most important people in our lives since our son or daughter was born? They may also include people from whom they've had reciprocal invitations, such as the friend whose child's wedding they attended or whose house they go to for dinner on a regular basis.

If you are paying for your wedding yourself, it's not too much to ask your parents to pick up the tab for the people they invite. Or you can ask them to make a general financial contribution so inviting these extra people won't be a financial burden for you.

LI: *What if your parents are paying for the wedding?*

JSB: If your parents are paying for the wedding, then they should have a say in who gets invited. For example, your parents who are involved in business relationships may believe that it's completely appropriate to invite their business associates to your wedding. Usually, the younger the bride and groom, the more likely it is that their parents will pay for the wedding.

LI: *Who else do you need to consider adding to the guest list?*

JSB: I believe you should invite the rabbi or minister to celebrate with you at the reception. In addition, you should be prepared to offer your vendors, such as the photographer, bandleader, and videographer, a staff meal.

LI: *What are A- and B-lists and where do they come into play?*

JSB: You may find it necessary to put together two lists of guests, especially if you committed beforehand to a certain number of people attending your reception. If not enough people from your original guest list, or A-list, respond, you'll need to fill the empty seats somehow so you're not paying for wasted food. Usually, the B-list comprises work associates and extended family.

"Nothing caused more angst for us than whittling our guest list down to a manageable number for our wedding, which we were paying for entirely. Our budget—and my preference—called for a 'small' wedding of 150 of our nearest and dearest friends. It was really tough, but eventually we came up with a list of who we wanted to invite. We allowed our parents an additional table of ten above and beyond that list so they could invite anyone they wanted who hadn't made the first cut."
Carreen, married 11/26/93

Guest List

The average number of wedding guests at an affair is 171, according to *Bride's Magazine*.

LI: *How should you handle your invitations if you decide to have two guest lists?*

JSB: Instead of following the old rule of sending out invitations four weeks before the affair, you should mail your A-list invitations at least eight weeks beforehand. Then mail out B-list invitations once the response date has passed. In addition, to avoid insulting anyone, you should have two response cards with two separate dates. That way someone on the B-list won't receive an invitation on which the response date has already come and gone. This has been known to happen, and it tells the guest straight out that he or she wasn't a first choice to be invited to the wedding.

LI: *Let's say you get your guest list settled and you decide to invite two hundred people. Can you expect all two hundred to show up?*

JSB: No. You should expect an 80 percent return. That means that 20 percent probably won't make it. That's why when you select a ceremony and reception site, it's important to keep in mind the number of guests you believe will *attend* your wedding, not how many you've *invited*.

Inviting Work Associates to Your Wedding

Marjorie Brody is president of Brody Communications, Limited, an Elkins Park, Pennsylvania–based business that specializes in business communications training. She is also a noted etiquette expert and author of Complete Business Etiquette Handbook *(Prentice Hall, 1995). Here she offers her tips for inviting (or not inviting) work associates to your wedding.*

* If you're friendly with only a few people at work, invite only those individuals. Be sure to ask them not to talk about your wedding at work, so you avoid offending anyone you didn't invite.

* If you have a group of people you work with, invite them all. It's better not to leave someone out.

* Don't try to include your work associates by inviting them to the ceremony only. That's rude. Someone who is invited to your wedding is invited to attend both the ceremony and reception.

* If you believe there will be long-term consequences of not inviting your boss to the wedding, invite him or her as well.

* If financial constraints prevent you from inviting anyone from work, be up front about your limitations. Tell your colleagues that you can't afford to invite anyone outside of immediate family and that you're being honest because you didn't want to hurt anyone's feelings. Most people will understand and appreciate your honesty.

Hair

Because I knew that I would be wearing a hat at our wedding celebration, I didn't bother to hire a hairstylist to do my hair. I figured, why bother paying someone to make my hair look gorgeous if it's going to be under a hat all day? In hindsight, I wish I had had a stylist do *something* to it. About halfway through our outdoor brunch, the weather became hazy, hot, and humid. My naturally curly hair started flipping this way and that. I tried to brush it straight so that the hair you could see under my hat wouldn't look wild and out of control, but I finally gave up hope and let Mother Nature do what she wished with my hair.

Even though it is usually the women of the wedding who worry about their hair, men should put some thought into it as well. Bill made the age-old mistake of getting a haircut the day before our brunch. Unfortunately, his regular barber wasn't available, and the guy who cut his hair took a little bit too much off. Because Bill didn't allow himself a week or two for his haircut to grow in and adjust, unfortunately now in all of our wedding pictures his hair is standing on end and looking not exactly as it should have for a formal event. Oh well, live and learn.

Wedding-Day Hair

Michelle Vincent is a stylist with Jacobson's Styling Salon in Ann Arbor, Michigan. She has been creating wonderful wedding-day hair for the past twenty-one years. Allure *magazine recently named Vincent one of America's hottest hairstylists. As she trimmed my hair, I asked for her advice on finding someone to do your wedding-day*

hair. If you're interested in hiring her to do your wedding-day hair, call 313-665-6111.

LI: *Why is it important to have someone do your hair professionally on your wedding day rather than doing it yourself?*

MV: You can do it yourself if you're really nervous and don't feel that you can trust someone to do it for you. But if you have a special look in mind, which most women do, then the best bet is to seek professional help.

We always suggest that before your wedding you have one or more dry runs with your hairstyles. That way you have a chance to get used to how it looks, and you can determine how long it's going to take to do your hair on your wedding day. Find a stylist who is going to experiment with a few different looks. If you want to wear your hair down, let the stylist play with it that way. If you want it up, let him or her try a few styles on you.

LI: *What advice would you give about finding a hairstylist to do your wedding?*

MV: If you find a stylist that you really like, stick with that stylist. If you go to a wedding and like the way the women's hair looked, find out who did their hair. Many times future brides will call us based on the work we did for a wedding they attended. We recommend that you come in, try us out, get a cut, and see how you like us. But you don't even have to go as far as having the new stylist cut your hair. We've had many brides come in who had us try out some hairstyles on them, and they hired us for the wedding based on that one experience. We were able to give them the style they were looking for, and that's why they hired us.

LI: *What sort of questions would a good stylist ask during that initial consultation?*

MV: The stylist should ask you for a photograph of the gown or, even better, a photograph of you in the gown, so he or she can get an idea of how you're going to look that day. For example, a dress with a high collar or long sleeves can radically affect the kind of hairstyles you might choose. The stylist should also ask you if you have any set ideas about your hairstyle.

LI: *What questions should you ask the stylist?*

MV: Just what styles the stylist would suggest and for his or her opinion. It's very important for the stylist to be honest about what styles he or she thinks will look good on you—and which won't.

LI: *At what point should you bring a stylist into the plans?*

MV: If you have a stylist whom you're comfortable with or if the store where you're buying your gown has a stylist on staff, it might be a good idea to have that stylist come in at the point of sale when you buy the gown and before you buy the veil. You don't have to hire this person to do your hair, but it might be helpful to have him or her help you choose a veil style that is right for your hair, face, and dress, and the hairstyle you want to wear on your wedding day. Oftentimes there are changes that are affected by the hairstylist's input. You may discover that the kind of veil that you liked on the rack isn't right for your face shape or for your hair length.

Here's a real-life example of how a hairstylist can work with a bride. I had been recommended to one bride by a friend. About six months before her wedding, she started coming to me to get her hair cut. That gave her the chance to get to know me and feel comfortable with my work. Then about two months before her wedding, she asked me if I'd do her hair for the wedding, and I agreed. So a few weeks later, she brought in her headpiece, and we tried out a few hairstyles. The next time she came in, we acted as if it were the day of the wedding and did a full dry run. I washed her hair, trimmed it as necessary, blew it dry, then put her headpiece on, and fixed her hair as it would look on the day of her wedding. Luckily, she'd chosen a headpiece that looked good on her, and our appointments together gave us the chance to find a style that looked perfect with her headpiece.

LI: *Why is it important not to get a new haircut the week of or the day before your wedding?*

MV: Don't do anything drastic the week before your wedding, because you don't want to take any chances that the end result will be a disaster. Besides, you need two to three weeks to settle into a new style, or you need a week or two for your hair to settle into a new haircut.

LI: *What if you color your hair?*

MV: If you color your hair, have your new color done about two weeks before the wedding. If you're only having a tint touch-up on your roots, then you can have that done the week of or a few days before your wedding. You want your color to look as fresh as possible.

LI: *Should you get photographed after your dry run to get used to your style?*

MV: If you're the kind of person who needs that visual reinforcement, then, yes, I would recommend that you have photographs taken of you with your new hairstyle. Oftentimes, we'll just use the store's Polaroid camera and then let the bride look at the style for a couple of days so she can decide whether she likes it or not. Some brides sort of freak out when they see their finished hair, because here they are sitting in jeans and a sweatshirt and their formal-looking hair looks silly with their casual clothes. If you have your wedding-day jewelry chosen already, you should bring it with you so you can try it on with your hairstyle. In addition, if you're hiring someone to do your makeup, you might want to schedule a practice run with the makeup artist so that it coincides with your practice run with the stylist. That way, you can get a more realistic idea of what you're going to look like on your wedding day.

You might take advantage of the dry run session by going to have your formal portrait done right after the session. What's great about that is you can see the results of your portrait long before the wedding, and it gives you time to decide if you want to make any changes to your hairstyle before the wedding day.

LI: *What should you expect on the day of the wedding if you hire a professional to do your hair?*

MV: First of all, you need to determine ahead of time at what time the stylist will arrive to do the hair and where he or she is going to go to do this. I've gone to the bride's home to do everyone's hair, and I've had them all come to the salon. Sometimes it's really fun when everyone comes to the salon. It can be more of a party atmosphere, which might actually relax you.

You have to remember that you are the last one to have her hair done. That's so you look the freshest when you take your first step down the aisle. Because you're the last one to have her hair done, you can socialize with your attendants and just have fun.

LI: *How much time should you expect the stylist to spend with you on the day of your wedding?*

MV: The stylist should spend at least an hour with you and about thirty minutes to forty-five minutes for each attendant.

LI: *How is the stylist's fee based?*

MV: It depends on the house prices—that is, what the salon charges for the services. However, if I go someplace else to do hair, I charge a higher fee. It's usually an increase of about $10 or $15 per head. If I have to drive a long distance to do the hair, I'll usually tack on a travel fee as well. If I spend time at the church or with the bride throughout the day, I'll charge an hourly fee or we'll work out a flat fee ahead of time. It's very important to discuss all the fees long before the wedding day so you'll know how much you're going to spend for the stylist's services. A good stylist will begin quoting you prices at that first practice session.

LI: *Is a tip included in your fee?*

MV: No. A tip tells me how I've served you. If you like what I've done, let me know with a tip. I've done weddings where they've tipped generously. A lot of people pay for everything in advance—including the tip—so that on the day of, they don't have to be bothered thinking about such mundane tasks as writing the hairstylist a check.

Hairdos and Don'ts

Here, Michelle Vincent offers her dos and don'ts for wedding-day hair.

Do eat before you go to the stylist. I don't want you to faint. It has happened.

Do remember to confirm your appointment in advance. Most salons confirm twenty-four hours in advance, but if you don't hear from them, you should call and confirm the appointment yourself.

Do get in writing the services your hairstylist will provide and what time he or she will show up—especially if he or she is coming to your home.

Do create a written schedule for your bridesmaids, especially if they're supposed to be at a salon or your house at a certain time to get their hair and makeup done.

Don't leave angry and go home and do your own hair. You should get your money's worth. If you don't like your hair, you should ask the stylist to give it another round. That's why it's important to go for a practice session so you know you'll get the hairstyle you want on the day of your wedding. You want to feel confident that the stylist will come through for you.

Don't feel that you have to stay with a stylist just because he or she is the person who cuts your hair or whom your best friend recommended. If you don't think a stylist can deliver for you on your wedding day, don't hire him or her. When in doubt, find someone else.

Hair to Die For

Jan Larkey, author of Flatter Your Figure *(Fireside, 1991), applies her figure-flattering tips to help you find a great hairstyle on your wedding day.*

- Bangs that create a horizontal line across the forehead can shorten a very round face or wide face and actually make you look heavier. On the other hand, they can enhance a long face by making it appear shorter. Therefore, think twice about bangs—especially if you have a round or wide face.

- If you have a short or round face, give your face some lift by showing your forehead. Or keep the sides of your hair flat while adding height to the crown of your head.

- Hair that is soft and curly and sits on the shoulders can look feminine and alluring.

- If you want to elongate your neck, wear your hair up.

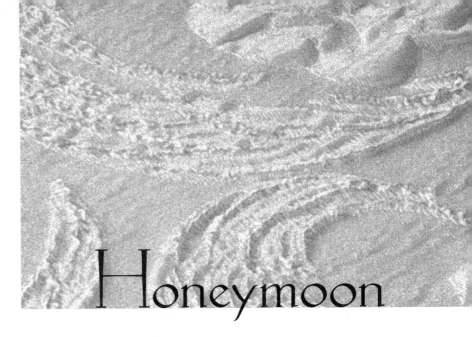

Honeymoon

The worst thing that could possibly happen did right before Bill and I left for our honeymoon—I lost our plane tickets. However, this wasn't discovered until just before we were to get into the car and drive to the airport hotel, where we would be sleeping the night before our 6:00 A.M. flight to the Caribbean. Luckily, we would be driving through our neighborhood on the way to the airport, so we stopped off at our apartment and searched high and low for the tickets. They were nowhere to be found.

We called the airline and discovered that we wouldn't have any problem getting on our scheduled flight; the airline would just charge us $100 to reissue the tickets. As ridiculous as we found that policy, what were we going to do? Not go on our honeymoon? So we continued on to the airport hotel, where we spent a fitful night going over in our minds where those damn tickets could be. The next morning, after getting our new set of tickets, we boarded the plane, exhausted but very much looking forward to our weeklong sojourn to St. Croix. We hoped our honeymoon would be a week of playing golf or sitting on the beach by day and drinking rum punch by night.

I guess ours was the Murphy's Law honeymoon, because when we landed in St. Croix, most of our bags didn't. Instead of being whisked off to our beachfront suite, we spent the first day of our honeymoon in the airport trying to figure out where our bags ended up. As dusk approached we finally decided to call it a day and head over to the resort. We had the airline's promise that if the bags didn't show up within twenty-four hours of our flight's landing, they would reimburse us for any money we spent replenishing our wardrobe and toiletries. Desperate for a change of clothing and a toothbrush,

Nuptials News

The average amount spent on a honeymoon is $2,964, according to *Bride's Magazine*.

83

According to *Bride's Magazine*, the following five places are the most popular honeymoon destinations:
Caribbean
Mexico
Hawaii
Florida
The Islands of the Bahamas

we went on a shopping spree at the resort clothing store and were able to change into new clothing by the time dinner was served.

Our bags, including our golf clubs, didn't arrive until late the next day, which prevented us from playing that first round of golf we'd been waiting to play. But from then on, our honeymoon was perfect. One day, my golf score beat Bill's, and I danced all the way back to the pro shop. Another evening, we took a sunset dinner cruise around St. Croix. Most days we relaxed and enjoyed our stay in the tropical paradise, and when it was time to head back home, we were tanned, rested, and relaxed—exactly as one should be after a honeymoon.

By the way, we eventually discovered our lost plane tickets. When we moved to Michigan a few weeks later, we found them behind our desk. They had fallen off and become wedged in a floorboard. We had a good laugh when we found them.

Deciding on a Honeymoon Destination

When it comes time to figure out what you want to do and where you want to go on your honeymoon, you shouldn't just spin a globe, close your eyes, and see where your finger lands. Instead, you and your future spouse should begin researching your honeymoon by jotting down a few items on a piece of paper.

First you need to find out what your likes and dislikes are. Here are some questions to ask yourselves: Where have you traveled to before? Where have you always wanted to go? Do you like the beach or do you prefer to spend a vacation skiing? It's best for you both to weigh what's important to you in a vacation, which will help you narrow down where you want to go or what kind of honeymoon you want to take. For example, if you decide that you would like to see a lot of islands on your honeymoon but you can't afford to stay at five different resorts on five different islands, then maybe a cruise is better for you.

A seasoned professional, namely a travel agent, can help you sift through this information and assist you in making the best honeymoon decision. Make an appointment with a travel agent about a year before your wedding. It's not uncommon for popular honeymoon destinations to be booked six to nine months ahead of time.

Besides your travel preferences, one of the most important factors affecting your honeymoon decision is your budget. Travel agents often liken deciding on which honeymoon you'd really like to take to buying a home. You tell the travel agent what your dream honeymoon would be, he or she tells you how much it will cost, and then you narrow it down until you find the trip you're happy with.

What's great about a travel agent is he or she can help you discover ways to cut costs on your honeymoon without compromising the quality of the trip. For example, he or she may suggest you go to that top-of-the-line resort but just not stay in the best room. Or instead of flying first-class, you go coach.

Another big consideration for newlyweds is how their money is going to be spent. If your budget for a honeymoon is $5,000, do you want to earmark some of it for airfare, another portion for hotel, and still another part of it for incidental expenses? Or would you enjoy your honeymoon more if everything was paid for up front and you never had to reach into your pocket while you were away? "This is the appeal of all-inclusive resorts," suggests Beatrice York-Blitzer who, with Myrna Ingram, is co-owner of Empress Travel in Wet Hills–Huntington, New York.

Some couples have the freedom of taking two weeks or longer to enjoy their honeymoon. Others have only a week's worth of vacation time. How much time you have to travel will also affect any honeymoon decision you make. For example, a couple living in New York who can take a weeklong honeymoon may find it's not in their best interest to select a Hawaiian honeymoon. "You'll lose about two days in travel time," says Ingram, "and a good travel agent will point this out. He or she should tell you the pros and cons of each destination you're considering."

A good travel agent will send you away from your first meeting together with a handful of brochures to study and possibly videos as well. If the agent doesn't have videos on hand, he or she may suggest that you go to the local library and check some out.

After your initial consultation with your travel agent, you can do the rest of your honeymoon planning over the phone. It make take two or more telephone conversations to hammer out all the details. However, once you decide on a destination, be prepared to start paying for your honeymoon. "Most tour operators or hotels want a deposit within seven days of a booking," says York-Blitzer, "and some airlines make you pay for the entire ticket within twenty-four hours of making a reservation." Deposits can range from $25 to $1,000, depending on the company you use. Then, at least sixty days before your departure date, you'll have to pay the entire balance for the trip. (During blackout periods, holidays, and high season, which is December to mid-April in the Caribbean, you may have to pay in full ninety days before departure.) If you won't have

Nuptials News

The average length of a honeymoon trip is eight days, according to *Bride's Magazine*.

the cash on hand, you can use a credit card to pay for your honeymoon. Not only will this help spread your payments out, but also some credit cards offer travel insurance.

Travel agents offer travel insurance as well, and York-Blitzer and Ingram highly recommend it to all their clients. "We just had a couple where the grandmother went into a coma on the day of the wedding, and they had to cut their honeymoon short because of the funeral," Ingram recalls. Luckily, the couple had purchased insurance. That means that whenever it is convenient for them, they will be able to take the remainder of their honeymoon at no additional charge to them. The only catch to travel insurance is it must be purchased at the time a deposit is paid.

Besides booking honeymoons, York-Blitzer and Ingram offer a honeymoon registry to help couples collect cash to cover their honeymoon expenses. For more information on the registry or to book a trip with them, call 800-291-3313.

Empress Travel's Tips for Finding a Trustworthy Travel Agent

* You should get a good feeling when you talk to your travel agent. The office should be organized and neat, and you should be treated politely.

* An agent isn't going to know answers to every question you ask, but he or she shouldn't brush off your questions either. If you ask the agent something he or she is not familiar with, make sure he or she gets back to you within seventy-two hours with a reasonable answer.

* Don't hire someone who works out of his or her home. You want someone who is affiliated with an agency and who is a member of an organization like the American Society of Travel Agents (ASTA).

* Find out if the agency has insurance that will cover you if an airline goes belly-up or a resort goes out of business.

Registering for a Honeymoon

More and more travel agencies are offering honeymoon registries as an alternative to traditional registries. This newfangled registry option makes a lot of sense if registering for china and silver isn't your cup of tea. Here, Larry Maloney, president of Forbes Travel in Pittsburgh, offers a few reasons for choosing a honeymoon registry:

* If you have a hard time deciding what you need for your household, let yourselves off the hook by registering for a honeymoon.
* By registering for a honeymoon, you can take a honeymoon that you might not have been able to afford otherwise.
* It's easy to work with a travel agent long-distance. You can register for your honeymoon and make your travel plans over the phone.

For more information about Forbes Travel's honeymoon registry, call 800-345-2984.

Internet Resources

When I got married, in 1992, I had never seen a modem, and I had no idea what the Internet was. Today, the Internet is mentioned in most news reports and daily conversations among friends and work colleagues. Writing E-mail is as common as making telephone calls, and when we refer to the Web, most people realize we're not talking about spiders.

Today, the Internet with its endless wedding-planning resources can be a bride and groom's best friend. With a mouse and modem, you can find information on everything from deejays to displays of wedding gowns. There are newsgroups dedicated exclusively to wedding planning on which you can post messages for other engaged couples and exchange ideas and inspirations for making your wedding festive and creative. There are thousands of World Wide Web sites dedicated to weddings, too. Not surprisingly, there is a lot of junk on the Internet as well. But if you use your search engines wisely, you can find some great Internet resources to make your wedding day perfect.

Surfing the Internet

Carl White is the creator of Way Cool Weddings, a website that features a different, unique wedding website each week. Besides working on Way Cool Weddings, White is a multimedia designer for a Philadelphia firm. Here he offers his advice for using the Internet to your wedding-planning advantage.

wedding wisdom

"I got tons of helpful hints and advice from the newsgroups as well as the wedding pages. Now I have my own links to websites I found helpful."
Amy, married 8/3/96

You can find anything about weddings on the Internet—from ideas on how to propose to information about store registries, such as JCPenney. You'll find the most thoroughly and visually enticing information on the World Wide Web, part of the Internet.

Of the wedding-related sites on the Web, most are commercial sites. That means that they were set up by a company that wants to get your business. In my opinion, it's best to stick with sites that have been set up by regular people. They can be very helpful, and if you ask them questions, most of these people will go out of their way to help you.

The best way to find websites that will interest you is to use a search engine. What a search engine does is scan pages of all websites looking for the word or series of words that you requested. For example, if you requested *wedding photographers in pennsylvania*, the search engine will look for and find all the websites that contain these words. Once the search is complete, it will create a list of the sites that fit the criteria. This list will usually include a brief description of the websites and a direct link to them. That is, one word in the description of each site will be underlined, printed in a different color, or both. If you click your mouse on that line, you'll be connected directly to that website's *home page*, the opening page of the website. A home page is sort of like a book's table of contents, because it tells you everything that's available at that site.

There are a number of search engines available. If you access the World Wide Web from a commercial on-line service, they may suggest a specific search engine for you to use, but you don't have to do that. Instead, if you know the Web address of the search engine you like best, you can type it in, go to that site, and search from there.

There are four search engines worth mentioning (note that all World Wide Web addresses start with *http://*).

Excite—http://www.excite.com
Yahoo—http://www.yahoo.com
Webcrawler—http://webcrawler.com
Alta Vista—http://www.altavista.digital.com

Currently there are about seven thousand websites related to weddings, and that number is growing every day. For that reason alone, you'll want to make your searches as specific as possible. For example, if you're searching for information on engagement and wedding rings, don't just search for the word *ring*. Type all three words. The more specific you can be, the better targeted your results will be.

Most search engines are not case-sensitive. What that means is if you want to search for honeymoon information and you don't capitalize proper names, such as *bermuda* or *florida*, the search engine will still find all the links to information on Bermuda and Florida.

Besides the World Wide Web, the Usenet newsgroups on the Internet can be a gold mine of wedding information. There are two newsgroups in particular of interest to engaged couples. They are

soc.couples.wedding
alt.wedding

Both were created by "real people" after they realized there was a dearth of wedding information available on the Internet.

Unlike websites, newsgroups are not interactive in real time. Instead, they act like a bulletin board. You write your message and then post it on the newsgroups' bulletin board. Then someone responds and posts a message next to yours. However, the soc.couples.wedding newsgroup has a website that includes FAQs (frequently asked questions, which were created to avoid duplicate postings) plus links to sites the creator finds interesting. The website for soc.couples.wedding is http://www.wam.umd.edu/~sek/wedding.html.

Recent *threads*, or lines of discussion, on both the alt.wedding and soc.couples.wedding newsgroups have ranged from What's on Your Don't-Play Music List? to Where Do I Find White Birkenstocks to Wear with My Wedding Dress? to How Much Should I Spend for a Photographer? Literally hundreds of messages are posted each day on these newsgroups. Most brides- and grooms-to-be find that a question posted in the morning will often have a handful of replies by the afternoon. Besides engaged couples, many newlyweds and not-so newlyweds read the newsgroups, so you can benefit from the experience of a range of people.

Way Cool Weddings

When Carl White and Kimberly McGowan were planning their September 1995 wedding, they decided to take advantage of the Internet to communicate with their guests. For starters, they gave guests the option of responding to their wedding invitations by E-mail. "Of our three hundred invited guests, nearly 15 percent responded that way," recalls White. To help guests with directions to their wedding and suggestions on things to do over the wedding weekend (besides going to the wedding, of course), the two designed Kimberly and Carl's Wedding, a website. In order to keep

"I began planning my wedding over a year ago, and the Internet resources that are available have grown tremendously since then. You can search the Bible (or any other religious book, for that matter) for specific readings and print them. You can find vendors and even wedding dresses at 20 percent to 40 percent discount. And other brides upload resources as well, such as shower games, nonreligious ceremony readings, and checklists. I ended up using the Internet extensively for my wedding, and it saved me so much time and so many headaches."

Rana, married 10/12/96

track of the guests who accessed the website, they created a guest book for visitors to sign. But a strange phenomenon began to occur.

"At that time, there were probably only six websites devoted to weddings, and anyone searching the Web for wedding information stopped at our site," he recalls. Within days of its debut, McGowan and White discovered "guest" signatures from all over the world, including Germany, Great Britain, and Singapore. "People we didn't know were leaving us messages to wish us good luck on our wedding," he adds.

With so much interest in their wedding, White and McGowan decided to broadcast their wedding on the Internet and announced just that on the website. Before they knew it, ABC News and Fox were on the phone asking if they could cover their wedding. The couple agreed.

On the big day, they set up a camcorder with a video capture card that simultaneously downloaded images from the wedding into White's computer and uploaded them to the Web. In all, more than thirty images from the wedding were sent out over the Internet.

"People were so receptive to us that we wanted to promote how fun it can be to use the Internet to tell about your wedding. That's where the idea for Way Cool Weddings came from," White remembers. On January 1, 1996, the site debuted. Its mission is to highlight wedding websites that are, in White's words, "designed well and fun to look at. I like a site that reflects the people's personality."

Each featured site sits in the spotlight for one week, and Way Cool Weddings offers a direct link to the site so interested parties can check it out. Currently, White considers a half dozen or so submissions each week. "Many people put all their wedding information on one page or they include gigantic photographs, which take too long to download," he says. Sites like that don't usually make the cut. "The best websites make it easy to get to know the couple getting married," he adds. "When you're clicking through the site, you feel as if you were a guest at their actual wedding."

To have White consider your wedding Web page as a possible Way Cool Wedding winner, E-mail him a brief description of the site along with the Web address to whitey@tribeca.ios.com.

Worthwhile Websites

Carl White recommends you check out some of the following websites as you plan your wedding.

Way Cool Weddings

http://www.waycoolweddings.com/home.htm

Each week this site features interesting wedding websites as deemed by Carl White. For example, one Way Cool Wedding documented the personal ad courtship and the New York City wedding that followed of a hip couple named Donna and Tom.

Kimberly and Carl's Wedding

http://tribeca.ios.com/~whitey/index.html

This is the original Way Cool Wedding site, which includes video of the big day, a complete guide to the wedding ceremony, and a guest book to sign.

Farmer's Almanac

http://www.rainorshine.com/weather/index/sites/njo#ofa

If you're worried about what the weather is going to be like for your June 30, 1999, wedding, this is the site that might give you a hint as to whether it'll rain or shine.

Automatic Wedding Speechwriter

http://speeches.com/auto.html

This is the sort of site the techno-savvy best man might want to check out—especially if he's having trouble writing his reception toast.

Wedding-Related Clip Art

http://barrow.uwaterloo.ca/~ghballin/wedpage.html

For those who dare to create a wedding website, this site offers hundreds of copyright-free images that can enhance any home page.

The Knot

Planning for a wedding can tie your insides up in knots, but if you know how to use certain Internet resources to your advantage, you should be OK in the long haul. One of the more creative wedding-planning sites to hit the information superhighway recently is America Online's The Knot.

Like the Internet newsgroups, The Knot offers bulletin boards where baffled brides- and grooms-to-be can post questions and get answers. But The Knot is more than just a place where you can query others like yourself. The Knot, subheaded Weddings for the Real World, includes the following six so-called channels of specific programming.

Decisions, Decisions. Here is where you'll find downloadable files, such as calendars and budget spreadsheets, to help with wedding planning. There's also a section called To-Be-Wed where readers are challenged to come up with and share their most creative alternatives to a traditional wedding ceremony and reception.

Turning Heads. This is wedding fashion central and includes color pictures of advertiser attire, such as cool Kenneth Cole shoes and nifty Nicole Miller dresses. You can also find information and advice on cosmetics and day-of beauty.

Sticky Subjects. If you're going to run into problems with your fiancé or your in-laws, this is the place to search for solutions. Every day, The Knot's staff creates a new How'd You Handle It?, a hypothetical sticky situation, and lets readers post their own answers. In addition, this area often has live chats with doctors and lawyers who can answer all your wedding jitters questions.

The Wedding Party. Should you choose chartreuse bridesmaid dresses and sky blue tuxedos? These dilemmas and more are solved through the eyes of fictional engaged couple Zack and Jessica, stars of The Knot's cyber-sitcom called First Comes Love.

The Great Escape. If you are having trouble deciding where to go on your honeymoon, you might find an answer here. Each day, The Great Escape features a small travel article called Postcard from . . . Recent destinations have include islands off Maine and some of the most romantic spots in Paris.

Material World. Not surprisingly, this area focuses on gifts—what to give and what to register for. In The Nest, the topic of conversation focuses on such mundane matters as applying for a home mortgage and fixing the kitchen sink. Furthermore, Trading Post offers a place to get rid of gifts couples really hate.

In addition to the regularly scheduled programming, The Knot also features The Knot Shop, a cyber-store that is open twenty-four hours a day, seven days a week. There are more than seven hundred items available for purchase, ranging from Black & Decker tools to Reed & Barton flatware.

America Online members can find The Knot by entering keyword: TheKnot. For America Online membership information, call 800-827-6364.

The Bride Wore a . . . Screen Saver?

Besides finding information about weddings on the Internet, some couples find true love. Take Dave and Denise Maiorana. They met in a chat room on America Online in November 1994. After about six weeks of chatting on-line, Dave drove from northern Virginia to Cleveland to meet Denise. They spent six months traveling on weekends to see each other. "After thousands of dollars in phone bills and many frequent-flier miles, I moved down to Virginia, and we got engaged and then married on August 10, 1996," recalls Denise. "Sometimes I look at him and can't believe the whole story is true." Well, you know what? It is.

Invitations

One of the best ways to set the tone for your wedding day is through the invitations you select. If you receive an engraved invitation on ecru card stock and with fancy black type, you can be pretty sure that the guys in attendance will be wearing tuxedos. Compare that with the invitation I used to invite friends and family to my celebration.

Once Bill and I decided to have a garden brunch, we selected an invitation that was bordered by spring flowers. We chose green ink and a green liner for the invitation envelope. What we hoped to convey was that we'd planned an outdoor party that was casual yet festive. When guests arrived in sun hats and Bermuda shorts, we knew our invitations' message had come through loud and clear.

Invitation Basics

Sue Winner is owner of Sincerely, Sue Winner in Atlanta, a business that specializes in wedding invitations and calligraphy. She sells invitations nationwide and promises a 20 percent discount off any invitation she stocks. For more information, call 404-255-3804. Winner recently went over the basics of wedding invitations.

Invitation Wording

There should never be an abbreviation on an invitation. (Exceptions include "Mr.," "Mrs.," and "St.," as in "Saint.") You have to write out every single word on the invitation, be it a middle name or a street address. Even the year is spelled out. For example, *1999* would appear as *one thousand, nine hundred and ninety-nine.* You have to remember that what is written on the invitation isn't complete sen-

Couples spend approximately $228 on invitations, announcements, and thank-you notes, according to *Bride's Magazine.*

"I nixed the idea of having a liner in our invitation because of the cost involved. We weren't sorry at all with our decision, because everyone complimented us on the simplicity of the invitation. I think the lack of a liner color and colored ink allowed guests to really focus on the wording of the invitation and the beauty of the invitation itself."

Nancy, married 11/16/96

tences, and an invitation is not the place to tell your life story. All you need to include is the particulars: who is getting married, when, where, and who is hosting the wedding. Keep in mind that etiquette states that the first names to appear on the invitation should be the names of the people paying for the wedding.

However, in today's world of blended families and divorce, I think it's perfectly OK for the couple to get a little creative. If you want to have the invitation read something like "Jennifer Smith and Roger Brown, together with their parents, request the honour of your presence at their marriage," it's a great way to get around divorce or any sticky family situations. Also, it's a terrific method for solving the problem of more than one person's paying for the wedding. However, if both sets of parents are contributing, you could add the names of all the parents involved after "together with their parents." The only problem that might arise from this wording is that the invitation could become too long to fit on the card stock.

Response Cards

Besides the basics of who, what, where, and when, you must also include a response card with an invitation. This will help you tabulate the head count for the caterer. However, even with a response card, some guests still don't understand that there's a meal involved and that they must respond in order for you to feed them. Instead, they think they can not respond to your invitation, show up on the day of the wedding, and everything will be OK.

To avoid problems with nonresponsive guests, you must include a "respond by" date on the response card. It may not inspire the guests to respond by that date, but at least it gives you license to get on the telephone and call the people who haven't responded by your set date.

You never put *number attending* on the response card. Believe it or not, by doing this, you're actually giving your guests license to bring as many people as they want to your wedding. The way you determine the number attending is by how many names appear on the response card. (The *m* followed by a line on the response card is so that the guest can write *Mr.*, *Mrs.*, or *Miss* before his or her name.) If you invite Mr. and Mrs. Smith and a response card comes back with "Mr. and Mrs. Smith" on it, you know two people are coming.

The way you let a guest know how many people you're inviting is by the names you write on the inner envelope of the invitation. For example, if you write "Mr. and Mrs. Smith," then the guest should know that he and his wife are invited to the party. If you write "Mr. and Mrs. Smith, Michael, Rachel and Donna Smith," then you're telling the guest that he and his wife are invited along with their three children. People often wonder what that inner invitation envelope is for, and that's it—to let the invited guest know exactly who in his or her family is invited to the wedding.

Just as there are guests who don't know enough to respond on time, there are some guests who ignore the name(s) written on the envelope and respond with the names of the people they want to bring. For example, if you've invited Mr. Smith only and a response card comes back with the names "Mr. Smith and Ms. Jones," you need to call Mr. Smith and point out the error. I suggest saying something like this: "Listen, we've had to cut our guest list to include people who are the most special to us. I hope you can join us for our wedding, but I won't be able to welcome your friend."

You shouldn't be shy about telling a guest this information. I know that in Atlanta today, for example, you can pay around $150 per person for a wedding. If someone brings a person you're not expecting, that puts you $150 in the hole. If more than one person does this, you've got a serious problem. To avoid any last-minute financial headaches, you've got to nip the uninvited-guest problem in the bud.

Besides uninvited guests, another big problem facing brides is response cards that come back with no name on them. One or two guests may have wanted to be so prompt about responding that they forgot to write their names on the response card. This has been known to happen. You can avoid this problem by keeping a list of all your guests with a number assigned to each person's name. Then you can pencil in the number on the back of the response card for that person's invitation. That way if a card comes back unsigned, you can cross-reference it with the number on the list and know from whom it came.

Calligraphy

Unless you have impeccable handwriting, you'll probably want to hire a professional calligrapher to address your invitations. There are two methods of producing calligraphy: by employing a calligraphy machine that uses a special pen and ink-filled cartridges and writes with a so-called mechanical hand; and by using a person who specializes in calligraphy, called a calligrapher.

Wedding invitations should be mailed four to six weeks before the wedding day. However, if guests will be traveling long distances to arrive, it is perfectly acceptable to send a wedding invitation sooner according to Sue Winner.

Invitations

"Check very carefully on
the response cards to
make sure that the
number of people coming
matches the number
invited. If it's higher, make
a nonaccusatory phone
call to the guest to find
out why the numbers
don't match up."

Heidi, married 10/19/96

Using a calligraphy machine is generally cheaper than paying a calligrapher and speedier to boot. It should take about two weeks to complete two hundred to three hundred invitations. You should pay by the line for this kind of calligraphy; my company, which offers this service, charges $.40 a line.

If you're going to hire a calligrapher to address your invitations, make sure you see the calligrapher's work and find out about his or her training. Calligraphy is an art form, but unfortunately anyone can take a calligraphy class at the YMCA. If you find someone charging $.50 an envelope, you should be suspicious. I know a woman here in Atlanta who charges $3.75 a line. That's a more appropriate price tag for an experienced calligrapher. Remember: you get what you pay for.

Invitation Printing

Today, thermography and engraving are equally accepted methods of printing for invitations, and few people can tell the difference between the two. However, the big difference is price.

One of the reasons that engraving is such an expensive process is it is a painstaking process. Years ago, a specialist called, not surprisingly, an engraver would do all the work of printing the invitation.

Here's what the process involved. The engraver would start off by holding a stylus in one hand and a plate of copper in the other. The engraver would cut the shape of the letters of the invitation into the copper backwards. Once finished, the engraver would clean the piece of copper and fill the crevices with ink. Then the engraver would take a piece of paper of a very high cotton content (for its absorbency), wet it, and put it on top of the copper plate. By applying pressure to the copper and paper, the engraver would force the paper to go into the copper and absorb the ink. That's how you get the lettering that is raised on the front and hollow on the backside of an engraved invitation.

One of the reasons that invitations are sent with a piece of tissue is to protect the engraved ink from running onto the other items in the envelope. Today, a machine does the job of the human engraver, but you still pay the same prices.

Thermography is more of a chemical process. Picture a long conveyor belt. At the first stop, the person running the thermography machine puts the shape of the lettering for the invitation into the machine. Then the operator applies a transparent coat of ink to the paper. At the next stop powder is sprinkled over the invitation. At this point, the machine heats the invitation so that anywhere the ink and the powder come into contact, they bubble up and form a raised letter. This creates the look of an engraved invitation. After the letters dry, a vacuum cleaner–like machine sucks off any residual powder left on the invitation. That's why some invitations printed with thermography arrive with a gritty feeling to them. All you have to do is use a dry dish towel or a hair dryer to get rid of the grit.

Invitation Style

According to etiquette experts like Emily Post, there are only a few kinds of acceptable invitations: paneled or not paneled, and printed on ecru or white paper. Personally, I think an invitation should reflect the couple getting married and the kind of wedding they're having.

Many people like traditional, plain, and simple wedding invitations that have a very formal look to them. Unless you're having a formal wedding, however, don't use them. It won't look right. Instead, you can keep a classic format or paper stock but use a more casual script or wording for a less formal wedding.

How you decide to have your invitation look is also reflective of your community. For example, if I received an invitation printed in black script on ecru paper for a Saturday night wedding in Atlanta, my husband would know to wear a tuxedo. But can the same be said for other cities? In fact, once we were invited to a Saturday night wedding in San Francisco by just such an invitation, and my husband ended up being the only one there wearing a tuxedo.

To avoid any confusion, you can add "black-tie" to the response card—not the invitation itself. Technically, a ceremony is never black-tie. And it throws off the balance of the invitation if you write "black-tie" in a lower corner of it. But you can *suggest* that a reception be black-tie.

In addition, never write "black-tie optional." That's redundant, because black-tie is always optional. You cannot command someone to wear a black-tie outfit to your wedding; you can only suggest it.

Assembling Your Invitation

Assemble your invitation so that all of its components are presented to the invited guest in a certain way. Here Sue Winner of Sincerely, Sue Winner goes over the basics of assembling your wedding invi-

"If you like a wedding invitation that a friend had, don't be shy about asking where she got it. A friend loved my invitation and asked if it would be OK for her to get something similar. I wasn't offended; I was flattered."
Wendy, married 11/19/95

Invitations

tation. It's important that you clear off a space on your dining room or kitchen table so that you have enough room to spread out all the parts of the invitations and a place to put them when they're assembled and ready to be mailed. Here's how to get started:

1. Have your addressed outer envelopes and your addressed inner envelopes standing in a box for easy access.

2. First place your wedding invitations, already folded in half, with the print side up on the far lefthand side of the table surface.

3. Next to the invitations, set down the stack of tissues you'll lay over the invitations.

4. The next pile includes the response envelope, the response card, and the reception card. Start by stacking the response envelopes with the print side down so that the flap is sticking up. (Make sure you've put a stamp on the envelopes already.) Next to the envelopes, place the pile of response cards and the reception cards.

5. Place at the far right end of your assembly line the outer and inner envelopes (with invited guests' names and addresses already written on them) and an empty box (in that order), into which you can place the assembled invitations. Now you can start putting them together.

6. Pick up the invitation and pick up the tissue and lay it over the printed portion of the invitation.

7. Then pick up the response card envelope and place the response card, with the print side up, under the flap but not in the envelope. Then place the reception card, print side up, on top of the response card. Lay this stack on top of the invitation (see diagram on how to assemble this component). Make sure the print on the invitation and the response card are parallel to each other.

8. Slide everything into the inner envelope with the invitation fold at the bottom of the inner envelope.

9. Turn the inner envelope over so that the printed names are facing you and then slide it into the outer envelope. The finished package should be put together in such a way that if you lifted the flap of the outer envelope, you would see the printed names on the inner envelope.

*1. A single-fold invitation
inserted into an envelope*

*2. Inserting a single-fold invitation
with an enclosure card*

*3. A twice-fold invitation
inserted into an envelope*

*4. Inserting a twice-folded invitation
with an enclosure card*

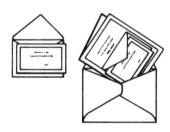

5. Enclosing a reply card and envelope

*6. Placing an inner envelope
into an outer envelope*

*Reprinted, by permission, from Crane's Blue Book of Stationery,
edited by Steven L. Feinberg, © 1989 by Crane & Co., Inc.*

10. Seal the envelope and place it in the empty box. Do the same for the rest of the invitations and, when finished, deliver them to the post office.

Questions About Invitations

If you choose to follow proper etiquette when wording your invitation, you'll soon realize that putting together a wedding invitation can be exceedingly difficult. Here are answers to some of the confusing questions you may face when writing your wedding invitation.

My father is a medical doctor. Do we include his title on the invitation?

Yes. Medical doctors are supposed to use their professional titles on wedding invitations. You should spell out the word *doctor*, unless your father's name is exceptionally long. Then you can abbreviate it.

My mother is a medical doctor. Do we include her title on the invitation?

For years, social convention said that even if a woman held a position in the medical community, she was to be referred to as *Mrs.* in social settings. However, times have changed. If your mother prefers to use her title on your wedding invitation, her name would appear on the first line of the invitation followed by her husband's. This is what it should look like:

Doctor Joan Ann Smith
and Mr. John Michael Smith

Be sure to include the *and* between their names. If you omit it, then you're telling the world that your parents are divorced.

What if both my parents are doctors?

You have two options for wording the invitation. You could list them as the "Doctors Smith" or put their names on separate lines like this:

Doctor Joan Ann Smith
and Doctor John Michael Smith

My husband and I are both medical doctors, but our parents are issuing the invitations. Do our titles appear on the invitation?

No. The only time a bride and groom's title, be it *Miss, Mr.,* or *Doctor,* appears on the invitation is when the couple themselves are issuing the invitation.

My parents and my fiancé each have a Ph.D. Should their title of Doctor *appear on the wedding invitation?*

No. Ph.D. is an academic title only. While your parents and fiancé may refer to themselves as "Dr. Smith" or "Dr. Doe" in the classroom, it is not proper to use the title *doctor* on a wedding invitation.

My mother kept her maiden name and never goes by Mrs. John Smith. How should her name appear on the invitation?

Your mother's full name should appear on the first line of the invitation, followed by your father's name. Remember to include the *and* before your father's name.

I hate my middle name. Does it have to appear on the wedding invitation?

Yes. A properly worded wedding invitation will include the first, middle, and last names of all the parties mentioned on the invitation.

Our ceremony starts at nine in the morning. Do we need to put P.M. *or in the evening on the invitation?*

First of all, you never put A.M. or P.M. on a wedding invitation. You say *in the morning* or *in the afternoon* or *in the evening.* Weddings that begin at eight, nine, or ten are always followed by *in the morning* or *in the evening* to reduce chances of confusion. Whether you follow weddings at other times of the day with a descriptor like *in the afternoon* is up to you.

> *Source:* Crane's Wedding Blue Book: The Styles and Etiquette of Announcements, Invitations, and Other Correspondences *by Steven L. Feinberg (Fireside, 1993), with permission from Crane & Co.*

Popular Invitation Wording

There are a number of ways to word your invitation. Who pays for the wedding most often determines how the invitation is worded. However, the marital status of your parents may affect it as well (see the chapter on divorced parents). What follow are a number of popular phrasings that you might find when leafing through invitation catalogs or invitation books at a stationery store.

If the bride's parents are paying for the wedding, you would use one of the following wordings.

Mr. and Mrs. John Michael Smith
request the honour of your presence
at the marriage of their daughter
Jane Marie
to
John William Doe
Saturday, the twenty-fourth of October
at five o'clock
one thousand, nineteen hundred and ninety-eight
St. Thomas Roman Catholic Church
Ann Arbor, Michigan

Mr. and Mrs. John Michael Smith
request the honour of your presence
at the marriage of their daughter
Jane Marie
to
John William Doe
son of Mr. and Mrs. William John Doe
Saturday, the twenty-fourth of October
one thousand, nineteen hundred and ninety-eight
at five o'clock
St. Thomas Roman Catholic Church
Ann Arbor, Michigan

Jane Marie Smith
and
John William Doe
will pledge their love as one
Saturday, the twenty-fourth of October
one thousand, nineteen hundred and ninety-eight
at five o'clock
St. Thomas Roman Catholic Church
Ann Arbor, Michigan
Our joy will be more complete
if you can share
this celebration with us

Mr. and Mrs. John Michael Smith

If the groom's parents are issuing the invitation and paying for the wedding, their names would come first on the invitation.

Mr. and Mrs. William John Doe
request the honour of your presence
at the marriage of
Jane Marie Smith
to their son
John William Doe
Saturday, the twenty-fourth of October
one thousand, nineteen hundred and ninety-six
at five o'clock
St. Thomas Roman Catholic Church
Ann Arbor, Michigan

This wording connotes that the bride's and groom's parents are paying for the wedding together.

Mr. and Mrs. John Michael Smith
and
Mr. and Mrs. William John Doe
request the honour of your presence
at the marriage of their children
Jane Marie
and
John William
Saturday, the twenty-fourth of October
one thousand, nineteen hundred and ninety-eight
at five o'clock
St. Thomas Roman Catholic Church
Ann Arbor, Michigan

Use the following wordings if the couple is paying for the wedding along with the parents.

Together with their parents
Jane Marie Smith
and
John William Doe
request the honour of your presence
at their marriage
Saturday, the twenty-fourth of October
one thousand, nineteen hundred and ninety-eight
at five o'clock
St. Thomas Roman Catholic Church
Ann Arbor, Michigan

Jane Marie Smith
and
John William Doe
together with their parents
Mr. and Mrs. John Michael Smith
and
Mr. and Mrs. William John Doe
request the honour of your presence
at their marriage
Saturday, the twenty-fourth of October
one thousand, nineteen hundred and ninety-eight
at five o'clock
St. Thomas Roman Catholic Church
Ann Arbor, Michigan

The bride and groom issue their own invitation if they're paying
for their wedding.

Jane Marie Smith
and
John William Doe
request the honour of your presence
at their marriage
Saturday, the twenty-fourth of October
one thousand, nineteen hundred and ninety-eight
at five o'clock
St. Thomas Roman Catholic Church
Ann Arbor, Michigan

Jane Marie Smith
and
John William Doe
invite you to share in the joy
when they exchange marriage vows
and begin a new life together
Saturday, the twenty-fourth of October
one thousand, nineteen hundred and ninety-eight
at five o'clock
St. Thomas Roman Catholic Church
Ann Arbor, Michigan

Jane Marie Smith
and
John William Doe
have chosen the first day
of their new life together as
Saturday, the twenty-fourth of October
one thousand, nineteen hundred and ninety-eight
You are invited to share in their joy
as they exchange marriage vows
at five o'clock
St. Thomas Roman Catholic Church
Ann Arbor, Michigan

Do-It-Yourself Invitations

With our society becoming more computer-savvy, it is now possible to write and design your wedding invitations on desktop. An excellent resource for do-it-yourself invitations is PaperDirect, a catalog that sells papers for all kinds of desktop projects.

At press time, the catalog offered three wedding invitation formats. Each format is available in white, cream, willow white, and almond cream colors.

* The formal format is a 7¼-inch-by-5⅛-inch folded card. The card can be free of decoration or come with a paneled edge or an embossed design.

* The modern format is a square 8-inch-by-8-inch card. It is available with a paneled edge or an embossed design on it only.

* The classic format is a 7¼-inch-by-5⅛-inch flat card. Like the formal format, the card can be free of decoration or come with a paneled edge or an embossed design.

In addition, the invitations come with response cards and envelopes, reception cards and envelopes, and inner and outer envelopes. Prices start at $20.95 for twenty-eight invitations and envelopes.

Beside invitations, PaperDirect sells supplies to make your own thank-you notes, table assignment cards, door hangers for guests' hotel rooms, and booklet covers for ceremony programs.

To request a PaperDirect catalog, call 800-A-PAPERS. All Paper Direct orders placed by 3:00 P.M. eastern time are shipped the same day.

Mail-Order Bride

Many couples today find invitations from mail-order catalogs to be a time-saving and cost-efficient option when purchasing invitations. In fact, Bill and I purchased from a catalog the floral-bordered invitations that we used to invite our friends to our garden brunch reception.

Here is a list of some of the more popular catalogs offering wedding invitations and other wedding accessories, such as printed napkins, aisle runners, and cake knives.

The American Wedding Album	800-428-0379
Creations by Elaine	800-323-2717
Heart Thoughts	800-731-3443
Invitations by Dawn	800-528-6677
Invitations Etc.	800-709-7979
Jamie Lee	800-288-5800
Now and Forever	800-451-8616
The Precious Collection	800-553-9080
Rexcraft	800-635-4653
Sugar 'n Spice Invitations	800-535-1002
Wedding Treasures	800-851-5974
Willow Tree Lane	800-219-9230

Kids at Weddings

*O*ne of the reasons Bill and I originally didn't want children to be at our wedding was based on the site of our reception—a yacht club, where the risk of a child's falling into the water and possibly drowning was very real. However, when we changed the venue to my grandfather's backyard, we decided that it would be nice to have children in attendance. There was no danger of their drowning; the backyard is huge, so there would be a lot of space for them to run around and play; and my grandfather's house sits at the end of a dead-end street, so there was no danger of the children playing in traffic.

So that our adult guests would be able to have a good time at the reception, we hired Bubbles the Clown to entertain the children. He stayed for an hour, and he was a big hit. He made balloon hats for all the children and taught them magic tricks. His presence gave the parents the chance to relax and enjoy their meals without having to worry about where their kids were. The kids, in turn, had a blast.

When Bill and I became parents, we were invited to a wedding where children were also welcomed. At the time, our daughter Jane was ten weeks old, so I knew she'd either cry through the ceremony or sleep through it. She did a little of both, but since there were other children at the church, nobody looked at me as if to say, "How dare you bring this infant to the wedding?" Everyone knew that Jane was as welcome as Bill and I were. When she started to cry and I had to abruptly leave the church in the middle of the service, instead of scowling, everyone smiled and nodded their heads at me.

So that Bill and I and the other parents could enjoy the wedding reception, which was held at a nearby hotel, the bride and groom arranged for two babysitters to watch all the children in a

wedding wisdom

"Here's a different way to use children in the wedding: have them go into the chapel ahead of the processional to ring bells to announce the arrival of the bride."

Sue, married 3/29/97

wedding wisdom

"We hired several babysitters who stayed with all of the kids at my sister's house during the wedding ceremony and through dinner. When we were done eating, the sitters brought the kids to the reception. This way the kids were able to join us during the fun part of the day, and we were able to get all of the family pictures that are so important on your wedding day."

Kim, married 8/25/90

wedding wisdom

"My opinion is that if we were going to have kids in the wedding, then why wouldn't we have them at the reception? The kids were all very well behaved, and they had a blast at the reception. We loved having them there."

Amy, married 8/3/96

suite. The hotel had supplied portable cribs for the little ones, and videos, cookies, and milk for the toddlers. Just as the reception was beginning, we dropped Jane off. It gave Bill and me the freedom to enjoy ourselves, and we were incredibly thankful that our friends had been so sensitive to our needs. To this day, that wedding remains one of the most pleasurable ones we ever attended.

Kids, Kids, Kids

Shelley Lindauer, Ph.D., is an associate professor of family and human development at Utah State University in Logan, Utah. Here she shares her thoughts on children at weddings.

I think you really need to think through why you want to have children in your wedding party or as wedding guests. You might think, "Oh, children are so cute," but how cute will a child be after sitting through a long church service? Children have very short attention spans, and they may lose their patience in the middle of the wedding ceremony or begin to cry. And this may not be the atmosphere you want to create for your wedding ceremony.

You may decide to have children in your wedding party because of what I call the cuteness factor. A little boy walking down the aisle in a miniature tuxedo is sure to get oohs and aahs from the guests— that is, if he does what he's told to do. Children are going to be children, and if they're not comfortable doing something, then they shouldn't have to do it. For some children, walking down a long aisle with hundreds of strange faces looking at them might be the most terrifying thing to happen to them in their young lives, and you need to keep this in mind.

I believe that if you decide to have children in your wedding you need to be flexible. For example, if the flower girl decides not to scatter the rose petals as instructed, let it go. Likewise, you have to keep calm if the ring bearer decides that he wants to sit with Mommy and Daddy in their pew during the service. You don't want to feel as if a three-year-old ruined your wedding.

I do believe that children can provide charm and levity to a wedding. But if you're not willing to take the child as the child and expect him or her to behave like one, then it's probably not a good idea to have the child in your wedding.

Another issue to consider is how many children you are going to invite. There's a good chance that many of your guests are parents, and you may feel that if you invite one child, you have to invite them all. But you don't. I think it's OK to invite children who are related—especially if they're going to be in your wedding party—and tell others that unfortunately their children aren't invited. If it makes breaking the news to them any easier, share your decision-making criteria with these parents long before the invitations are sent. Tell them that you are inviting only children of relatives, and while you would like to invite their children as well, circumstances dictate that you must limit the number of children in attendance. Hopefully, your honesty will prevent any headaches.

However, if you do decide to extend an invitation to all children, you'll need to plan ahead so that the children are duly entertained during both the ceremony and reception. For example, at weddings I've attended, most parents whose children were well behaved throughout the ceremony had brought toys for the children to play with or books to read. I'm not saying everyone would do that with their children, so maybe you could do that for them. When your ushers are handing out programs at the entrance of the church, maybe they can hand out coloring books and crayons or a small toy to the younger ones in attendance to keep them occupied during the service. Sure, it will be an added expense, but it might guarantee quiet during the ceremony.

What will surely guarantee that there are no screaming children around when you exchange vows is if you provide child care at the church, synagogue, or wherever you're getting married. I've been to many weddings where child care was provided during the service and then the children rejoined their parents afterward and came to the reception. This is an excellent option, because you're not expecting a child to sit through a long service. Or you could provide child care for the service and for the reception as well but give parents the option of bringing the children to the reception for part of the time. Receptions usually have more moving-around space than a church does, so if children run around, it won't seem so out of place as it would during the wedding ceremony.

If you decide to offer child care, you'll want to let parents know ahead of time that it is available. A great way to do that is to slip a note into the invitations. It might say something like "Child care will be provided for children under two at the service. Child care will also be available during the reception." Then you might include a separate reply card or RSVP telephone number, with a "respond by" date, so you can get a sense of how many parents and kids will be taking advantage of your child care offer.

A great way to guarantee that children don't run wild at your reception is to plan ahead so that they feel as if they belong. For

wedding wisdom

"We really wanted children to be in our wedding, as they are such a big part of our lives. I mean, at the time, I was working as a teacher. So I decided to have my kindergarten class sing throughout the ceremony. The children rehearsed for several weeks for their big debut. The guests were enchanted by their performance. Later on, we had a special reception for the children and their families only. We had a miniature wedding cake, and it worked out beautifully."

Julie, married 6/24/90

Kids at Weddings

"We had three children involved in our wedding, two eleven-year-old girls and a thirteen-year-old boy. One girl manned the guest book while the boy handed out programs at the ceremony. The other girl also helped hand out programs at the ceremony, and then at the reception she was in charge of the gift table and securing any cards that became separated from their gifts."

Amy, married 10/12/96

"The key to including children is to be flexible and have fun with it. Don't include them if it will upset you if they don't 'perform.' My four-year-old flower girl decided as we left the house that her shoes were uncomfortable, so she went down the aisle shoeless. Then, halfway down she stopped to make faces at her brother. I didn't get upset; I thought it was funny."

Carreen, married 11/26/93

example, you'll probably want to offer some kind of developmentally appropriate entertainment, such as a clown or a magician. In addition, if children will need high chairs or booster seats, you should make sure enough are available and speak to your banquet manager or caterer well in advance about providing them. And when it comes to food, offer the kind that kids love, like macaroni and cheese or chicken fingers. Think about it this way: if the kids like the food you offer and spend time eating it, it will keep them busy for a while and prevent them from getting into trouble. Plus, with food in their stomachs, they'll probably be a lot less cranky.

Besides a clown or magician, keep in mind that your band or deejay can also provide entertainment for the children. Kids love music, and don't be surprised if many of them end up out on the dance floor. You might even suggest that your band or deejay play some music just for the kids. We went to a wedding recently where every once in a while the band would play a song that got all the kids on the dance floor, like the Bunny Hop or something by Raffi.

If you think of all the contingencies ahead of time, like child care, child-friendly food, and appropriate entertainment, you should be able to have kids at your wedding without worrying about their turning into tiny terrors.

Dos and Don'ts for Including Children

Kathy Moore is a certified bridal consultant and the owner of Ambiance Party Services in Garner, North Carolina, a full-service wedding- and special-event planning company. Moore has planned many weddings where children were involved. She has some definite feelings about when it's appropriate to include children in a wedding— and when it isn't. You can reach Ambiance at 919-779-9303.

* Don't include children under age four in your wedding. They can be very unpredictable.

* If you choose to include a child in your wedding, do try to include at least one of the child's parents as well. It will make it less frightening for the child, and if he or she needs to be comforted, Mom or Dad is right there.

* Do have an alternate plan if a child decides not to do what you want him or her to do. For example, assign someone to help coach the child who won't walk down the aisle.

* Do provide babysitting services or entertainment for children.

* If a child misbehaves, don't feel as if the child has stolen the show from you. This is your day, and no matter what, you are the center of attention.

Shelley Lindauer's Tips on Child Care

* Always hire someone whom you consider reliable. A family friend is a great option, of course. However, if you're having your wedding in a place where you don't know anyone, call a local college with an education program or a local daycare center. Oftentimes, teachers at the center will provide child care on the weekends on a freelance basis.

* Make sure that the space you've selected for the child care is adequate. Twenty toddlers in a small hotel room may not be appropriate, because there won't be enough room for them all to play. Instead, you might want to consider moving up to a suite. If you're having child care at the church or synagogue, see if there are any classrooms you can use.

* If infants are going to be involved, make sure there are portable cribs available. Cribs can help keep the infants safe from older children, and it's a great place for them to sleep. Most hotels can provide cribs along with fresh sheets.

* Be sure to provide things for the children to do, be it Barney tapes or coloring books.

Kids at Weddings

Long-Distance Planning

Most of the people I know who have gotten married recently planned a wedding from afar. One couple in Michigan planned a wedding in Oregon (the bride's home state) and then a second reception in Indiana (the groom's home state). Another couple planned an upstate New York wedding while the bride was attending graduate school in New Hampshire and the groom worked in Connecticut.

Our friends John and Penny did a long-distance wedding as well. At the time, John was living in New Jersey and Penny was in New York, but their wedding was to be held in Penny's hometown in southern California. Even the bridal party was scattered. For example, my husband, Bill, the best man, lived in Michigan. The other ushers lived in Massachusetts, New York, and Arkansas. To keep everyone in touch with how the wedding planning was going, John would send a group letter every once in a while to tell the guys such pertinent information as the name of the tuxedo shop where they would be renting their attire and the name of the hotel where everyone would be staying.

I guess Bill and I were lucky. Not only did we plan a wedding that would occur in the state where we both lived, but also we happen to have grown up in the same town and so we had our reception in the very town where we attended elementary, middle, and high school. Having our family and friends nearby made all the planning so much easier, but I guess the truth is we're an anomaly. Statistics say that most brides and grooms today marry someone they met at college or on the job—someone who most likely didn't grow up in the same town, as Bill and I did. Oh, well. We've always been unconventional people. It's nice to know that we've bucked the trend in this area, too.

Far and Away Weddings

Alan and Denise Fields have made a name for themselves as advocates of smart shopping. Their highly successful book Bridal Bargains *has more than 300,000 copies in print and has helped brides and grooms become aware of possible rip-offs in the bridal business. A few years ago they wrote a book that strayed from their common consumer advocacy theme to the topic of long-distance planning. That book, called* Far and Away Weddings *(Windsor Peak Press), has also been a strong seller. You can contact them with wedding-related questions at adfields@aol.com. I recently spoke to Alan Fields about the trend of planning weddings from afar.*

LI: *Why did you decide to write* Far and Away Weddings?

AF: There are a couple of different trends that are driving this concept. Number one, today, brides and grooms aren't always living in the same city where they grew up. The reason? Most brides and grooms are older, and they may have gone away for college or moved away for a job. They usually have a set of friends in the city where they live now and then relatives back home. What ends up happening is they have to coordinate a long-distance wedding. Either everyone comes to them where they live now, or they go back to their hometown to get married. Logistically, it can be a nightmare. We have heard from a few couples who say, "I live in New York, and I'm trying to plan a wedding in Miami. How do I do this?"

Sometimes couples decide that they don't want to travel to their hometown to get married, and they also don't want to get married where they're living now. So they pick a location in between. This choice has led to the other major trend in long-distance weddings. It's called the *destination wedding.*

I believe that the rise in destination weddings, where the couple might pick a neutral or offbeat location at which to get married, is a backlash against the wedding excess of the 1980s. During that decade, weddings grew to be grandiose affairs, and people remember that. When it comes time to plan their wedding, they don't want to do the standard wedding.

Another reason for a destination wedding is if this is a second wedding for one of the people. That person may have already had a big wedding, and this time they want to do something different.

So they fly off to Hawaii to tie the knot, or they rent out a bed-and-breakfast in Vermont and invite only their closest friends to be with them when they get married.

LI: *What are the pros and cons of planning a long-distance wedding?*

AF: Cost is one factor that could be one of the major advantages of planning a long-distance wedding. For example, you may live in New York but decide to get married in Maine. Anyone can tell you that a wedding in a rural setting is going to be cheaper than one in New York City.

It can be cheaper to go home for your wedding as well, rather than staying in the city where you live. And while it may be harder to plan your wedding from afar, you'll be saving so much money that it's worth the extra effort. Say you live in Los Angeles, but your hometown is Portland, Oregon. I can guarantee an Oregon wedding will cost about half of a Los Angeles one.

One of the reasons that cost becomes such a strong determining factor in the location the couple choose is that couples are paying for their own weddings today. We estimate that approximately one-third of all couples pay for the wedding themselves. Another one-third split the cost with both sets of parents, and the remaining one-third still rely on the bride's father to pay for everything. People who pay for their own wedding end up coming to the conclusion that by having their wedding in a cheaper city, they can still have enough money in the bank afterward for part of a down payment for a house.

The major downside of a long-distance wedding is the logistics of trying to plan a wedding when you're in city A and the wedding will be in city B. People underestimate the time it takes to plan a wedding. The Association of Bridal Consultants estimates that it takes ninety to one hundred hours to plan a wedding. Even planning a wedding nearby has its ups and downs, but when you add distance to the equation, you start running into unforeseen problems. For example, vendors you call may not want to return long-distance calls, and that makes it difficult for you to do research.

Some brides end up visiting the town where the wedding is being planned, and in a whirlwind tour of the town, they take two or three days to plan everything. It can be exhausting, but sometimes it's the only way to get things done.

Other couples decide on a surrogate wedding planner, such as the relative who happens to live in the town where the wedding will take place, or hire a wedding consultant. Problems can arise in using the help of a relative who has a hidden agenda. For example, if the bride's mother is doing the planning, she may end up making her daughter's wedding more of the wedding she never had. Or the consultant she hires may institute what's considered a regional tradition without consulting with the bride. One bride from Florida was planning a wedding in Pennsylvania. Apparently at all weddings in this Pennsylvania town, a keyboard player plays during the sit-down dinner. That wasn't what the bride wanted for her wedding, and she ended up fighting about it with the consultant she had hired.

If you're going to delegate the planning of your wedding to someone else, you have to be really comfortable with this decision. For example, if you are a real control freak and detail-oriented, having someone else making decisions for you might become a problem. There are certain questions you have to ask yourself to determine whether you can handle someone else's planning your wedding. For example, how good do you feel as a person who delegates responsibility? Do you trust the person you're delegating to? Can you let go of control of certain decisions?

One of the things couples forget is that a wedding is sort of a good dress rehearsal for the rest of your life. In your relationship with your spouse, you're going to have to learn to compromise on certain things. Having someone else help plan your wedding may be a good way of learning to compromise.

Of course, long-distance planning has been eased a bit with the use of faxes and E-mail. I don't know if a long-distance wedding could have been done twenty-five years ago. I mean, in today's technological world, you can have a contract or menu faxed to you instead of waiting for it in the mail.

LI: *When you're planning a long-distance wedding, do you need to start planning sooner than a bride who is planning a wedding nearby?*

AF: We were talking to a bride in New York City who was planning a wedding in Vermont, and she found that all the wedding photographers she was considering were booked a year in advance. Therefore, you probably do need more time. It seems obvious that even in small towns, you need a year in advance to plan a wedding, because of the logistics of doing it over a long distance.

Part of the process depends on the schedules of you and your fiancé, especially if you work. You need to set aside some time to visit the place where you're going to have your wedding, and you probably don't want to use up your vacation time traveling to this destination. However, it may be necessary to coordinate a trip back to plan the wedding with another event or holiday, if you're going to be going there anyway.

LI: *I know with many choices you make for your wedding that it's important to see what you're buying, whether it's a photographer's work or the bridesmaid dresses. How does planning from afar affect these decisions?*

AF: You might have only two days back in the city where the wedding is going to be, and you have to prioritize what's important to see during that trip and what things you can let go. It will be impossible for you to meet with every single vendor you might hire, so decide which ones you absolutely must see. For example, if photography is very important to both of you, you should arrange to meet with two or three photographers during your visit. However, if a florist has been recommended by a friend you trust, then you probably don't have to schedule an appointment with the florist.

LI: *Why might hiring a consultant make sense for a long-distance wedding?*

AF: If you know ahead of time that you're not going to have a lot of opportunity to visit the destination where you're going to have the wedding, then the consultant can save you from running around like crazy when you do get to town.

When you hire a consultant, you're usually purchasing two separate services. The first is someone who can plan the event, which can save you money in long-distance phone calls and delivery service charges. The second is someone to do day-of and on-site wedding planning. The same consultant can wear both hats, or you may find that you have to hire separate individuals.

If you live in Boston and you're getting married in Pittsburgh, I suggest hiring a consultant in Pittsburgh. Not only will this person know of reputable vendors in the area that he or she can suggest for you, but this person can handle minute yet important tasks for you as well. For example, after you've selected your bridesmaid dresses, you can send the consultant a fabric swatch to take to the florist. Then the consultant can work with the florist to make sure that the flowers the florist is creating are appropriate for the dress color.

Of course, you may not feel the need to hire a wedding consultant to do this. However, I believe that if you are having more than 150 guests at your wedding and you have very few resources in the town, you should seriously consider hiring a consultant. If you think family isn't reliable or if they're going to be too busy to help you plan your wedding, then you also need to hire a consultant.

Sometimes it's good to have a wedding consultant around to make decisions, especially if your parents are going to have strong opinions about the choices you make. Then you and the consultant can play Good Cop, Bad Cop; and when you decide on something that your parents don't agree with, you can say, "Well, it's out of our hands. It's what the consultant told us was best, and I'm paying the consultant for her expert advice."

If you can't justify hiring a consultant, think about it this way: you're saving money by having a long-distance wedding. Why not use the extra money and put it toward a consultant? You'll end up ahead in the long run.

LI: *Even if you decide to hire a consultant, aren't there certain wedding decisions that shouldn't be made from afar?*

AF: Yes. Two things that you'll want to decide on in the town where you live is your apparel and invitations. Those are critical things that you can do on the home front. For example, it's not unheard-of for brides to have problems with bridal retail shops. Therefore, you really want to be in the same town or one nearby the store where you buy your dress. This way you can be close by if there are any problems with your dress. Then when it's ready, you can get it to the wedding site, either by taking it on the plane or shipping it. We would recommend taking it on the plane. However, if carrying it on the plane is impossible because of all the bags you'll have to carry, then we recommend sending it by UPS or FedEx so that the package can be tracked. In fact, our book *Far and Away Weddings* offers tips on transporting a gown.

Invitations are another major decision that we strongly recommend you make in person. It's one of those things that you should see beforehand. Plus, since you'll probably end up stuffing and sending them yourself, you might as well keep the entire task limited to one location—where you live now.

I guess if you really wanted to, you could also do your flowers at home as well. Of course, you won't be able to use real flowers, so you might want to think about silk or dried flowers. You can find high-quality silk flowers done by a professional florist that look pretty much like the real thing. When they're done, you can ship them to the wedding location as well.

LI: *Are there any additional tips you might offer for planning a long-distance wedding?*

AF: You might want to consider having your wedding in an off-peak month, on an off-peak day, or at an off-peak time of the day. Then you won't have much local competition for popular days and good vendors. For example, in the Pacific Northwest, June isn't as popular as August. Besides not having to compete with local brides, you may find that prices are cheaper and merchants are less harried. It does help to lessen the stress.

Also, if you get a contract for wedding services that is written with a local bride in mind, don't hesitate to modify the terms to fit a long-distance wedding. For example, we recently spoke to a bride who lived in California but got married in Houston. Her Houston-based photographer had recently contacted her because she had signed a contract that said she would return proofs within ten days or she would be charged for the proof set. Well, when the photographer said ten days, he didn't take into consideration the transit time between Houston and California, and it ended up that she had received the proofs only after the deadline had passed. Now the photographer was trying to enforce that part of the contract. That ten-day limit would be fine for a local bride, but give me a break. It could take up to five days to ship the photos to California, and that doesn't give the couple very long to look at their photographs.

In addition, make sure that you use a credit card when making a deposit or paying for services, as you should with all the wedding vendors you hire. When you live out of town, the vendors know that if something goes wrong, you won't be there to yell in their faces. However, if you use a credit card and vendors fail to deliver the goods, you have a lot more leverage—namely the backing of the credit card company. You can dispute the charge, and it will force the vendors to deliver what was promised, because they know that if they don't, they won't get paid.

Planning from Afar

When Sharon Naylor, author of 1,001 *Ways to Save Money and Have a Dazzling Wedding* (Contemporary Books, 1993), was planning her own wedding, she did it from afar. Here are her tips for pulling off a fabulous long-distance wedding.

* Keep good notes on what's being done and whom you might have delegated something to. That way if something happens with your flowers, you can look in your notes and see who it was who was supposed to be handling them and what you jotted down from your last conversation.

* Keep in touch with major players in the wedding, such as the bridal party or your mother-in-law—especially if one of them is doing some of the planning for you. I did a lot of commu-

nication with my bridal party and family by letter, because I didn't have access to E-mail. But I'm sure people today use E-mail for the same purpose.

* If you're going to travel to the wedding destination at all beforehand, plan to get as much done as possible during that trip.

* Learn that when planning a wedding from afar, you're going to have to give up some control. If you accept that fact from the very start, you'll save yourself from getting upset later when you realize you can't control everything—especially over long distances.

* Confirm everything ahead of time, including the names of the vendors you've hired and the date the deposit was sent.

* Only hire people who were recommended to you by someone you trust or whom you've seen in action at other weddings.

Makeup

While you definitely want to look beautiful on your wedding day, the morning-of is not the time to experiment with a new eye shadow color or try on false eyelashes for the first time. Just as you should visit your hairdresser and try out your wedding-day hair ahead of time, you should practice with your wedding-day makeup before the wedding day. Unless you're really good at applying makeup, I would suggest having it done professionally at least once so you can pick up tricks for making your eyeliner look straight or finding a lipstick that doesn't make your teeth look yellow.

Recently I had to have a professional photograph taken, and I knew that I couldn't afford to hire a makeup artist to do me up before the photo session. I was low on my Clinique base anyway, so I scheduled a makeover at my local Clinique counter. I got pointers on putting on eye shadow to enhance my eyes and concealer to cover up under-eye circles. When you look at the end results of that photo session, I don't look as if I'm wearing a lot of makeup. But that's the key—you can look great with makeup on without looking as if you spent hours applying it.

Doing It Yourself

Gina Hart is a makeup artist at Cappelli Hair Face Body, a spa in Bloomfield Hills, Michigan. As a professional makeup artist, she has the upper hand on the average person who attempts to apply her own wedding-day makeup. If you decide to do your makeup yourself—and decide that your attendants are adept enough at makeup applications to do their own as well—here are her tips.

wedding wisdom

"When considering who will do your makeup and hair, take a picture of yourself after a tryout. Sometimes it is hard to tell just by looking in the mirror if you like the look and if it will photograph well. By taking a picture, you'll know exactly how you will look if you hire that person to do your hair or makeup. In fact, I ended up trying two different people before I found the right one."

Wendy, married 11/19/95

* Keep in mind that you have to do a little more than street makeup for your wedding. Otherwise, you're going to look washed out in your photographs.

* Many women don't like to wear foundation, but you need to even out your skin tones, and that's what foundation does. Therefore, you'll need to wear it on your wedding day.

* Concealer is also a must, to cover up any blemishes or dark circles under the eyes.

* You should always apply powder to your finished makeup. It helps the makeup set, and it will keep you from looking shiny right away.

* Avoid looking as if you have a face and neck of two different colors. Make sure that your base looks as natural next to the skin on your neck as it does on your face. You may have to select a base that is somewhere in the middle of the color of your face and neck to pull off this natural look.

* Don't do what the cheerleaders in your high school did—apply a coat of petroleum jelly to their front teeth—to avoid getting lipstick on your teeth. That's gross. Instead, to ensure that your lipstick will stay put, dust some translucent powder on your bare lips. Then apply a coat of lipstick and blot with a tissue. Add another coat of lipstick and blot again. Then outline the lip and fill in any empty spaces with a lip pencil that matches your lipstick.

* Of course you want to play up your eyes on your wedding day, but don't do it by applying bright blue or green eye shadow. All you and your guests will see is the color of your makeup, not your face as a whole. Instead, I like to build the intensity of the eyes by layering neutral colors, such as browns with a little green mixed in.

* If you're afraid you're going to look washed out in your pictures, don't automatically turn to bronzing powder. While in person it can give you a sun-kissed look, in your wedding photographs you're going to look all red.

* Don't use bright lipstick. Find a color that looks natural on you.

* If you know you're going to cry at your wedding, invest in waterproof mascara to prevent it from running.

* Even your guy can benefit from a little makeup. If your fiancé tends to get dark circles under his eyes or has blotchy skin, invest in some foundation and concealer for him.

* Keep a pressed powder compact on hand throughout the wedding day so you can blot oily spots on you and your new husband's face.

Hiring a Pro

* Ask friends, relatives, and colleagues if they can recommend a makeup artist. If not, call a reputable salon in the area and ask if they have a professional makeup artist on staff who specializes in wedding makeup.

* Make sure that the makeup artist you hire is polite and cooperative and that your personalities click. You'll already be under enough stress on your wedding day; you don't want a makeup artist to add to your stress.

* A makeup artist should be willing to travel to your wedding location if necessary so you don't have to worry about getting to a salon. However, you should expect to pay some sort of travel fee to compensate the makeup artist for his or her time on the road.

* Expect to have a preliminary makeup consultation one month before your wedding.

* Tell your makeup artist whether you are having a day or evening wedding. Time of day can greatly affect the look the makeup artist selects for you and your attendants. For example, makeup for daytime weddings should look more natural, while makeup for a nighttime affair will be bolder and more dramatic.

* Let the makeup artist know whether you're wearing a white or ivory gown and try to take a swatch of fabric with you to your consultation. For example, if you're wearing a white gown, your makeup colors will probably be cooler, and black mascara is a must so that your face doesn't look washed out. Compare that with makeup requirements for an ivory gown, where colors will be warmer and more from the earth tone family. The same goes for your attendants. Be sure to let the makeup artist see a fabric swatch of the attendants' dress

beforehand. Because every woman has a different skin tone, the makeup artist should know ahead of time how to custom-create a makeup look that will complement each attendant best in her dress.

* If there's a certain makeup style you like, take a photograph with you to show your makeup artist. However, you have to keep in mind that each woman's makeup will vary according to her skin type, her natural coloring, and the color dress she wears on her wedding day.

* Your makeup artist will probably suggest that your face be thoroughly cleansed, toned, and moisturized before your wedding. If you regularly get facials, schedule one for about one week before the wedding. This will guarantee that your face has been deep-cleaned. However, if you've never gotten a facial, now isn't the time to get your first one. You don't want to take a chance of your skin having an adverse reaction to the skin-care products used in the facial.

* Finally, make sure you settle on a makeup style that looks natural. You don't want to look like someone who just stepped out of a glamour portrait on the day of your wedding.

Source: Wendy Cromwell, a professional esthetician and makeup artist at Robert Andrew DaySpa Salon in Gambrills, Maryland.

Music

Nothing quite sets the mood for a wedding ceremony and reception like the music you choose for each. For example, a string quartet playing classical tunes from the balcony of a church will create a completely different atmosphere from a Spanish guitar being played for an outdoor ceremony. Likewise, a jazz trio playing background music during dinner connotes a more relaxed atmosphere than a deejay who spins Top 40 tunes to entice guests onto the dance floor.

Obviously, because we eloped, we didn't have to think about having ceremony music, it just wasn't appropriate. But when it came to planning the music for our garden brunch, Bill and I decided to keep it simple. We were already spending an arm and a leg to throw the party—we didn't want to blow more cash on a band. Plus, at our backyard brunch, there really wasn't any need to have dancing music.

Luckily our friends Steve and Arlene gave us a five-CD player as a wedding gift, which Bill and I decided to use to provide music for our guests. Our friend John lent us a set of speakers, which he and Bill placed strategically throughout the tent. Then Bill and I selected five of our favorite CDs (including Harry Connick Jr.'s *When Harry Met Sally* and the all-star *Deadicated*), placed them in the CD player, and, by hitting shuffle, were able to get five hours of music for our brunch.

Everyone loved the varied selection, and most of our guests commented that it was the first time they'd attended a wedding and had actually been able to talk to their neighbor throughout the meal. Usually, they had to shout over the loud music. Hearing comments

wedding wisdom

"We went the nontraditional route and had bagpipes at both the ceremony and reception."

Julie, married 3/8/97

like that confirmed that we had made the best music decision we possibly could have.

Ceremony Musicians

Brenda Anna is a violinist and manager of the Riversdale Chamber Ensemble, a group of freelance professional musicians who regularly perform at weddings in the greater Washington, D.C., area. Her group has been playing together since 1982, and they've been hired for hundreds of weddings. I asked her what you need to keep in mind when hiring musicians to play at your wedding ceremony. For more information on the Riversdale Chamber Ensemble, call 301-699-5079.

How much you can spend on your ceremony musicians will often determine whom you hire. I've heard everything from $35 for student performers to $125 and up for professionals. But don't let the price the performer charges sway you in your decision making. Of course, a student is going to be cheaper, but a student can also be a risky hiring decision.

For example, I've heard of students who backed out of a wedding at the last minute because they had exams to study for. Another time I heard of a student performer who was unfamiliar with the sequence of events in a wedding and didn't start playing "The Wedding March" (otherwise known as "Here Comes the Bride") on cue.

Just because someone is a student at the Peabody Conservatory in Baltimore or at Juilliard in New York City doesn't mean he or she will be great for your wedding—unless, of course, the musician comes highly recommended from friends who used him or her at their wedding. As with any other professional you'll hire for your wedding, having a glowing, firsthand recommendation is always a good sign.

If you can't get a firsthand recommendation, a local university could turn out to be a gold mine. While students aren't always the best bet, a professor might be. In fact, some teachers play in symphonies during school breaks. In addition, many schools keep a list of alumni who've gone on to professional music careers that you could ask to access. You might also look in the phone book for the local chapter of the American Federation of Musicians, a union that can put you in touch with members. A local symphony is also a good resource. For example, I play in the Alexandria Symphony, and many times people will call the symphony offices and ask if anyone there does weddings. I've gotten a number of jobs that way.

If you do decide to use your local symphony as a resource for musicians, keep in mind that December is the busiest season because of holiday concerts. Therefore, if your wedding is planned for that month, call at least six months in advance. At other times during the year, a three-month lead time should be sufficient.

Recommendation or not, I would ask to hear a demo tape from different groups you're considering—that is, if you haven't already heard them play at a wedding. Otherwise, a demo tape, especially one that features such traditional wedding songs as Pachelbel's *Canon* and "The Wedding March," will give you a good sense of how well this group plays.

When you're thinking about a group to play at your ceremony, try not to become wedded to the idea of specific instruments that you want. Unless you're a professional, you really can't make a good decision about what instruments sound best with each other. I had a bride once insist on having a violin, flute, and trumpet. To her it sounded like a nice combination, but there were too many high-sounding instruments. You don't want all instruments in the same register, and you should listen to your musician if he or she makes a suggestion, like adding a cello to the group.

In addition, if you're having an outdoor ceremony and really want a string quartet, you may find that the musicians you interview would suggest a flute or oboe instead. This isn't because of some prejudice against stringed instruments. Instead, musicians know that stringed instruments don't sound as good outside as they do indoors. Instead, wind instruments work better in an outdoor setting. Again, listen to the suggestions the musicians make. They're professionals, and they know what they're talking about.

Once you decide on a group to play at your ceremony, you should talk about specific tunes you want played at certain times during the ceremony. This is another area where the musician can make some valid suggestions on music. For example, I recently did a wedding where the couple wasn't interested in having all classical music during the ceremony. So I suggested we add some more contemporary tunes, like music from *Phantom of the Opera*. They agreed, and it sounded wonderful. I send all my clients a list of possible ceremony selections to help them choose what they want to have played.

One thing that brides and grooms often do that drives musicians crazy is specifying each and every tune we are to play before

"We hired a trio for our indoor ceremony. It consisted of a violin, cello, and flute. I have to say that their demo tape did them an injustice. I enjoyed the demo tape, but they played more wonderfully in person. It was really beautiful."

Amy, married 8/3/96

Music

the ceremony begins. Maybe they want to print all the musical selections in the program or they're simply control freaks. Instead it's better to give the musicians an idea of the kinds of music you'd like them to play before the bridal party arrives, and then leave the selections up to them. If you tell me I can play a specific list of tunes only and the bridal party ends up arriving late, then there will be dead space with no music. Likewise, if the ceremony gets started early, we may have to abruptly stop a tune in the middle of playing, which will sound awkward. Instead, give the musicians the freedom to bring a variety of appropriate music to play before the bridal party arrives. Of course, you should feel free to suggest some specific songs, but try to avoid dictating every single preprocessional music selection.

As soon as you find a group to play for your ceremony, put down a deposit and get a written contract. Of course, you should make sure there is certain information in the contract to protect you, such as what kind of attire the musicians should wear and what happens if the group has to cancel. However, don't be surprised if the musician adds certain items to the contract as well. For example, if you want me to play at an outdoor wedding, I might add to the contract that you have to provide a sheltered area under which I can play. You may not realize this, but direct sunlight can damage stringed instruments. In addition, if your ceremony is after dark or in a dimly lit church, I'll make sure electrical outlets will be provided to plug lamps in so I'll be able to see the music.

Just keep in mind that the right combination of musical instruments can really make your ceremony a wonderful one.

Brenda Anna's Helpful Hints

* Before you begin interviewing ceremony musicians, find out if your church or synagogue has any restrictions on outside musicians. For example, some churches insist that if you're going to have organ music you use the house organist. You'll usually have to pay a nominal fee for this service.

* It is possible that you envision your musicians sitting one place during the ceremony but, in fact, there isn't enough room. You may need to have your musicians come with you to the ceremony site to scout a location for them. In addition, keep in mind that if you hire a cellist, he or she will need a lot of elbow room to properly play the instrument.

* One of the worst places you could put the musicians is where they can't see who is coming down the aisle. These visual clues tell the musicians what music to play. Try to place the musicians in the front of the ceremony site or off to the side, if possible. If necessary, designate someone as the musicians' liaison, who can signal them when the bridal party arrives or when you are ready to walk down the aisle.

Music for Your Wedding

The University of Virginia Music Library in Charlottesville, Virginia, has a World Wide Web site at http://www.lib.virginia.edu/MusicLib/wedding.html that offers a list of suggested music for your wedding along with sound bites of certain selections. Following is a list of some of that suggested music, reprinted with permission.

Preservice Meditation: Organ and Instrumental Works

Bach, Johann Sebastian—"Air" (on a G string) from *Orchestral Suite in D Major, BWV 1068*

Bach, Johann Sebastian—"Jesu, Joy of Man's Desiring" from *Cantata no. 147*

Bach, Johann Sebastian—Preludes and fugues for organ

Bach, Johann Sebastian—"Sheep May Safely Graze," from *Cantata no. 208*

Bach, Johann Sebastian—"Sleepers Wake"/"Zion Hears the Watchman Singing" from *Cantata no. 140*

Boèllmann, Léon—"Prière" from *Suite Gothique*

Buxtehude, Dietrich—Organ works

Elmore, Robert—*Three Meditative Moments Based on Moravian Hymns*

Franck, César—Organ works

Handel, George Frideric—"Largo" from *Xerxes*

Handel, George Frideric—"Pastoral Symphony" from *Messiah*

Haydn, Franz Joseph—*Musical Clock Music*

Micheelson, Hans Friedrich—*Das Holsteinische Orgelbuchlein*

Pachelbel, Johann—*Canon* (originally for three violins, cello, and harpsicord; has been arranged for keyboard instruments)

Pachelbel, Johann—Organ works

Peeters, Flor—"Aria" from *Trumpet Sonata, op. 51* (also arranged for organ solo)

Vaughn Williams, Ralph—"Rhosymedre" from *Three Preludes on Welsh Hymn Tunes*

Widor, Charles Marie—"Adagio" (4th movement) from *Organ Symphony no. 5, op. 42, no.1*

Preservice Meditation: Vocal Works

Bach, Johann Sebastian—"Jesu, Joy of Man's Desiring" from *Cantata no. 147*

Bach, Johann Sebastian—"Sheep May Safely Graze" from *Cantata no. 208*

Bach, Johann Sebastian—"When Thou Art Near" ("Bist du Bei Mir") from *Anna Magdalena Clavier Book*

Bach, Johann Sebastian/Gounod, Charles—"Ave Maria"

Dvořák, Antonín—*Biblical Songs*, especially "God Is My Shepherd" and "I Will Sing New Songs of Gladness"

Franck, César—"Panis Angelicus"

Handel, George Frideric—"Where'er You Walk" from *Semele*

Malotte, Albert—"The Lord's Prayer"

Schubert, Franz—"Ave Maria"

Vaughan Williams, Ralph—"The Call" from *Five Mystical Songs*

Processional and Recessional

Bach, Johann Sebastian—"Gravement" from *Fantasy in G Major* (middle section), *BWV 572*

Bach, Johann Sebastian—"Prelude in C Major, *BWV 553*" from *Eight Little Preludes and Fugues*

Boèllmann, Léon—*Suite Gothique*

Buxtehude, Deitrich—*Fugue in C Major, BuxWV 174* ("Jig Fugue")

Campra, André—"Rigaudon"

Charpentier, Marc-Antoine—"Processional"

Clarke, Jeremiah—"The Prince of Denmark's March" (attributed to Henry Purcell as "Trumpet Tune")

Clarke, Jeremiah—"Trumpet Tune"

Daquin, Louis Claude—"Grand Jeu et Duo"

Dunstable, John—"Agincourt Hymn"

Handel, George Frideric—"La Rejouissance" ("Rejoicing") from *Music for the Royal Fireworks*

Handel, George Frideric—Sections from the *Water Music* suites, especially "Air" from Suite no. 1, "Alla Hornpipe," and "Solemn Processional"

Haydn, Franz Joseph—"Praise We Sing to Thee" ("St. Anthony's Chorale")

Langlais, Jean—"Pasticcio" from *Organ Book*

Marcello, Benedetto—"Psalm XIX"

Mendelssohn-Bartholdy, Felix—"Con Moto Maestoso" from *Organ Sonata no. 3*

Mendelssohn-Bartholdy, Felix—"Wedding March" from *A Midsummer Night's Dream* ("Here Comes the Bride")

Mouret, Jean-Joseph—"Rondeau" (Theme from *Masterpiece Theatre*)

Purcell, Henry—Trumpet tunes and voluntaries

Rodgers, Richard—"Processional" from *The Sound of Music*

Stanley, John—"Trumpet Tune"

Wagner, Richard—"Bridal Chorus" from *Lohengrin*

Wesley, Samuel Sebastian—"Choral Song"

Widor, Charles Marie—"Toccata" (Finale) from *Organ Symphony no. 5, op. 42, no. 1*

Willan, Healey—"Finale Jubilante"

Listen Up

To help her brides decide on musical selections for their wedding ceremony, bridal consultant Charlene Hein, president of Everlasting Memories by Char, Lakewood, Colorado, suggests they listen to the following CDs:

O Perfect Love . . . and Other Wedding Songs (Intersound, Inc., 1994)

There Is Love (Scotti Bros., 1992)

The Ultimate Wedding Album (The Decca Record Company, 1995)

The Wedding Album (Sony Music Entertainment, Inc., 1991)

Wedding (Dominique Entertainment, Inc., 1994)

Your Perfect Wedding (Scotti Bros. Records, 1994)

Reception Music: Disc Jockeys

"In the last fifteen years or so, the wedding market has become very accepting of deejays," says Laurence Elliott, president of Fascinating Rhythm Disc Jockeys and vice president of the National Association of Mobile Entertainers, a trade association representing deejays. "Deejays are no longer just people who stand behind turntables and play music. We're more sophisticated than that." Elliott says that today's wedding deejays do dance steps with guests to encourage people onto the dance floor, and if you want, a deejay can bring a lighting system to create a more concertlike atmosphere.

What you'll pay for a deejay depends on where you live. "That's why you have to call around and see what people are charging," says Elliott, whose company might charge anywhere from $300 to $1,300 to do a wedding. He says it's important to interview three to four deejays, not only to compare prices but to compare personalities as well. "You have to find someone whom you like and who will listen to your needs. This is your affair," he adds. "You don't want to hire someone who is going to tell you how he or she is going to run things."

It is especially important to meet the actual person whom you might hire for your wedding. Sometimes companies represent a number of deejays, and at your initial meeting you'll speak with a salesperson who will tell you about the company in general terms. Then he or she will discuss different people the company represents. Make sure you get to meet with a specific entertainer, not just a representative.

Be sure any deejay you interview specializes in weddings. "That way they're fresh with music and in touch with what crowds want," he says.

A great way to see what a deejay is like at a wedding is to view a videotape of the deejay at work. "Videos can show you what the deejays wear, what kind of equipment they use, and what they act like when they're working," Elliott says. However, he says, sometimes a video may not suffice. "If the deejay charges $300, a videotape viewing should be OK. But if the deejay charges you $1,000 or more, you might want to take a look at his or her work in person so you can see the difference. There's got to be a reason this person costs more."

Keep in mind there are some valid reasons that some deejays charge more than others. For example, the market drives deejays' rates. If they're doing business in a major metropolitan area, like New York, they're probably going to charge more. In addition, how many people the deejays bring with them, what kind of lighting equipment they use, and if they have costumes or favors to hand out are all going to affect the price tag. "A deejay's having two people working with him or her may be a simple explanation for why this deejay costs $1,200," Elliott adds.

If you like what you see and hear, be sure to ask the deejay for references. "If the deejay refuses, it's a red flag," says Elliott, who suggests hiring someone else. "A deejay should come highly recommended. I live by a simple philosophy of What have I done for you lately? If I've done well for you, you'll recommend me to others."

As with any other vendor, get a contract with your deejay. One important item to include in the contract is when the deejay should arrive. Elliott suggests at least one hour before the affair begins so that when the first guest arrives, the deejay isn't still setting up.

What you might not want to include in the contract is a specific list of songs you want the deejay to play. "A list of songs is very difficult to adhere to. First of all, it doesn't allow the deejay any flexibility of playing things that the crowd seems to like dancing to," says Elliott, "and you've got to keep in mind that in a normal four-hour affair, you can play only eighty songs." Therefore, handing the deejay a list of 120 songs you want played will only lead to disappointment.

About two weeks before your affair, you should sit down with your deejay and map out the reception from beginning to end. Here is where you can make any special requests, such as the one song you want played for your first dance. "In a situation like that, it's OK to specify a song," Elliot says. Then you can put together a list of song categories that you'd like the deejay to play at certain times during the evening. For example, during dinner you might suggest that he or she play jazz and then between courses switch to disco or country to encourage dancing. "That way the deejay has guidelines so he or she knows how to play music that will make you and the groom happy," adds Elliott, "and that the crowd will like."

The National Association of Mobile Entertainers has more than twenty-four thousand members and is happy to refer interested parties to members. For a free referral, call 215-676-4544.

Reception Music: Hiring a Band

One of the most remarkable differences between a disc jockey and a band is a deejay is going to play music that sounds like it does on the radio. The band, on the other hand, is going to play music that sounds similar to what you hear on the radio but with a slight twist to it. If you like the aura of live entertainment and would prefer your music not to be a carbon copy of the music you listen to at home, then a band is right for you.

Here are some tips to keep in mind when hiring a band to play at your wedding reception.

* As soon as you book your wedding date, book a band. Good bands get snapped up as much as a year in advance.

* If you're planning your wedding a year ahead of time, you don't want to have to worry about where your band is going to be in a year. What that means is you should only hire a band that has been in business a number of years and has a good reputation in the area where you're going to have your reception.

* Your banquet manager at your reception site can be a great source of information on local entertainers. You may find that the name of a certain band keeps coming up when you talk to various people in the wedding industry. This is the sign of a good band, and you'll probably want to check this band out.

* Pick a band that specializes in weddings. A band that plays clubs on Friday night and weddings on Saturday nights may not have a clear direction and could be unfamiliar with the way wedding receptions go.

* If you go to a company that represents a number of bands, make sure you get to meet with individual bandleaders. This is the only way to know if you like the person who will be playing at your wedding, and that's an important thing to consider.

* Ask to listen to an audiotape of the band at work. If videotapes are available, ask to see them. While the quality of sound on a videotape can't do a band justice, it will give you a sense of what the band looks like when they are performing.

* Find a bandleader who is flexible. If you or your groom-to-be is a fledgling songwriter and has written a love ballad, the bandleader should be more than willing to get a copy of the music and learn it for you.

* If a band promises to give you continuous music throughout the affair, find out what their definition of continuous music is. It may sound silly, but it means different things to different bandleaders. Some bands will play for the entirety of the reception; others will play for forty-five minutes and then put a tape on for the remaining fifteen minutes of the hour and call that continuous music.

* Tell the bandleader what kind of music you like and want to have at your reception—and what music you don't want them to play. For certain special events during the evening, like the cutting of the cake, inform the bandleader of specific songs you want played.

* On your contract, be sure to include the time the band is to arrive and begin playing, the name of the bandleader you like, and how the band members should dress. Most professional band companies will send their musicians out in attire that's appropriate for a black-tie affair. However, if you're having a casual reception, tuxedos would look out of place. So tell your band what kind of clothing they should wear.

* A good band is worth its price tag. A reputable six-piece band in New York City may charge $3,700; one in Nashville will probably cost less. Think about hiring a band in terms of buying a car. If you find a brand-new Mercedes and it comes with a really cheap price tag, you have to wonder what's wrong with it.

Source: Michael Taylor of Hank Lane Music and Productions, a co-op of ten bands that provides music for weddings in the New York metropolitan area. For more information, call 212-767-0600.

Songs to Play at the Reception

Each year *Mobile Beat Magazine* surveys its readership to find out what the most requested songs at weddings are and then places the songs in corresponding categories, such as dance, ballads, and all-time favorites. For more information about this, write *Mobile Beat Magazine*, P.O. Box 309, East Rochester, New York 14445. Following are the Top 10 songs in a variety of categories from the 1995 list. Reprinted with permission.

All-Time Favorite Songs

1. "Old Time Rock & Roll" (Bob Seger)

2. "Y.M.C.A." (The Village People)

3. "Electric Boogie" (Marcia Griffith)

4. "The Twist" (Chubby Checker)

5. "Mony, Mony" (Billy Idol)

6. "Hot, Hot, Hot" (Buster Poindexter/Arrows)

7. "Wonderful Tonight" (Eric Clapton)

8. "Shout" (Isley Brothers)

9. "Chicken Dance" (Emeralds/Various)

10. "Locomotion" (Kylie Minogue/Grand Funk)

Dance Songs

1. "Gonna Make You Sweat" (C&C Music Factory)

2. "Show Me Love" (Robin S)

3. "The Sign" (Ace of Base)

4. "Twilight Zone" (2 Unlimited)

5. "Move This" (Technotronic)

6. "Baby Got Back" (Sir Mix A-Lot)

7. "Rhythm Is a Dancer" (Snap)

8. "Whoomp! (There It Is)" (Tag Team)

9. "Push It" (Salt-N-Pepa)

10. "Mr. Vain" (Culture Beat)

Ballads

1. "Wonderful Tonight" (Eric Clapton)

2. "Unchained Melody" (Righteous Brothers)

3. "Unforgettable" (Natalie Cole)

4. "Can't Help Falling in Love with You" (Elvis Presley)

5. "I Will Always Love You" (Whitney Houston)

6. "I Swear" (J. M. Montgomery/All-4-One)

7. "Power of Love" (Celine Dion)

8. "After the Loving" (Engelbert Humperdinck)

9. "Have I Told You Lately" (Rod Stewart/Van Morrison)

10. "When a Man Loves a Woman" (Bolton/Faith)

Oldies

1. "The Twist" (Chubby Checker)
2. "Shout" (Otis Day/Isleys/Dynatones)
3. "Old Time Rock & Roll" (Bob Seger)
4. "Twist and Shout" (The Beatles)
5. "Mony, Mony" (Tommy James/Billy Idol)
6. "Brown-Eyed Girl" (Van Morrison)
7. "Runaround Sue" (Dion)
8. "Pretty Woman" (Roy Orbison)
9. "Tequila" (Champs)
10. "Louie, Louie" (Kingsmen)

Bridal (or First-Dance) Songs

1. "Everything I Do" (Bryan Adams)
2. "I Swear" (J. M. Montgomery/All-4-One)
3. "I Cross My Heart" (George Strait)
4. "Power of Love" (Celine Dion)
5. "Have I Told You Lately" (Van Morrison/Rod Stewart)
6. "I Will Always Love You" (Whitney Houston)
7. "Here and Now" (Luther Vandross)
8. "Unchained Melody" (Righteous Brothers)
9. "When I Fall in Love" (Celine Dion/Clive Griffin)
10. "Unforgettable" (Natalie Cole)

Country

1. "Boot Scoot Boogie" (Brooks & Dunn)
2. "Chattahoochie" (Alan Jackson)
3. "Friends in Low Places" (Garth Brooks)
4. "Achy Breaky Heart" (Billy Ray Cyrus)

5. "Crazy" (Patsy Cline)

6. "Baby Likes to Rock It" (The Tractors)

7. "I Swear" (J. M. Montgomery)

8. "Trashy Women" (Confederate Railroad)

9. "The Dance" (Garth Brooks)

10. "Watermelon Crawl" (Tracy Byrd)

Classic Rock

1. "You Shook Me All Night Long" (AC/DC)

2. "Old Time Rock & Roll" (Bob Seger)

3. "Paradise by the Dashboard Light" (Meatloaf)

4. "Mony, Mony" (Billy Idol)

5. "What I Like About You" (Romantics)

6. "Brown-Eyed Girl" (Van Morrison)

7. "Taking Care of Business" (BTO)

8. "Some Kind of Wonderful" (Grand Funk)

9. "Centerfold" (J. Geils Band)

10. "Satisfaction" (Rolling Stones)

Alternative Rock

1. "Love Shack" (The B-52's)

2. "Two Princes" (Spin Doctors)

3. "Mr. Jones" (Counting Crows)

4. "Come Out and Play" (Offspring)

5. "Basket Case" (Green Day)

6. "What I Like About You" (The Romantics)

7. "Bizarre Love Triangle" (New Order)

8. "Losing My Religion" (R.E.M.)

9. "Melt with You" (Modern English)

10. "Smells Like Teen Spirit" (Nirvana)

Disco

1. "Y.M.C.A." (Village People)
2. "Stayin' Alive" (Bee Gees)
3. "Celebration" (Kool & the Gang)
4. "I Will Survive" (Gloria Gaynor)
5. "We Are Family" (Sister Sledge)
6. "Disco Inferno" (The Tramps)
7. "Play That Funky Music" (Wild Cherry)
8. "Le Freak" (Chic)
9. "Super Freak" (Rick James)
10. "December 1963" (Four Seasons)

Rap/R&B

1. "Whoomp! (There It Is)" (Tag Team)
2. "Shoop" (Salt-N-Pepa)
3. "Baby Got Back" (Sir Mix-A-Lot)
4. "It Takes Two" (Rob Base)
5. "Push It" (Salt-N-Pepa)
6. "Can't Touch This" (M. C. Hammer)
7. "Hip Hop Hooray" (Naughty By Nature)
8. "Wild Thing" (Tone Loc)
9. "Regulate" (Warren G)
10. "Tootsie Roll" (69 Boyz)

Music

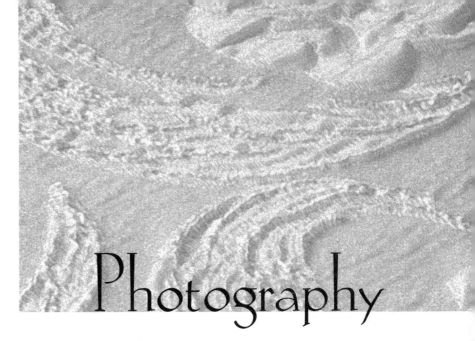

Photography

Capturing your special day on film is one of the most important parts of your wedding memories. Making sure you find a photographer who can record your event in the way you want it is as important as finding a good caterer and a wedding gown. When my husband and I were planning our wedding, we decided that we didn't want a traditional photographer who would use soft-focus filters and set up enough lights to make our wedding ceremony resemble a Hollywood production. Instead, we preferred to go with a photographer who specialized in photojournalistic photography—that is, recording the event more like it really was rather than setting up shots and then asking us to hold unnatural poses for minutes at a time.

But just because a photojournalistic wedding photographer was perfect for my wedding, it doesn't mean it will be for yours. You and your future spouse need to discuss exactly what you expect—and don't expect—from your photographer. And you'll need to figure out what your idea of the perfect wedding album is. For some couples that is shots of the two of them looking like glamorous screen stars. For others, like Bill and me, that meant behind-the-scenes candid pictures that looked more like documentary photographs than traditional wedding pictures.

How to Find a Picture-Perfect Wedding Photographer

Ann K. Monteith is a professional wedding photographer and author of The Business of Wedding Photography *(Amphoto, 1996). Here are her tips for finding a picture-perfect wedding photographer.*

Nuptials News

Many wedding photographers are members of the Professional Photographers of America (PPA), a trade association in Atlanta with approximately fourteen thousand members. You can call PPA for a free referral to wedding photographers in your area. For more information, call 800-786-6277.

* One of the best ways to find a wedding photographer you'll be happy with is through other people who have had really good experiences with that photographer. While the photos themselves are important, the service you get from the photographer is crucial. Remember: the photographer is one of the people your family will be with from the beginning of the day to the end of the day.

* Make sure you like the photographer you consider hiring. You want someone who is a good listener and seems to understand your vision of your wedding day. In fact, a good wedding photographer may ask as many questions of you as you do of him or her.

* When you visit a photography studio and look at samples of wedding photographs, make sure you ask to see a complete album of one wedding. This will give you a good indication of what the photographer can do. For example, does the photographer seem to handle portraits as well as candid pictures? Also, make sure that a studio isn't trying to show you the best work of all of its photographers.

* When you look at sample books, make sure you ask how much they cost. You want to get a good sense of what you get for what price tag. If the photographer offers packages, ask to see written descriptions of each package. Find out if there are any extra charges for having additional photographs printed after your wedding is over or once your album is delivered.

* Ask the photographer to map out the wedding day for you—how he or she sees the timing of the day. Make sure that all the photographs you want taken can get done without anyone's feeling rushed. If you've already booked your church and reception location and your schedule doesn't leave you a lot of time between the ceremony and reception to take pictures, ask how the photographer would work with you on that.

* Ask the photographer how many breaks he or she expects to take. Because a professional photographer is on duty throughout the wedding, you should be prepared to offer him or her a meal. This person will be with you all day and will get hungry.

* Find out how the photographer feels about your guests' taking pictures. Some photographers don't want guests taking

photographs when they do, because they feel it cuts into their chances for reprint business. More important, cameras flashing all over the place when the photographer is trying to set up an exposure can throw his or her camera off and literally ruin the photographs you've paid him or her to take.

* If you're going to look at preview photographs (formally called *proofs*) of your wedding photographs, find out what methods the photographer uses. Many photographers still present the preview set of photographs as prints. However, some upload the images to CD-ROM, copy them onto a videotape, or show them to you in a slide presentation. Make sure the photographer uses a presentation method you're comfortable with. For example, if you're not very technologically oriented, you probably won't care to have a photographer hand you a compact disc of photos instead of a box of prints. Also find out how long you'll have to keep the preview photographs for your perusal. Some photographers ask for them back in a short period of time.

* Finally, if you find a specific photographer at a studio with whom you click, have his or her name added to your contract. That way you're guaranteed that this will be the person who shows up on your wedding day. Also make sure your contract includes price and payment information, specific attire the photographer should wear, and the time the photographer should arrive at your home, church, or wherever you've agreed to meet.

Traditional Wedding Photography

I recently had the opportunity to chat with David Bentley, owner of Bentley Studio in suburban St. Louis. Bentley has been in the business for more than two decades and has photographed hundreds of weddings. His portrait work has won numerous awards, including Kodak's Gallery Award for Photographic Excellence. Bentley's ability to take gorgeous wedding photographs has brides and grooms all over the Midwest flying him in to shoot their weddings. For more information, contact Bentley Studio, Le Chateau Village, 10403 Clayton Road, Frontenac, MO 63131, 314-991-2502. Here he talks about the basics of finding a traditional wedding photographer.

LI: *What makes a good traditional wedding photographer?*

"We did all our formal pictures before the ceremony. The nicest thing is that we got to be with our guests the whole time at the reception without any disruptions for formal photographs."
Elena, married 8/17/97

Photography

149

According to a 1996 Photo Marketing Association survey, there are certainly popular places where wedding portraits are photographed. Of the couples surveyed, they had their portraits taken at the following locations:

church
   (51.6 percent)
in an outdoor setting
   (28.3 percent)
professional studio
   (21.4 percent)
department store
   (21.2 percent)
bride/groom's home
   (14.8 percent)

DB: Understand that traditional wedding photography is more than just posed pictures. An album of all posed pictures is a portrait album, not a wedding album. In my opinion, a wedding album includes some posed pictures, but it also includes a good body of unposed, candid pictures. In a finished wedding album, the posed pictures that we take are supposed to introduce the characters of the wedding. Then we go to mostly unposed pictures to show what happened to you and your family that day.

LI: *So why would you hire a traditional photographer over a photojournalist?*

DB: My clients want images with a greater degree of predictability. They want posed pictures that are flattering to them. All brides want to look beautiful, and all grooms want to look handsome. They want to know that I will take the time to set up photographs so that their hair looks perfect or the bride's gown looks just so. And they like knowing that if there's a blemish on their skin that shows up on film, I will retouch it on the finished product.

LI: *What about the issue of packages?*

DB: I always ask my clients what their ideas of wedding photography are. Do they want photos of each of their guests? Pictures of tables at the reception? Beautiful pictures in the park? I also ask about their photography budget, and then we put together a package that best serves their needs. For example, if they're having five hundred people to their reception but they can afford only a twenty-four-page album, then I might suggest a package that doesn't include pictures of all the guests. If the bride and groom have no preconceived notions of what kind of photographs they want, a package can help them make a decision. You need to look at the photographer's menu of packages and see what fits the bill.

LI: *Aren't some wedding photographers rigid when it comes to their packages?*

DB: Yes, and they'll probably do your wedding in a cookie-cutter format as well. So you want to stay away from a photographer who is inflexible about his or her packages or has his or her own vision of how weddings should be photographed. Nothing in my packages is written in stone. You can change elements of the packages around to fit what you want financially and artistically so that no one is disappointed in the end.

LI: *What sort of questions should you ask a traditional photographer to make sure he or she doesn't take a cookie-cutter approach to your wedding?*

DB: Ask the photographer how long he or she expects to spend taking formal photographs and when he or she usually takes them during the day. Is the photographer willing to be flexible about the timing of the formal pictures? For example, I had a couple who didn't want to see each other before their wedding but they also didn't have time on their wedding day to have formal portraits taken without taking time away from the reception. So what did we do? Moved the appointment for the formal pictures to another day, after they returned from their honeymoon. I believe that a photographer's time budget can be spread around in whatever way serves the client and the photographer best.

Besides your asking the photographer questions, the photographer should also ask you questions that will help him or her take great pictures—questions about the size of your family, the marital status of your parents, the kind of attire you and your attendants will be wearing, and any special people who will need to be photographed that day.

LI: *How many photographs should you expect the photographer to produce?*

DB: I tell my clients to expect double the amount of images that will be in their wedding album. So if they've ordered a forty-page album, I'll deliver eighty images. But keep in mind these are eighty different pictures, all of which are of a quality that I believe would be worthy of being placed in the finished album. So make sure that your photographer doesn't present you with a bunch of duplicate pictures or ones in which people's eyes are closed. Ask to see proofs from a finished album that the photographer has done so you can get an idea of what to expect.

LI: *How long should it take for the photographer to deliver your proofs?*

DB: Each photographer is different, but I think three weeks after the wedding is a reasonable time to expect to see your proofs.

LI: *What if the photographer puts a time limit on how long you have to look at your proofs?*

DB: You should ask your photographer up front if he or she expects you to return the proofs and in how short a period of time. In my case, I let the clients keep the proofs. In fact, most of my clients don't contact me about putting their album together until two to three months after the wedding. For some photographers, returning the proofs and getting the albums made is their way of making money. With me, I get half of my fee before the wedding and the

Engaged couples in the Northeast are more likely than couples living elsewhere in the United States to have a formal wedding portrait taken, according to the *1996 Photo Marketing Association U.S. Consumer Photo Buying Report.*

Photography

151

other half when you pick up the proofs. So make sure you ask the photographer how his or her getting paid will affect your ability to look at your proofs and order your album.

LI: *What if you want pictures made after you've already paid the photographer?*

DB: At my studio, everything after the fact is à la carte on the menu—meaning you'll have to pay additional fees for additional services. Make sure you find this pricing information out ahead of time. That's why it's so important to get package information in writing. This way you'll know what the original fee will cover and what it won't.

LI: *What else do you need to know to find a great wedding photographer?*

DB: Hire someone who has been in business for a while and will probably be in business for years to come. You never know when you'll need reprints of your wedding photographs, and you want to know that your photographer will be around in the future. Also make sure you hire a wedding photographer you like. If the photographer's vision of your wedding doesn't match yours, then maybe you need another photographer.

David Bentley's Photography Package

A typical photography package from Bentley Studio costs $3,160 and includes the following (reprinted by permission):

* engagement session for the couple
* formal bridal portrait session
* two four-by-five-inch black-and-white photographs for publication
* eighty images of mixed sizes in a custom leather album
* photographer's services for seven consecutive hours
* complete proof collection

Photojournalistic Wedding Photography

Sardi Klein, a New York City–based photographer, has been shooting Manhattan weddings for more than twenty years. She also teaches photography at the School of Visual Arts and Cooper Union. Her real specialty is photographing weddings in a nontraditional way. Here's what Klein had to say about finding a photojournalistic wedding photographer.

Couples who hire me to shoot their wedding would rather have candid pictures of their friends and family enjoying the party than tons of posed pictures. People hire me because of my selling point—I do take some nice formal pictures, but mostly I take a lot of candid pictures. They tell me, "I'm not getting married for the photographer, and I'm not arriving at my wedding two hours early to take pictures. I'd rather forgo the formal pictures and spend more time at my party enjoying myself with my friends." After the fact, when I deliver the pictures and negatives to my clients, most of them confess that they didn't even know I was at their wedding. That's how discreet I try to be.

Make sure that if you decide to go the freelance, photojournalistic route that you find someone who specializes in weddings. I know a couple who hired a freelance photographer who'd worked for *Life* magazine to shoot their wedding. They had great pictures of themselves but none of their friends or the bride's grandmother, who died a week later. Local art schools or colleges can be a resource for low-cost freelance photographers, but, again, make sure they've shot weddings before.

A great way to make sure your photographer doesn't miss certain images is to give him or her a shooting schedule and family tree before the wedding begins. I have people tell me who the important people in the family are and who's connected to whom. I also ask if there are any family feuds, so I know who can't be photographed with whom. Then, to make sure I can put a face with a name on a list, I ask the bride and groom to assign at least one person at the reception to me so that person can walk around with me and point people out.

In addition, when putting together the shooting schedule, I ask the bride and groom to let me in on any traditions or special items at the wedding that may not be obvious to me. For example, I recently photographed a wedding where the couple was of Latvian descent. At Latvian weddings, the father gives a piece of black bread to the groom during the ceremony, and it's a big deal. If someone didn't point this out to me beforehand, how would I know its significance and that I should record it? Also I'll want to know if a close friend baked the cake or the bride's sister did the centerpieces. That way, I'll know to shoot a number of photographs of something I might not normally concentrate on.

I always ask the couple if there are any photographs they can't live without. I learned to do this after a client complimented me on all the photographs I'd taken of her and her mom and dad but then told me that she really wanted a picture of her with her dad alone by the fireplace. She didn't speak up on her wedding day about that shot, and I didn't know enough to ask.

Sardi Klein's Tips for Getting Great Wedding Photographs

* Many guests have a tendency to blink just as I'm snapping a picture. It seems like they're watching my finger on the trigger and then blink as I press down. To avoid their blinking, I try two different things. I might have them look at the bride and groom, so they can't watch my finger. Or I'll ask them to keep their eyes closed. Then, when I count to three, I tell them to open their eyes and smile.

* Many overweight people who are self-conscious of their double chins will try to stretch their necks to make themselves appear thinner. What ends up happening is they seem as if they're looking up to God. When I have a heavy person in a group shot, I may ask him or her to stand sideways. This way, when the overweight person brings his or her neck around to look at the camera, it stretches and straightens out a double chin and makes him or her appear thinner.

* Eyeglasses will always reflect my flash unless the person tilts his or her head down, and then you're stuck with someone's literally looking down his or her nose at you. Usually, I'll ask a person to take two different pictures—one with the glasses on and the other with the glasses off. If the bride and groom like the picture with the glasses on, I can always retouch the little dot the flash caused.

* If you plan to dance it up at your wedding, make sure your photographer gets all your formal photographs before the band starts playing. Your hair and makeup will look fresher and neater before you start dancing and sweating.

* Try not to have any guests near where you're taking formal pictures. Some photographers put a clause in their contract that says no guests can take pictures when formal pictures are being done, because the bride and groom are easily distracted by all the different flashes. If keeping the bride and groom isolated isn't possible, I'll make a brief announcement to the shutter-happy guests. I tell them that if they start taking pictures when I do, then the bride and groom are most likely going to end up with photographs of themselves look-

ing every which way except at me. I ask them to hold off on their picture taking until I've had the chance to take five or so images. Then they can take as many as they want. The end result? I take my pictures faster and the bride and groom get great pictures.

One-Time-Use Cameras: Letting the Guests in on the Fun

Sometimes it's impossible for a wedding photographer, no matter how well prepared, to capture everything that goes on at a wedding, especially from the guests' perspective. That's why supplying the guests with one-time-use cameras is a great option. Kodak recently introduced a Wedding Party Pack that includes five one-time-use cameras each complete with flash and a fifteen-exposure roll of film already loaded in the camera. These cameras are a special wedding edition and are packaged in an attractive cardboard case that is decorated with wedding-type flowers.

The pack also includes tent cards that say "Share the memories with us! Pick up a camera and capture the fun!" You can place these cards on reception tables to help inspire guests to play amateur shutterbug.

Don't worry about offending your professional photographer by giving your guests these one-time-use cameras. Says Terence McArdle, a spokesperson for Eastman Kodak, "Most photographers don't see these cameras as competitive but rather as a way of getting things that a professional photographer isn't hired to do." In fact, says McArdle, some professional photographers offer Wedding Party Packs as part of their package deal.

To find a retailer near you that sells Kodak's Wedding Party Pack, call 800-242-2424.

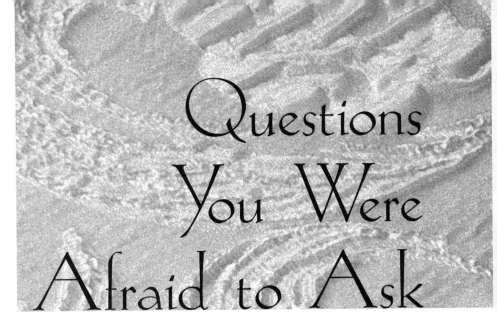

Questions You Were Afraid to Ask

*E*veryone has heard of the term *cold feet*, but what does it really mean? For some jittery brides and grooms, the definition could become frighteningly obvious if they start to question the decisions they're making, as most brides and grooms do at some point in the wedding-planning process. These questions could range from "Do I really want to have such a big wedding?" to "Am I really ready to get married?"

Just because you start to ask questions doesn't mean you're actually having cold feet; quite the opposite is true. Having questions is completely normal.

So that you won't freak out if any questions start popping up in your mind in the months before your wedding, here are the answers to some of the questions you were probably afraid to ask.

I recently spoke with Dr. Everett Worthington, a professor of psychology at Virginia Commonwealth University in Richmond, Virginia. Dr. Worthington has done extensive research on family and marriage issues, and has written sixteen books and more than one hundred articles on the topic.

LI: *What if you get cold feet?*

EW: I hope that you would not feel compelled to go on with the wedding if you really didn't feel that this was the thing for you. The consequences of divorce are simply too high to go through with the marriage because it's easier than backing out. You want to make sure you feel good about marrying this person.

On the other hand, many times cold feet are caused by simple nervousness, and that's perfectly normal. It's a big change that

Nuptials News

According to *Bride's Magazine*, the average length of an engagement is 12.1 months.

you're about to make, and with any big change, you're going to feel uncertain about what's going on. You're going to feel anxious to some extent. In order to get over your nervousness, you may have to make your own judgment about to what degree is this person not right for you versus your natural uncertainty as to whether you ought to get married at all.

Ask yourself, "Why am I worried about this? Are there things that I think have revealed themselves so far that might indicate that we're not going to do very well?" For example, if you have had a lot of conflict before getting married, chances are you're going to have it after the wedding. Have you noticed negative things that you've been hesitant to admit to yourself but are gnawing at you? When people are engaged, they get stars in their eyes, and it's easy to overlook things or say, "I'll change my partner when we get married." But you can't change someone, and you've got to feel confident that you're marrying this person because you love him or her for who he or she is right now.

The inability to resolve a number of issues can be a big problem. You want to ask yourself, "What's our balance between positive and negative interactions?" One researcher found that the major predictor of divorce is the ratio of positive to negative interactions in a day-to-day relationship. A ratio of 5 to 1 shows that the marriage is stable and satisfying. But if the ratio is less than 5 to 1, chances are the relationship won't endure for more than four years.

These positive and negative interactions aren't just about agreeing on everything but on whether you kiss, laugh together, have fun on a date, or do anything you consider positive. This is day-to-day interactions. Also ask yourself, "Are we able to discuss things? Are we able to talk in a way that's satisfactory?" Communication is the cornerstone of a solid relationship.

LI: *What if one of you isn't in the mood to have sex on your wedding night?*

EW: In general, people make love all the time when they're not in the mood for it. One of the things that I've found is that if you're not in the mood and you don't make love, your mood doesn't improve. Often if you're not in the mood and you do make love, it does improve.

To violate the norm of the expectation—that you're going to make love on your wedding night—is pretty serious. When you don't understand each other sexually, it can cause problems. If you have saved having sex for the wedding night, you probably see losing your virginity that night as a pretty strong cultural norm. When you go against that, it can be a blow to the relationship. If you've been living together, you've already established a relationship and know that you don't make love every night.

In general, making love, whether it's the wedding night or any other time, is more than hopping into bed and having intercourse. Foreplay starts long before you ever get near the bedroom, with touches, looks, talking, and just gentleness with each other. Lots of stuff goes on during the wedding day, and it's a high-tension time. You probably won't leap out of the car, jump into a motel room, strip down, and hit the bed naked. You should count on wooing your partner a little bit, getting your partner in the mood, perhaps taking the initiative to try to focus on how you're going to seduce your partner. Then, by the time you're ready to make love, you will be more in the mood.

LI: *What can you do if you fear that you won't be a good spouse?*

EW: Not everyone is a good husband or wife. Being one doesn't happen because you were born to be a good husband or wife. Becoming a good husband or wife happens because you make it a high priority and really work at it. It's a lot like tending a garden. If I want to grow a garden of beautiful vegetables, it requires putting a lot of energy into that garden. If I think it's great fun to garden but I don't put energy and work into it, I don't get any beautiful vegetables. I may just end up with a patch of weeds.

It can be great fun to have a wonderful marriage relationship, but it requires a lot of work and creativity on the part of both the husband and the wife. You have to understand that being a good spouse is something that's learned. It's like learning to do any skill. Yes, you are someone's wife the day after your wedding, but you're going to be better at being someone's wife the more effort you put into it.

LI: *It's possible for newlyweds to not like their in-laws. How can you have a relationship with them that's civil and cordial?*

EW: I think you ought to value your partner's parents, especially if your spouse feels really positive about Mom and Dad. If he or she is really close to his or her family, you're going to have to figure out how you're going to live with those folks and keep a good relationship without spending 100 percent of your time worrying about it.

You need to be honest with your spouse and talk about how you'll manage the in-law problem. There might be times that one of you goes to visit your family and the other doesn't go. As long

Nearly 2.4 million marriages occurred in the United States in 1994, according to *Bride's Magazine.*

Questions You Were Afraid to Ask

According to U.S. Census Bureau statistics, there were 3.7 million unmarried couples households in 1994. That means there were seven unmarried couples living together for every one hundred married couples in the United States.

as every once in a while the other shows that he or she values the in-laws and minimizes the contacts so there are no outright arguments or disagreements, he or she should be OK. If I don't like my boss, I have to figure out how I can do my job and interact with my boss in a way that I don't really anger him. It's the same fundamental human problem with in-laws.

Just because you don't see eye to eye doesn't mean you have to have a heart-to-heart talk every time you differ with someone. On the other hand, if something your in-laws said or did is going to eat at you, then there's got to be a way to resolve the issue, and that may involve talking it out with them.

Wedding planning can be very stressful, and it doesn't help when the parties involved don't get along. Sometimes stress skews your ability to see things clearly. For example, someone may do something, like make a joke, that under ordinary circumstances people would find funny. But when people are under stress, they may not laugh at things and instead be insulted by them. It's the stress that causes this change in behavior. For example, if your future mother-in-law does something that annoys you, when you're stressed out you won't say, "Oh, isn't that annoying." Instead you'll probably say, "Oh, my mother-in-law is possessed, and she's out to get me."

In the heat of wedding planning, you ought to give your future in-laws the benefit of the doubt unless they do things to you time and time again. Then it's probably best to avoid them for a while rather than fight with them. If you pick a fight, you will inadvertently put your spouse directly in the middle, and you should never force your spouse to divide his or her loyalty.

LI: *If you live together before marriage, will you end up divorced?*

EW: Some people reason that living together may affect the divorce rate, because when you live together, you're not committed to each other. You're usually together on a basis of "we'll see if this works," and that attitude continues after marriage. It's as if some people say, "Yeah, we're married, but it may not work out, and then I'm out of here."

To try to go against the statistics, ask yourself, "What can I do to make sure that I know that I'm committing to this person for life?" You need to try to think intentionally of how you can make that commitment for life real. I say that because if you just say commitment, what does it mean? You're only committed for as long as you feel like you love each other, which is an attitude that contributes to divorce.

According to *Bride's Magazine*, 63 percent of brides and grooms are getting married for the first time; 37 percent of them are remarrying.

You can feel more committed by simply talking about it and saying out loud, beyond your wedding vows, that you are making a commitment for life. Commitment is not related to time but rather to exclusivity. You want to discuss ahead of time that you've adopted an attitude that this relationship is going to last forever, that you're going to make it work, and that when things get bad, you're still going to make it work instead of bailing out.

Reception

Originally Bill and I were going to have our wedding reception at a yacht club a family member belonged to. What was great about this location was it was on the waterfront; it came complete with tables, chairs, linen, china, and so forth; and because of our family association, it would have cost only about $500 to rent. There were some bad things about this location as well, which led us to find an alternative reception site. For one thing, because of its waterfront locale, we couldn't invite any children, and we really wanted to. There was the danger of their slipping off the dock and falling into the water. Even worse, the fire code said the building could hold no more than 125 people, and our guest list had already creeped up over the 150-person mark.

These deterrents led us to the idea of having our reception in my grandfather's backyard, something I'd actually dreamed about since I was a child. While the yacht club may have been filled with bad karma, it did lead us to the caterer we eventually hired. We'd chosen her not only because we loved her food but also because she was located only a few blocks from the yacht club. We figured her proximity to our reception site was a good thing—and what a good thing she turned out to be.

When we decided to change reception sites, she didn't fight us. Instead, she offered suggestions on how we might alter our menu to better suit our garden brunch (as opposed to the menu she'd created to fit the atmosphere of the yacht club). In addition, now that we were throwing the party in a backyard, we needed a tent, tables, chairs, linens, plates, silverware, glasses, and so on. "No problem," our caterer said. "I'll research it for you and just add it to my bill."

Nuptials News

According to *Bride's Magazine*, the average wedding reception costs $5,957.

Finally, because we would no longer have a stocked bar and bartender supplied by the reception site, we turned to our caterer for advice. She suggested we limit our bar to wine, champagne, gin, vodka, and fruit juices and stock it ourselves to save money. She, in turn, would supply bartenders at cost.

All in all, thanks to the creative genius of our caterer, Bill and I were able to pull off a reception that people still talk about to this day.

Reception Styles

The kind of wedding you're planning to have often determines where you'll have your reception. Here, Lois Pearce, a master bridal consultant and president of Beautiful Occasions in Hamden, Connecticut, offers some ideas to keep in mind when selecting a reception site. Beautiful Occasions plans a variety of wedding-related events, from rehearsal dinners to receptions. For more information, call 203-248-2661.

- If you are looking for a high-style reception, with chandeliers, marble floors, a great dance floor, several courses of food service, and good china and crystal, a hotel ballroom will probably fit the bill.

- Your best bet for entertaining a large number of people—say two hundred or more guests—is a hotel ballroom or reception hall.

- One of the benefits of going to a banquet hall or hotel is that they are used to having events. Therefore, you don't have to worry about their having a sufficient number of electrical outlets for the caterer and band, enough fire extinguishers on hand, or handicapped access. In addition, sites like this supply all your linens and china for you.

- It might make sense to hold a smaller wedding reception in a more unusual locale, such as on the patio of a country club, in a museum, or at a park.

- If you decide to have your wedding in an offbeat location, your caterer can act as your event planner. He or she can find vendors to provide tables and chairs, dishes and glasses, table linens, and more.

Reception Sites: Hiring a Hotel or Hall

The Loews Ventana Canyon Resort in Tucson, Arizona, offers a variety of locations for ceremonies and receptions, including two grand ballrooms. Staci Barton is the catering sales manager at Loews. Couples who decide to get married at the resort, have their reception at the resort, or both, work with Barton on all aspects of planning the reception. For more information, call 520-299-2020. I recently spoke with Barton about what you need to keep in mind when hiring a full-service hotel or hall for your wedding reception.

LI: *How do you decide if a hotel or reception hall is right for your wedding reception?*

SB: You need to get as much information as possible about the place, and the best way to do that is to call ahead and make an appointment with the catering manager. I can't tell you how many people just walk in and start asking questions. I may not have time to talk to them then, but if they make an appointment with me, I can give them my full attention, answer their questions, and take them on the tour of the property.

LI: *When you call to make the appointment with the catering manager, where should you be in the wedding-planning process?*

SB: You should definitely have a date in mind so I can check availability. For example, in the summer of 1996, people started calling about dates in 1998. While that is pretty far in advance, popular dates do book up. For example, here in Arizona, June isn't very popular because the temperature gets up to 120 degrees. However, dates in September through November get snapped up fast.

In addition, you should have an estimated number of people you think will attend. The size of your guest list will help me determine whether it's more appropriate to show you a space designed for an intimate wedding dinner for fifty or a dinner dance for five hundred.

LI: *What can you expect to discuss during this initial meeting with the catering manager?*

SB: Not only will I show you various spaces in the hotel, but I'll also talk about menu choices and the prices for each. In a full-service establishment like the Loews Ventana Canyon Resort, your per-

Reception

head menu price will include food (of course), room rental, dance floor, chairs and tables, and most things that go on the table, such as linens and china. What I'll show you are our standards, but if you want a different color linen or another kind of china, it will cost you more.

LI: *What food items aren't covered in the per-head fee?*

SB: Wedding cake is normally a separate cost, and alcohol isn't included in your menu price.

LI: *What if you don't want Loews or your reception hall to provide your wedding cake?*

SB: Like many other reception sites, we charge a cake-cutting fee if you bring in your own wedding cake. It's $1.50 per person.

LI: *Can a place like Loews provide anything else for you?*

SB: If they want, I'll put together a list of reputable local vendors that they can call themselves. However, I don't ever want you to feel as if I'm pushing our florist on you. Some sites will do this—that is, require you to use their florist, photographer, and cake baker. Make sure you ask about this up front. What I try to do is encourage my couples to shop around so they feel that they're getting the best deal.

LI: *What if you decide that you do want the catering manager to do all the planning for you? How much will the catering manager do?*

SB: I love clients who hire me to work as the wedding coordinator. I provide the photographer, the florist, and anything else they need. Many couples don't realize that a catering manager is supposed to act as a wedding coordinator if necessary.

LI: *Why might you choose a hotel over a hall for a reception?*

SB: Of course, I'm biased on this one, but the great thing about a hotel—especially if your wedding is taking place over an entire weekend—is we can provide accommodations for your guests. We can work out a deal where your guests get dinner and accommodations on Friday night, they attend your wedding on Saturday, and then they come together again on Sunday for a farewell brunch.

The benefit to the bride is we can offer her a changing room free of charge, and she can take advantage of our on-site beauty salon for her wedding-day hair and makeup.

On-Premises Caterer Versus Off-Premises Caterer

Teresa Yodice, president of Hearts of Palms Catering in Brightwaters, New York, has catered everything from a backyard luncheon wedding for forty to a two-hundred-person-plus grand affair in a Manhattan mansion. For more information about events and weddings catered by Hearts of Palm, call 516-968-4047. Here she explains the differences between an on-premises caterer and an off-premises caterer and why you might want to hire one over the other.

* I'm called an off-premises caterer because I am not associated with a specific reception facility. I bring my services to the premises. Not surprisingly, an on-premises caterer is one that works exclusively with a reception site, be it a hotel or a hall.

* The benefit of using an on-premises caterer is many of the decisions are already made for you, and if you are uncertain about what you want, this can take some of the hassles out of the decision-making process. For example, you won't have to worry about finding a company to provide linens or a wedding cake because the on-premises caterer will do that for you. Your biggest decision may come down to whether you want prime rib or chicken. For someone with a lot on her mind, having limited selections may be a big relief.

  When you come to an off-premises caterer like me, either you already have a space chosen or you want me to help you find an independent space to rent. Couples who hire me probably have a set idea in their minds about where they want their reception and what kind of food they want served, and as an independent caterer, I can be very flexible.

* An on-premises caterer can act as your party planner by supplying you with a photographer, florist, and more. And you know what? So can I. You can hire me to be your party planner, and I'll get you everything you need for your wedding day. Or you can simply hire me to make the food that your guests will eat.

* While the price of hiring an off-premises versus an on-premises caterer probably won't vary too much in the long run, you may find that there are more hidden costs with an off-premises caterer. For example, an on-premises caterer will probably offer you a package deal and price list of what ser-

Reception

According to the
Association of Bridal
Consultants, the trend in
wedding receptions is
toward light fare and
buffet-style food stations
with a wide variety of
foods. More couples are
including ethnic foods in
their menu as well.

vices he or she includes in the per-head price, such as the meal and the linens. Your final cost probably won't vary too much from the price you're quoted.

Compare that with an off-premises caterer, who is providing all services à la carte. Therefore, such a caterer will have to spell everything out for you, from the cost of appetizers to the cost of alcohol. If the off-premises caterer you meet with isn't up front with you about all his or her costs, find someone else.

* Find out where tipping comes into the picture. Some caterers, like an on-premises one, might add a set gratuity into the total price as a way to cover their service costs. With me, it's up to you. If you find my service extraordinary, then feel free to tip me. I suggest offering an extra hour's wage for each staff person working at the reception.

* Finally, don't walk away from your meeting with your caterer feeling robbed. You want to feel good about the check you write to pay for your reception, so make sure you feel good about the decision you make when hiring your caterer.

How to Have a Mouth-Watering Menu and a Reception Your Guests Will Remember

The Chicago Caterers is a full-service custom caterer that has been in business since 1979 and prides itself on cutting-edge cuisine. They will cater any special event in the greater Chicago area, as well as Wisconsin, Michigan, and Indiana. For more information call 630-355-1208. Jon Wool, a sales manager at The Chicago Caterers, shares his ideas on how to create a mouth-watering menu and have a reception your guests will remember long after your first anniversary has passed.

A wedding celebration should reflect who you are, what your history is, and how you like to entertain in your spare time. I recently worked with a couple who had fallen in love on a corporate retreat to Hawaii, and they wanted their reception to reflect the genesis of their relationship. For them, we created a South Pacific menu that featured fresh seafood. Even our service staff got into the act by dressing in white linen pants and colorful shirts.

You want to find a caterer with a good reputation who can create a menu that suits your taste. The number-one way to find a caterer is through word of mouth, and most couples find that only caterers or catering halls with tried-and-true track records will get recommended to them again and again.

You may find that the caterer of your dreams works for a catering hall. Or you may find that the caterer who can create your ideal menu from scratch is an independent contractor. The decision of which kind of caterer you hire is up to you. But the bottom line is you want to hire someone who listens to your ideas and who can help make the reception of your dreams come true.

This past summer, a couple with very particular tastes hired us for their wedding. They instructed us on everything from where the lobster tail for the main entree was to have come from (Africa, not Maine) to the ingredients for their wedding cake. They arrived for our first meeting armed with sketches and story boards. While they were an extreme, it's great when you are as clear as possible to your caterer about what you want for your wedding reception.

What you need to take into consideration when planning your menu is the time of day and season of your reception. People tend to eat lighter in the early part of the day and in the summer. That doesn't mean you'll offer a smaller quantity of food, just lighter fare. Compare that with meals served late in the day or in colder weather. Then, you'll want to stick with heavier sauces and flavors of the season, such as pumpkin and squash in the fall.

While time of day may affect your menu, it probably won't affect your bottom line. Brunch may seem as if it could be cheaper but not if you offer a large variety of food. In addition, you may think a sit-down dinner would be more expensive than a buffet; that's not always true. For example, on food alone, a sit-down meal is cheaper, because you know you need, for example, only five ounces of roast beef for each guest as opposed to buying an entire side of beef to carve at the buffet. However, when your guests are sitting down for a multicourse dinner, you need more china, silver, and glassware and a larger service staff.

Of course, budget is a big determining factor for the menu you create for your wedding. That's why it's important to talk about it up front. If I know what your budget is, I can come up with appropriate sample menus.

In fact, a good caterer will follow up your initial meeting with a letter that is a synopsis of your conversation and includes three or four sample menus that display a variety of items that are all within your budget. Along with the menus should be a rough estimate of

Reception

"We helped our guests determine who could keep the centerpiece on the table by asking the couple who was married longest to take it home. At some tables there was only one married couple, so the decision was easy. But at other tables there were couples who had been married thirty and forty years, which sparked a bit of conversation and competition."

Holly, married 8/25/96

how much the caterer's services will cost for the reception you discussed.

If you like what you see, it isn't too much to ask to taste some of the dishes the caterer suggested. We do tastings in our facilities (as opposed to in someone's home), because if they don't like what they taste, we can jump back into the kitchen and ask the chef to make an adjustment on the flavor.

Before you put a deposit down for your caterer, find out if he or she meets a few critical criteria. For example, does the caterer have insurance? This is just in case someone slips and falls. In addition, is the caterer licensed to serve alcohol?

Make sure that once you hire your caterer, you get everything down on paper. You want a description of the menu, who the service staff will be and how many there will be, and how much the caterer will charge for specific items, like the wedding cake, linens, and overtime. Simply said, make sure everything in the agreement is spelled out ahead of time. The only thing you should have to think about on your wedding day is enjoying the food the caterer has made for you.

Renting Equipment

If you decide to organize your reception yourself, you may need to find vendors from whom you can rent certain types of equipment. Following are suggestions on finding rental services that are right for your reception.

* Today, just about every type of special-event equipment you can imagine is available for rent—including tents, canopies, food service equipment, grills, tables, chairs, candelabra, dance floors, and more.

* To find a rental company in your area, look in the yellow pages under Rental Services for stores that carry party or special-event rental equipment. Look for the American Rental Association logo in the company's advertisement, or call the American Rental Association at 800-334-2177 for a referral.

* Before you call a company, decide on a date, time, location, and approximate number of guests. Set your budget, meal type (e.g., dinner and reception dance or brunch buffet), and decide what ambiance you want to create. These choices will determine the number of square feet per person you should plan for and will guide the rental center's event planner (most

every center has one) in helping you choose the right equipment.

* Because June is a very busy rental month, you should contact a rental center at least six months in advance of a June event. At all other times of the year, three months should be sufficient lead time.

* If you're planning to rent a tent, find out if there are underground sprinklers, wires, cables, or any other restrictive items that might prevent the rental personnel from setting up the tent.

* Like most other businesses, rental companies vary in size. Special-event rental operations range from a small department in a general rental store to a huge party rental business with a number of locations. Don't worry about company size. Just find the firm that best fits your needs.

* Ask to see the center's selection of inventory. Are products seemingly state of the art or outdated?

* Always ask for references so you can find out how the company served others in the past.

* Get a rental contract that spells out the store's rental price and general policy. For example, most rental centers are responsible for the general maintenance of their equipment and will immediately replace anything that breaks down.

Source: The American Rental Association, headquartered in Moline, Illinois, an international trade association of more than 6,800 independent rental dealers and equipment manufacturers throughout the United States, Canada, and overseas. Reprinted with permission.

Seating Arrangements

There's nothing more embarrassing at a reception than when a guest can't find a place to sit or a couple have to sit at separate tables because they can't find a table to accommodate them together. "That's why it's so important to have seating arrangements," says Bev Dembo, president of Dembo Productions, a full-service consultancy in Glencoe, Illinois.

Doing seating arrangements is admittedly a huge task, and many brides decide to have open seating simply to avoid it. Dembo has

wedding wisdom

"Let your parents and his parents do the seating for their friends and relatives. You and your fiancé should just worry about seating your friends."
Wendy, married 11/19/95

wedding wisdom

"We put the place cards for our reception in gold frames, which doubled as favors for guests to take home with them."
Jenelle, married 5/17/97

Reception

"I discovered during our wedding planning that the reception site needed a fire marshall's permit for anything bearing a flame, including the votive candles I wanted to use as centerpieces. Be sure to check with your reception site, since they either will already have votives that are preapproved, or can help you plan to get some that will pass inspection easily."

Carolyn, married 9/14/96

a terrific solution to seating-arrangement anxiety—creating three separate lists that cross-reference and correspond.

"You should start off with an alphabetical list of all your guests," she says. That may require combining your list with your parents' and in-laws' list, but the extra effort will pay off in the long run. "This list is hugely helpful in recording responses and getting a final count on the number of guests attending."

Next you want to have a table sheet, on which you'll arrange where certain guests will sit.

Finally, you'll need to get a layout sheet from your catering manager or create one with your caterer. This sheet will tell you where the tables will be arranged throughout the reception.

All three sheets should include the same information. So, say Sally Smith is sitting at table 12 with her husband, Bob Smith, and Sally has requested a vegetarian meal while Bob wants beef. All that pertinent information should appear on the alphabetical list, the table sheet, and the layout sheet. What's great about having this cross-referencing system is it pretty much guarantees that all your numbers match up, none of your guests will arrive at the reception and not find a place card for them, and if one of the three lists is lost, the other two will fill in the blanks.

When plotting who sits at what table, keep in mind that the tables closest to you and your groom are the most important ones and should be reserved for important people, such as parents. Another seating arrangement consideration to make is for the tables closest to the band or deejay. "You may want to put the younger people there," Dembo suggests, "not older people whose hearing aids will amplify the sound."

Another seating suggestion Dembo has is for you and your groom to sit by yourselves, instead of at a head table with your attendants or parents. "There is a new movement that allows the bridal party to sit with their spouses," she says. In addition, if you newlyweds sit alone together, you don't have to choose which parents will be at your table—an important decision to consider when you're dealing with divorced parents.

If against Dembo's best advice you decide to forgo assigned seating, at least consider this suggestion. "Have about ten extra seats," she says, "so that someone who doesn't know where to sit won't have a hard time finding an open seat."

Dembo Productions will consult on any event in the greater Chicago area. For more information, call 847-835-5000.

Registering and Gifts

When Bill and I began discussing registering, we decided that it wasn't right for us. We reasoned that since we'd lived on our own and had all the household items we needed, it didn't make sense for us. But had I known then what I know now, we probably would have registered for unusual items, like tools and compact discs.

Even though we didn't register at a store, we did create a gift wish list, which we gave to our parents. We also spent time thinking about the gifts we would give our attendants. We wanted something that rang true to the best man's and the maid of honor's personalities and conveyed our true thankfulness for their having been involved in our wedding. Bill decided to buy a silver frame from Tiffany for his best man, and I treated my maid of honor to a day of beauty at a local spa.

Commonly Asked Registry Questions

Deciding where you're going to register—and what you're going to register for—is undoubtedly a big decision. Like most brides- and grooms-to-be, you're probably uncertain about specific aspects of the registry process, ranging from how soon before the wedding you should register to whether it is OK to register in more than one place. You may need answers to some of the following questions.

Why should I register?

There are a number of reasons for registering, some that might seem selfish and others that are definitely altruistic. For starters, if both of you have never lived on your own before, you probably need items to furnish your home. By registering for kitchenware, house-wares, bath and bedding items, even furniture, you and your future spouse are guaranteed to get your new home off to a great start.

But even those who have established homes should feel comfortable registering. A wedding is the perfect opportunity to select items that you might not otherwise be able to afford or have never allowed yourself to indulge in. For example, if you've got a kitchen fully stocked with casual dinnerware, take advantage of your guests' expectations that you'll register, and go out and choose a formal china pattern, along with silver flatware and crystal stemware.

Ideally, registering makes gift giving easier on your guests. Because today's wedding guests do expect couples to register, don't feel guilty about it. Instead, realize that by taking the time to select gifts that you really want and need, you're making it much simpler for your friends and family to purchase a shower or wedding gift. It lets them feel confident that they're buying stuff that you'll be happy receiving, and they will appreciate knowing that.

Should I register in a department store or a specialty store?

The answer to this question really depends on what your needs are. Many younger brides and grooms choose to go the department store route because they need a store that can take care of all their furnishing needs. Because most department stores allow you to register from almost any area of the store—including housewares, bedding, furniture, and luggage—you can get literally everything you need to furnish your home. For people with eclectic needs, this kind of one-stop shopping can be a real convenience.

Specialty stores come in handy if you've already got most of your basic necessities and want to jazz up your home with unique items. Or if you feel the selection available in department stores is too limited, specialty stores, such as Williams-Sonoma and Crate & Barrel, can offer you cookware, dishes, and other housewares that are a little beyond the ordinary. Then there are specialty stores that cater to the offbeat and specific interest—such as camping stores, wine outlets, and lingerie boutiques. If these are the places that you'd really like to see your guests shop to get you wedding gifts, then by all means, register there.

Is it OK to register in more than one store?

Most of the brides I know did register in more than one store—usually a department store to take care of their basic home necessities (and because that's where their families expected them to register) and then a specialty store or catalog for more unusual items.

By registering in more than one store, you're giving your guests additional options in buying you gifts. Plus, since your friends and family may be scattered all over the country, it's great to choose one or two stores that can be accessed anywhere in the country, either via an 800 number or at store locations in almost every state (like JCPenney). This way, you're guaranteeing that your guests won't have a tough time getting a hold of your registry list and buying you what you'd really like.

I'm planning on registering in more than one store. Should I simply write duplicate lists for each store or split the items up between the two stores?

There are a number of issues to consider before you even write up lists and submit them to the stores where you'll be registering. First, you should find out about each store's return policy. If, for example, the store will take back any merchandise, whether it was purchased at the store or not as long as the store sells the same item, then you should have no qualms registering all your items there. That way, you know in advance that if you get duplicates you won't have any trouble returning things.

You should also consider how many people on your guest list will actually be able to access the registry list at the stores where you've registered. If most of your family lives on the East Coast but you and your friends live in the Midwest and you've decided to register at department stores in both locations, then you should probably split the list between the two stores. For example, request six place settings of china at one store and six at another, instead of twelve at both; this way, should everyone decide to buy you china, you won't end up with twenty-four place settings altogether.

However, sometimes guests will buy gifts from another store. Maybe they found your wish-list items on sale somewhere else, or they couldn't get to the stores where you registered. This practice can easily throw your registry plans out of whack, because you won't be able to keep track of what's been bought off your registry. Luckily, most stores will let you update your registry over the telephone—they understand that gift buyers often shop around. So, as soon as a gift arrives and you know it didn't come from the place where you registered, call the store and let them know. Most establishments will deduct the item from your list in a timely manner.

My fiancé and I have lived on our own for a long time and have everything we need for our home. Is it still OK to register?

Of course it is. Just because you have your basic household needs doesn't mean you shouldn't register. You might be surprised to learn

"We wanted our gifts to be unique and tailored to the interests of each attendant. We decided to design individual baskets filled with thematically similar gifts. For example, one attendant was a fisherman so we filled his basket with fishing supplies. Because we were married at a California winery, we included a bottle of California wine as well. The baskets were a big hit."

Julie, married 6/24/90

Registering and Gifts

that you can register for such wacky items as a barbecue pit (at Barbecue Hall of Flame in Houston) and a boat (at BOAT/U.S. Marine Centers nationwide).

Since your guests and loved ones expect that you'll register (and it will make their gift buying easier), take some time and really think about what you and your spouse-to-be would love to receive.

For instance, if a romantic Caribbean honeymoon seems beyond your bank account, then register for one (see the honeymoon chapter for more information). If you've been salivating over a new set of camping gear for your regular treks to the mountains, check out camping stores and catalogs, such as Campmor and L. L. Bean, which both allow you to register for very outdoorsy items. Or if you've been thinking about updating your CD collection, then Tower Records might be the perfect place for you.

Should I register in the town where the wedding is, where I live, or where I'll be moving to after we get married, or all of these?

Think about what will be the easiest for all your guests. Remember: even though they're buying gifts for you, you should make accessing your registry as painless as possible for them. One bride, who lives in Chicago but grew up in San Francisco (where her wedding was held), registered at two places. She chose a well-known Bay Area store for her friends and family still living there plus a nationwide housewares store that guests in both Chicago and San Francisco could easily access.

Should I consider registering in a store that's not nationally accessible?

If you're marrying the boy next door and all your wedding guests live within a fifty-mile radius of each other, then sure, why not? But the truth is most families are spread out across the country these days. Plus, if you and your groom-to-be went to colleges in faraway locales, you've probably developed a network of friends living in many different places. Thankfully, most stores, no matter how small and where they're located, are capable nowadays of dealing with out-of-town guests. They can describe your registry list over the phone, fax it or mail it to them, and then arrange to have a purchased gift wrapped and shipped.

I really don't want to register, but everyone tells me I should for my guests' convenience. Should I just register for the heck of it and then return everything for cash?

In a situation like this, you should approach registering the same way as a couple who has lived on their own for a long time or perhaps been married before. That's because I definitely don't advocate the practice of requesting gifts just so you can return them for cash. Not only is this in extremely poor taste, but what happens when you have a wedding guest to your home at a future date and he or she begins asking about his or her wedding gift? (Yes, we know this is tacky, too, but guests are bound to do it.) One bride I know did return all her gifts for cash. Then, six months later, she had a friend coming to stay with her for a week who specifically requested that she eat dinner on the plates she'd bought the couple. Well, of course, those plates had long ago been returned to the store, so, in a panic, the bride went back to the store where she'd returned the plates and bought them all again—at a higher price, I might add. She learned her lesson.

How much homework should I do before registering?

Some couples like to spend weeks poring over advertisements and articles in bridal magazines and compiling folders full of china patterns, serving dishes, and table linens so that they'll be well prepared when they finally go to register. Others just like to wing it once they get to the store. It really depends on your personality and what your needs are.

However, it doesn't hurt to do at least a little homework, especially if you choose to go the nontraditional route and register in an offbeat store. In this instance, you'll need to spend time thinking about the kinds of things you really want and will really use and researching which stores will serve you best.

Even if you register for china and silver you should at least have an idea of what you don't like. For example, one woman's fiancé told her from the get-go that he refused to choose a china pattern that would have baskets of fruit or colorful flowers on the center of the plate, things he found distracting when eating. When they eventually checked out different dishes, they were able to tell the bridal consultant specifically the kinds of plates they didn't even want to look at and within a matter of minutes were shown a number of patterns that had plain centers and simple borders. It didn't take them long to find a pattern they both liked.

Do I need to meet with a bridal consultant?

There are very few stores out there that require that you meet with a bridal consultant. So it's really up to you whether or not you want someone walking you through the store and helping you make gift selections. If you know very little about the quality of china, crystal, and silver, then you'll probably want to talk with someone who

Of couples registering, 84 percent register for china, 82 percent register for cookware and small appliances, 81 percent register for flatware, 78 percent register for bed linens, 73 percent register for stemware, and 51 percent register for home electronics, according to *Bride's Magazine*.

Registering and Gifts

"Return the gifts you don't
like or can't use. Don't let
sentimentality stand in
the way of practicality.
This is advice from
someone who has moved
four times since her
wedding—carrying along
three unused crystal ice
buckets, all in their
original wrapping."

Leslie, married 10/30/88

can educate you on products in the store plus help you select patterns. Some stores have arranged it so that the bridal consultant can actually design a dining room table right in the store so you can see how pieces look when they're sitting on a table (as opposed to on a shelf).

Bridal consultants are there to educate you, help you make the selections that are right for you, and, ideally, speed up the registering process. If you don't mind a little hand-holding, use them to their fullest potential.

How soon should I register?

As soon as your sweetheart pops the big question, your mind will probably begin racing with all the things you'll need to do before the wedding day. For many newly engaged couples, registering is right up there with setting a date, finding a location, and buying a gown. However, if you're going to have a very long engagement (more than a year), you might want to hold off on registering until six to twelve months before your wedding. (Besides, even if you're having more than one shower, they probably won't occur until a few months before your wedding anyway.)

Why should you wait? Because the items you choose for your registry list may be out of stock or, heaven forbid, discontinued by the time you're ready to walk down the aisle. One couple I know registered more than a year in advance, around Christmastime, for a spring wedding that was two calendar years away. First off, many of the items on their registry list were gone from the store by the time the warm weather rolled around, primarily because the store had stocked seasonal holiday items. Then, to make things even worse, the following year their china manufacturer decided to stop producing their pattern. Thankfully, the bridal consultant at the store alerted them to this change and suggested they come back in and reregister. In hindsight, the couple realized that if they'd been less eager to register as early as they did, they could have spent just one day, instead of two, at the store picking out their china pattern and other assorted gifts.

If I decide against all odds to register a year in advance, how can I be sure that the items I've registered for will actually be available when my guests go to buy them?

Ask questions. When you choose a china pattern, a bath towel, or a brand of cookware, make sure you find out from the bridal consultant or store manager if the item is seasonal or about to be discontinued—they do know these things. If the answer is "yes," then you'll probably want to choose something that isn't going to be gone by the time your guests get to the store. A best bet, at least in the china department, is to pick a pattern that the manufacturer has just debuted. Chances are it won't go out of stock or be discontinued any time in the next few years.

Nonetheless, you should always find out what kind of stock replenishment options the store has available to it. If a situation arises where your wish-list items are out of stock, find out if the store can call its other locations to see if they have your items in stock and if shipping products from one store location to another isn't a big deal. If this scenario is impossible, determine how long a special order from the manufacturer will take. Some stores have secure relationships with their suppliers and can get merchandise in stock in under two weeks; others might make your guests wait as long as twelve weeks.

Are registry seminars that some stores offer really worthwhile?

If you feel you need a crash course in decorating and using items for entertaining, then, yes, these seminars can help. But salespeople can also go for the hard sell here, so don't be swayed into registering right then and there, which is what they want you to do. You should shop around first and make sure the store(s) where you do decide to register will best meet you and your guests' needs.

Perhaps the best part about going to seminars is that many include drawings for prizes donated by participating manufacturers. So you might just go home with a nifty gift. People walk away with things like an all-expenses-paid honeymoon, an espresso maker, and a sterling silver serving tray. Also, many stores give you a goodie bag just for attending. These bags often are filled with manufacturers' brochures and sometimes small gifts—I got a silver-plated frame from one seminar. This way, even if you don't win anything in the drawings, you'll have lots of fun stuff to go through once you get home.

Should I pick out items that I really like—and are really expensive? Or should I vary the price range of items on the registry list?

I can't say this enough; so I'll say it again: even though you'll end up benefiting from any gifts your guests buy you, you want to make their gift giving as painless as possible. Unless your last name is Rockefeller, you might want to avoid registering only for items that are completely out of most normal people's price range—including

"We made a last-minute decision to register at Crate & Barrel two weeks before our wedding. We ended up getting everything on our registry, and so many people told us what a positive buying experience it was for them."
Amy, married 8/3/96

Registering and Gifts

According to *Bride's Magazine,* on average 171 gift givers per couple buy something off the registry.

a $250-per-place-setting pattern of china, a silver pattern in which a fork costs $85, and a down comforter made exclusively in Sweden that costs $5,000.

Your guests are going to spend what they're comfortable with—not what you want them to spend. So by all means register for a few expensive things if you think someone might actually buy them for you, but be sure you vary your registry list so that your graduate student friends and your retired aunts and uncles alike will be able to find something they'd like to give you and can afford to buy. Besides, if you register for only outrageously priced items, like a $250-per-place-setting china pattern, and you get only one or two place settings, you and your spouse will have to finish off the set yourselves, and that could cost a pretty penny.

It used to be that you should register in time for an engagement party, but is that still true?

Definitely, especially if your family is accustomed to throwing such a bash, which in some social circles rivals the wedding itself. Also, it's now common for couples to have not only an engagement party thrown in their honor but also two and three showers as well. So make sure you find out from your parents what sort of party planning is down the road and be sure to register at least a month in advance of the first get-together.

Do I need to register in time for my first shower?

Yes, yes, yes. Plus, since many of today's showers have a theme, such as lingerie, kitchen, or even the backyard, you'll want to register well in advance of these events so your guests have ample time to get to the places where you've registered and pick out a fun gift for you.

How long does it take to register? How much time should I set aside?

The time you'll actually spend in a store registering differs from store to store. At a small boutique, you can probably expect the whole process to take about forty-five minutes to an hour. At a department store or superstore that encompasses fifty thousand or so square feet, plan on as long as three hours.

How can I persuade my fiancé to go register with me?

Face it: some people just don't get into the idea of registering. Probably the best way to make sure your future spouse enjoys the registry experience as much as you do is to choose a store where you'll both have fun looking at the stuff. For my husband, whose heart really beats fast at the first hint of sawdust, the best place for me to take him would have been a home-improvement store. If your guy loves the outdoors, consider registering in a store that caters to an outdoorsy lifestyle. If your fiancé is really into sexy lingerie, suggest registering at a lingerie shop. Remember: you're registering for both of you, so make sure you find a place that offers items that you'll both enjoy.

What is the proper etiquette on getting the word out about where we've registered? Some of the stores have given me "We've registered at . . ." cards. Can my maid of honor insert these in shower invitations? Can I put them in wedding invitations?

Miss Manners and other etiquette doyennes find the idea of inserting these cards in any invitation so distasteful that if they could, they'd probably delicately remove their white gloves and smack you across the face if you did such a thing. But thankfully, etiquette restrictions in various social circles have relaxed in recent years, and it's actually become quite commonplace to insert registry cards in shower invitations. Inserting them in wedding invitations is still considered a no-no, but, honestly, do whatever feels comfortable for you.

I recently received a shower invitation where the maid of honor had written at the bottom of the invitation itself, in lovely calligraphy, the names of the two stores where the guest of honor and her fiancé had registered. It was so unobtrusive that it was hardly offensive; in fact, I rather liked having the information given to me directly. This way, I didn't have to bother the maid of honor with questions about where the bride was registered. Instead, I had all that information at my disposal and I could head right out and buy the bride-to-be her shower gift.

If, however, you are uncomfortable with having your maid of honor insert a card or include any other registry information in the invitation, rest assured that the word *does get out* about where you're registered. Mothers and mothers-in-law are notoriously good about spreading the registry gossip.

Should I have the store where I've registered mail catalogs to my guests?

Having the store do this unsolicited is probably a bit too pushy. But if the option is available, you might want to let your maid of honor know, since she'll probably be getting the word out about your registry and answering any questions your guests have about where you've registered. Or you can have her insert a note in the shower invitation, along with the registry information, that catalogs are available upon request.

Reprinted from The Bridal Registry Book *by Leah Ingram (Contemporary Books, 1995).*

Places You Never Knew You Could Register

For many couples, the thought of registering for traditional china and crystal is about as appealing as going in for a root canal. Here are ten stores that would probably appeal to less-than-traditional couples.

* Barbecue Hall of Flame, Houston (713-529-1212). Here you can register for a barbecue pit and cuts of exotic meat to cook in it.

* Intimate Bookshop, Chapel Hill, North Carolina (919-929-0414). Wish lists here often feature *New York Times* best-sellers.

* Lover's Lane, Westland, Michigan (313-728-5100). Lingerie and Kamasutra products are hot with couples who register here.

* Metropolitan Museum of Art Shop, New York City (212-650-2909). Any art reproductions, jewelry, books, and decorative items the store sells can be added to a registry.

* Real Goods Trading Corporation, Ukiah, California (800-762-7325). If you're into alternative-energy products, this place is for you.

* Sherry-Lehmann, New York City (212-838-7500). This wine seller lets you register for any vintage the store stocks.

* Tower Records, New York City (800-648-4844). Music lovers can request works by their favorite artists.

* Backroads, Berkeley (800-462-2848). You can register to take one of this company's to-die-for trips to any destination in the Backroads catalog.

* BOAT/U.S. Marine Centers, Alexandria, Virginia (703-461-2850). Boat owners and nautical nuts can ask for any of the more than four thousand boating items these stores stock.

* L. L. Bean, Freeport, Maine (800-341-4341). This legendary cataloger of outdoor and adventure gear has a registry that's perfect for active types.

Register for Home, Sweet Home

Nowadays couples need not limit their registry requests to tangible gifts. While you can't exactly register for a home, you can register for your mortgage—or at least a down payment on a house. Here are three programs of interest.

BankAmerica Mortgage (800-272-6791) This bank sets up a savings account in your name to which friends and family send cash contributions. You needn't use this Uniondale, New York, bank as your mortgage lender, but if you do, the bank will waive the usual $100 closing costs. Currently, only residents of the following states can participate in BankAmerica Mortgage's program: Arizona, Connecticut, Delaware, Maryland, Massachusetts, Michigan, New York, New Jersey, Pennsylvania, and Virginia.

Federal Housing Administration (800-CALLFHA) There are approximately thirty Federal Housing Administration lenders across the country that will set up a mortgage registry program for interested couples. The Housing and Urban Development office unveiled this program in late 1996 as a way to increase home ownership among young people.

Universal Lending Corporation (303-758-1013) This Denver-based bank's home ownership bridal registry program is available to Colorado residents only. For couples that sign up, the bank provides a gift letter and envelope that can be passed along to guests who decide to contribute to the mortgage fund.

Gifts for Attendants

Your attendants have spent a lot of time and money planning your wedding and buying their attire. It only makes sense to thank them for their support and dedication. The most important thing to keep in mind is that an attendant's gift should reflect the gift recipient. Think about his or her likes and interests before setting out to shop for the gift. Even though *Brides Magazine* estimates that the average amount spent on an attendant's gift is $163, most consultants agree

"We had a decorated birdcage for guests to insert the 'nest egg' cards (monetary gifts) in. This is our alternative to a wishing well, which is often used to collect cards and prevent loss and theft of them at wedding receptions. Having some sort of card receptacle is a must!"

Julie, married 3/8/97

Registering and Gifts

that a reasonable amount to spend is between $20 and $50. The best time to present your attendants' gifts is at the rehearsal dinner.

Here are some general gift suggestions.

* If someone in your bridal party is a theater buff, why not buy him or her tickets to a play?
* A sports fan will probably enjoy a subscription to *Sports Illustrated*, if he or she doesn't already have one.
* A very feminine woman will appreciate a feminine gift, such as a basket of specialty soaps.
* Your young flower girl may enjoy a bridal Barbie doll; the young ring bearer will probably get a kick out of receiving a wallet with $5 inside it.

Source: Cheri Rice, master bridal consultant and owner of The Personal Touch Bridal Agency, a full-service consultancy serving the greater Minneapolis area. For more information, call 612-421-4525.

Gifts for Each Other

Whether or not you decide to give each other a wedding gift is entirely up to you. "I believe it's nice to give gifts that are made with precious materials, such as gold, silver, and platinum," says Lynn Ramsey, president of the Jewelry Information Center, a nonprofit trade association that represents the fine jewelry industry, "because precious materials last a long time. And isn't that what marriage is all about?"

Ramsey says an excellent option is always fine jewelry, such as shirt studs or fine cuff links for him and a cultured pearl necklace for her. A groom might express his love for his bride with a set of heart-shaped earrings, and a wife can show her husband that she's looking forward to having the time of her life with him by presenting him with a classic-styled dress watch.

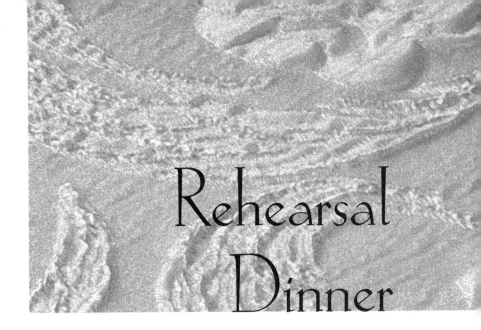

Rehearsal Dinner

*R*ehearsal dinners sometimes are the most relaxing time during the entire wedding. The bride and groom arrive giddy and flushed having just practiced walking down the aisle, and friends and family who are joining them for dinner have a chance to talk in a more intimate setting. It also gives the bridal party time to get to know one another.

This was the exact scenario at the rehearsal Bill and I attended for the wedding at which Bill was the best man. After months of hearing about the other ushers in the groom's regular update letters, we finally got to meet them. It was also a great chance for us to catch up with the groom's parents—people Bill and I had known since junior high school. In addition, it was the first time most of our friends were meeting our then ten-week-old daughter, Jane, so the rehearsal dinner was really special for us.

Rehearsal Dinner Basics

During her work as an accredited bridal consultant, Lois Pearce, president of Beautiful Occasions in Hamden, Connecticut, has planned many rehearsal dinners. Here she explains the basics of a rehearsal dinner.

LI: *What purpose does the rehearsal dinner serve?*

LP: The rehearsal dinner functions as a time for the bridal party to get together for a social event before the actual wedding day. Many times brides and grooms don't get to see their attendants

Nuptials News

According to *Bride's Magazine*, the average rehearsal dinner costs $409.

"We decided to have the rehearsal dinner a week before the wedding. I'm glad we did, because after the rehearsal itself, we really weren't in any shape to socialize. Instead, we went and had a quiet dinner together and that was really nice."

Amy, married 8/3/96

before the actual wedding rehearsal. Some of the attendants may have flown in from out of town that very day and gone directly to the church. The dinner is also the time when the bride and groom can thank their attendants for being in the wedding.

LI: *Does the dinner have to occur on the day before the wedding or on the actual day of the rehearsal?*

LP: Rehearsal dinners are usually held the night before the wedding because that's the time when everyone is in town. If your wedding is on a Saturday evening, the church rehearsal may be on Friday night. But, the rehearsal dinner could be held on Thursday, if everyone is in town by then. I recommend that with a Saturday wedding the rehearsal dinner be held on Thursday. That will still be in advance of the actual wedding enough that you won't be so on edge that you can't relax and enjoy yourselves. Plus, if there are any last-minute errands to run on Friday, you won't have to worry about the rehearsal dinner's cutting into your already busy day.

LI: *I've heard of rehearsal dinners being as formal as a wedding. What form should one take?*

LP: The rehearsal dinner does not have to be a formal affair if that's not what you want to do. It could be a picnic, or it could be dinner in a restaurant.

The more common route is to have a rehearsal dinner at a restaurant or even sometimes the church fellowship hall, since everyone will be at the church for the rehearsal anyway.

LI: *Do you invite only the bridal party to the rehearsal dinner?*

LP: I have found that rehearsal dinners nowadays include out-of-town guests as well. For example, you may feel that invited wedding guests who've traveled a long distance to attend the wedding should be entertained in the days leading up to the wedding. Instead of leaving them in a hotel room to order room service, you might invite them to the rehearsal dinner as a means of hospitality.

LI: *Isn't it expensive to invite more than just the bridal party to the rehearsal dinner?*

LP: Absolutely. An average rehearsal dinner, with just bridal party and family, can be about twenty-five people. If you're going to include guests, that brings up the number attending by ten or fifteen people, and it's not unheard of for a rehearsal dinner to be for fifty people or more. A rehearsal dinner could rival a small wedding. For example, here in Connecticut, dinner can range from $20 to $45 per person. That means you could end up spending $2,000 or more for a rehearsal dinner alone.

LI: *What can you do to keep costs down?*

LP: If you're going to have your rehearsal dinner in a restaurant, create a predetermined menu. That way you'll have an idea of how much each dinner will cost you and then you won't have to worry about someone's ordering lobster. If lobster isn't on the menu, no one can ask for it. Another benefit to having the menu selected in advance is that you'll probably get faster service.

LI: *Who pays for the rehearsal dinner?*

LP: Traditionally the groom's family is responsible for covering the rehearsal dinner, and I haven't seen too much variance with that.

LI: *Besides eating dinner, what goes on at a rehearsal dinner?*

LP: During dinner the father of the bride usually makes a toast. He offers good wishes to his new son-in-law. Then the groom usually makes a toast to the bride.

If the bride and groom are going to distribute any gifts to their parents and their bridal party, they'll do so at the dinner. It's really the best opportunity to give your attendants gifts, especially if they're wearing specific jewelry with their wedding-day attire.

LI: *Don't the guys usually head out to the bachelor party right after the rehearsal dinner?*

LP: It is no longer traditional to have the bachelor party right after the rehearsal dinner. In fact, many grooms are not in favor of bachelor parties anymore. Instead they may get together with their friends and go to a sporting event or out to dinner and a movie. I will say this, though: if there is a bachelor party after the rehearsal dinner, the ladies should find something similar to do.

LI: *Should you buy a special outfit to wear at your rehearsal dinner?*

LP: The bride usually wears something special to the rehearsal dinner, just as she would wear something special to her shower. However, what you choose to wear depends on you and your attitude. You might choose a suit or a simple dress.

LI: *Doing arranged seating for a wedding reception can be headache enough. Do you need to worry about doing the same for the rehearsal dinner?*

LP: Your rehearsal dinner may be the place where your families meet for the first time. If your families aren't from the same town, the dinner is the first opportunity for them to get together. It is advisable to seat your parents and your fiancé's parents together so they can discuss you two and get to know one another. However, if your parents and your fiancé's parents have met before and have had trouble getting along, I would advise against seating them together. Instead, you might want to seat the parents with their respective families. Also, you might not want to seat divorced spouses together.

Ask your attendants to bring their spouses to the rehearsal dinner, and seat them together.

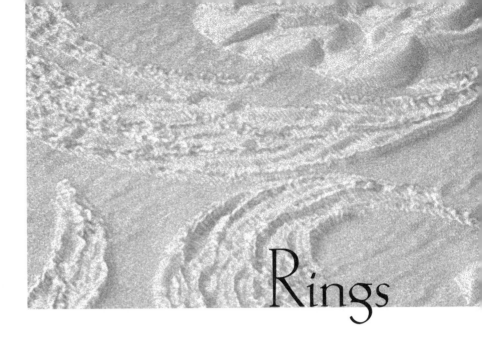

Rings

*E*loping was such a last-minute decision for Bill and me that we actually didn't have rings to exchange at our wedding ceremony. It was a weird feeling, too, especially when you grow up knowing that someday you're going to say, "With this ring, I thee wed . . . " In fact, when it came to the part of the ceremony when we should have exchanged rings, we had to sheepishly admit to the justice of the peace performing the ceremony that we didn't have any.

Since we were married on a Monday, the next day we headed to New York City's infamous Forty-Seventh Street to buy wedding bands—well, actually, to buy me a wedding band; Bill had decided to wear his grandfather's. We spent the entire day walking up and down the street trying to find the perfect wedding band to go with my diamond ring, which had been handed down to me from Bill's mother. The diamond was actually purchased by Bill's grandfather for his grandmother, more than fifty years previously. Because the setting of my diamond ring is antique in nature, it was quite a challenge to find a band to go with it. But finally we did.

I chose a simple white gold band with a raised center and notched edge, mostly because it fit perfectly behind my engagement ring. We ordered it, paid for it, and then returned a week later to pick it up. Finally, we were both able to wear wedding bands and look like the married couple we actually were. In fact, because I didn't have a wedding band for more than a week, most of my friends didn't believe that I'd gone ahead and eloped. But now there was no doubting it. Bill and I really were married.

Nuptials News

Almost 70 percent of all brides-to-be receive a diamond engagement ring, according to the Diamond Information Center.

Ring Rudiments

When you think about it, you're going to be wearing your wedding band for the rest of your life. Therefore, it's wise to research the rings you buy and to make sure the purchase you make is one you can live with forever. It's never too early to start shopping for your wedding band.

"Generally, it's a good idea to shop for your wedding band when you buy your engagement ring," suggests Lynn Ramsey, president of the Jewelry Information Center, a trade association representing jewelers nationwide. "Some jewelers can show you sets, in which the engagement ring and wedding band match." Or by buying more than one ring, you might be able to work out a deal with the jeweler.

As you would with any other major purchase, you want to shop around and compare prices of various jewelers. You also want to look through your favorite bridal magazines so you can zero in on the styles of rings you like. Taking tear sheets from magazines with you when you visit jewelers can be helpful as well, especially if you think you may have trouble describing the kind of ring you have in mind.

One of the ways to know if a jeweler is showing you a quality ring is to look for markings of trademark and content or quality on the shank of the ring. Ramsey says that reputable jewelers will sell quality rings only. However, there are some jewelers that will sell substandard rings. "That's why you want to look for the markings on the ring," she adds.

What these markings tell you is the make of the ring and whether it's 14-karat gold or 18-karat gold. "The trademark tells you that the manufacturer is standing behind its product," adds Ramsey.

Trademarks come in all shapes and sizes, and there's no uniformity to them. For example, if the ring manufacturer is the Tucker Company, its trademark could be "T" or "TC"—whatever it chooses. Nonetheless, you want to make sure that any ring you buy has both a trademark and a contents marking on it.

Of contents markings, here are two of the most common you'll find on gold rings:

"14K," meaning 14-karat gold. It's actually 58.3 percent gold.
"18K," meaning 18-karat gold. It's 75 percent gold.

You won't find rings made of 24-karat gold, Ramsey says, because the metal is too soft to hold shape.

According to Ramsey, platinum is quickly becoming the metal of choice for engagement rings and wedding bands. "It's the purest and hardest of all metals," she says, "and it has a wonderful luster to it." It also complements diamonds nicely.

Platinum rings are usually made of 90 percent platinum and 10 percent iridium and marked "irid plat." Or they're made from 95 percent platinum and 5 percent ruthenium and bear the marking "plat."

If you don't find a ring you like in a jewelry store, you can always design your own ring. "Many couples choose to design their own wedding bands," says Ramsey. Not all jewelers are set up to do custom-made jewelry, so call around first before visiting any shops. Having your rings made can be a more expensive option but one where you know that you'll end up with a ring that is uniquely yours.

Finger Swelling

Women and men who live in warm climates or work with their hands may find that their fingers swell, which can be a problem when trying on wedding rings. Gary Gordon, owner of Samuel Gordon Jewelers in Oklahoma City, offers these ring-buying tips.

* If you normally experience finger swelling during your menstrual cycle, let your jeweler know so that he or she can size your ring one-sixteenth of a size bigger to accommodate for the regular swelling.

* Hands can be a lot like feet and become more swollen at the end of the day. If you find that your fingers get puffy at day's end, try to go ring shopping in the morning when they will be less so.

* If you or your fiancé discover finger swelling after you've purchased and started wearing your rings, please do not hesitate to return to your jeweler to have him or her resize your rings.

Ring Insurance

As soon as your boyfriend slips the rock on your finger, you should get it insured. Don't worry; having an engagement ring insured does not require a call to Lloyd's of London or anything like that. Instead, you can add a rider to your homeowner's insurance to cover the value of the ring—especially if it's more than $5,000.

How do you know how much your ring is worth? According to most insurance companies that issue homeowner's insurance, the

"We were shopping in the mall one day, and I found the ring set that I fell in love with. Two weeks later, he proposed with *the* ring that I'd seen at the mall. When it was time to start looking for his wedding band, he mentioned that he kind of felt left out. Here I had this beautiful ring to show everyone that I was engaged, and he wanted something to show for it, too. So we went and found him an engagement ring! It matched my ring, and then we found a matching wedding band. Now we have two sets of rings that match."

Amy, married 8/3/96

receipt for the ring isn't enough, says Mark Bass, a certified financial planner at Pennington, Bass & Associates in Lubbock, Texas. "I would encourage you to get an appraisal from the place where you purchased the ring," he says, "and then get another appraisal from an independent jeweler. This way, you'll have an estimated range of value."

The reason having an appraisal is so important is in case of loss. Your insurance company will reimburse you only for the amount your ring is worth, which is not necessarily what your fiancé paid for it. "I'd rather have an appraisal and a disagreement with my insurance company about how much the ring is worth," says Bass, "than not have any appraisal at all and not get any money for the lost ring."

Another time an appraisal is important is when the engagement ring is handed down, as so many are, because there is probably no receipt. "When there's no receipt, you want an appraisal certifying the value of the ring," says Bass. "Remember: an insurance company won't insure the sentimental value of the ring, but it will insure the amount that is stated on the appraisal."

How to Buy Diamonds

In today's world it doesn't seem too ostentatious for a woman to wear a diamond wedding band long before her tenth wedding anniversary—the traditional time when a husband gives his wife such a ring. In addition, you may feel that because your fiancé gave you a diamond engagement ring, it is only right for you to give him a diamond wedding band in return.

If you find yourself in the market for a diamond, be sure to keep the four Cs—cut, color, clarity, and carat weight—in mind. Following is a description of each.

Cut

A well-cut diamond (that is, one whose cuts are neither too deep nor too shallow) will refract and reflect as much light as possible. The better the diamond has been cut, the greater its brilliance, sparkle, and fire will be.

Color

Most diamonds are colorless, although there are naturally occurring subtle shade differences that may make a seemingly colorless diamond not so at all. In fact, the less color a diamond has, the more valuable it is. Color is usually graded from D to Z, with D being the best.

While colorless diamonds are exceedingly rare, so are those with a strong natural color. These are called "fancies" and can be intense yellow, red, pink, or blue.

Clarity

Thanks to nature, every diamond is unique. Each one possesses its own individuality, possibly due to the minute traces of other minerals trapped during the crystallization process.

These natural characteristics, called inclusions, are better described as nature's fingerprints. The number, color, nature, size, and position of any inclusions determine the clarity of the diamond.

The fewer inclusions a diamond has, the more light it will reflect and the better its clarity. Fewer inclusions means a more valuable diamond.

Carat

The carat is the unit of weight used to measure the diamond. When it comes to diamonds, bigger isn't always better. In fact, a diamond's carat weight has no bearing on a diamond's cut, color, or clarity—the true measurements of how valuable a diamond is.

Source: The Diamond Information Center, reprinted with permission. To receive a copy of the brochure "How to Buy Diamonds You'll Be Proud to Give," write Diamond Information Center, 466 Lexington Avenue, New York, New York 10017.

Cleaning Your Diamond

While it's best to have your diamond ring cleaned on a regular basis by a professional jeweler, finding time to do so isn't always possible. The Diamond Information Center suggests two methods of cleaning your diamond at home.

Detergent Bath

Prepare a small bath of warm sudsy water with any of the mild liquid detergents you use in your home. While the ring is soaking, brush it with a small soft brush, such as a toothbrush. Then rinse it under warm running water. Pat it dry with a soft, lint-free cloth.

Bride's Magazine says that the average couple spends $2,807 on an engagement ring and $2,152 on wedding rings for both the bride and groom.

Rings

The Cold-Water Soak

Soak the ring in a half-and-half solution of cold water and household ammonia. Let it soak for thirty minutes. Lift it out and gently tap around the front and back of the mounting with a small soft brush. Swish the ring in the solution a second time and then rinse it under warm water. Drain it on a piece of tissue or paper towel.

Showers

We broke all the rules for my bridal shower. To begin with, Bill and I were already married when we found out I was getting a shower. I didn't think it was necessary, but my mother told me that most of the women in my family and my female friends expected it— even though I was already married. What was I to do? Refuse to go? The other major faux pas with my bridal shower was the fact that my mother planned it. Parents are never supposed to plan showers, because it might look as if they're begging people to give the bride gifts. (Come to think of it, she planned my baby shower, too.) Oh, well, I guess Mom was never one for following Emily Post etiquette.

Nonetheless, the bridal shower turned out to be a lot of fun. It was held in a seaside restaurant with giant windows overlooking the water. It was a chance for me to see some of my girlfriends whom I hadn't seen in a while, and I think it was a great joy for my mother to plan the whole shebang. (Mom eloped, too, and I think she didn't want me to miss out on any of the festivities she did.)

What was also great about the shower was it gave my mother-in-law the chance to get involved in the wedding plans as well. She was responsible for buying party favors for all the guests (romantic-looking note cards), and I believe she helped my mother track down guests who were delinquent about responding.

By the end of the day, Bill and I had received more towels and bed linens than we knew what to do with. In fact, we started joking that we were going to be able to open a bed-and-breakfast because our linen closet was so well stocked. My wishing well— the place where guests deposited token gifts of a certain theme—

"My mother planned a shower for us and hired a violinist to play background music throughout the party. The music set an elegant tone, and all the guests commented that the musician was a truly memorable touch."

Julie, married 6/24/90

turned out to be a big hit, too. Because I'm a writer, my mom had asked everyone to bring a little something related to writing. I still have some of those boxes of crayons and writing tablets that people bought as gag gifts. I'm sure my children will end up enjoying them as much as I enjoyed receiving them at my bridal shower.

Bridal Shower Basics

Donna Schonhoff is a certified bridal consultant and state coordinator for the Association of Bridal Consultants in Shelby Township, Michigan. Her company, La Donna Wedding Expressions, can handle all wedding-planning tasks, from finding a reception site to helping you choose a honeymoon destination. The company's phone number is 810-731-8400. Here she explains the basics of the bridal shower.

Years ago, bridal showers were a lot like afternoon tea. A small group of women gathered at someone's house to enjoy finger sandwiches and beverages and toast the future bride with household gifts. The event was quite low-key and always the textbook definition of proper etiquette. The purpose behind the shower was altruistic: friends and family reasoned that the happy couple needed all the help they could get in setting up their new home together, and the shower would be the perfect chance to give them a basic supply of housewares and linens.

Today, everything has changed. Brides sometimes have more than one bridal shower, and gifts they receive are no longer simple pot holders and dish towels. Today's shower gift is usually a place setting or two of china, which can easily set a guest back $100 or more.

The other critical element of the bridal shower that has changed is the setting. It's so costly today to put on bridal showers because you rarely ever hear of their being put on in homes anymore. Sometimes, bridal showers are so large that one hundred people might attend. Because of the size and scope of the once-simple bridal shower, popular places to hold them now include restaurants and even banquet halls. Sometimes, showers can rival the weddings themselves.

One bride's extremely large bridal party rented out a banquet room at a local Chinese restaurant to accommodate the sixty or so women in attendance at her shower. Not only did they enjoy a four-course Chinese meal, but also there was a deejay and dancing after the meal. The bride received so many gifts that almost one entire table had to be cleared of plates and glasses to hold all the boxes.

All of the bride's attendants chipped in to pay for the festivities. However that is a rarity these days. Traditionally, it's the maid of honor who organizes the shower, but it can be very costly; the maid of honor must spend her own money for a dress, shoes, a gift for the couple, and various other wedding-related items. If she has to add a bridal shower to the list, she might end up broke.

Although it's against Emily Post–like etiquette rules for the parents to throw a shower, mothers usually end up shelling out the money for it anyway, because it's so costly. The wedding party may chip in to pay for part of it, but in no way should they feel responsible for paying for the whole thing.

Another of the rules that has been broken in recent times is the one that said that a bride is to have only one shower. In fact, having more than one shower used to be the rule of thumb. The bride's girlfriends would give her a small shower where the invited guests were the bride's friends. Then her mom would give her daughter a shower, where the mom's friends would be invited. Finally, the groom's mother would have a shower for her side of the family. One of the benefits of having more than one shower is it gives the bride the chance to spend time with different people in smaller doses—instead of being overwhelmed by a flock of well-wishers at one large shower.

You should finalize your registry selection long before any showers might occur, because guests will probably use the registry as a guide to gifts. In addition, all the bridal showers should take place long before the wedding invitations go out.

By having the bridal shower before invitations are sent, you have the chance to write all your thank-you notes before you have to worry about writing and assembling your wedding invitations. Plus, you don't want guests to feel bombarded by receiving invitations to two events for you. In addition, you will have many things to take care of in the weeks leading up to the wedding. If you're having all these showers it will eat into all your free time.

Bridal Shower Themes

Plain and simple bridal showers rarely happen anymore. At a couple's shower, the bride and groom are included along with their male and female friends. Other showers sport themes that help perk up the party atmosphere and give guests creative gift ideas. Here Donna Schonhoff shares a few shower themes.

Kitchen Shower

One of the main things a newly married couple has to do is furnish their kitchen, especially if they're moving from Mom and Dad's home into their own. Or they may have lived on their own before but never owned matching plates and glasses. A kitchen shower is a great opportunity for guests to help the happy couple stock their cabinets.

Besides buying kitchen-themed gifts, guests at a kitchen shower may be invited to share their favorite recipes. Oftentimes, they receive a blank index card with their invitation and instructions to fill in a recipe. Then, at the shower, all the recipe cards are collected and placed in a recipe box, which is presented to the bride.

The shower decorations, party favors, and invitations all reflect the theme. For example, table centerpieces might be teakettles with fresh flowers in them, and the walls might be decorated with aprons sporting the happy couple's names and wedding date. Favors could be a small wooden spoon or a wire whisk, and the invitations might feature a chef's hat.

Personal Shower

Think of this as a sexy shower for the bride where lingerie and other personal items are de rigueur. To get invited guests in the mood, the shower invitations could have a piece of lace inside or some other romantic theme to them. The wording on the invitation could suggest straight-out that guests buy something to add to the bride's trousseau.

Potpourri sachets make great favors at a personal shower, and the centerpiece might be gift bags filled with soaps, lotions, and bath gel. To determine who gets to take home each centerpiece, guests might play a fun game, in which, for example, the lady with the reddest nails or the one wearing a black bra wins.

Hobby Shower

Whatever sports or hobbies the bride and groom enjoy are the theme for a hobby shower. For example, if the couple enjoys hiking or spending time in the mountains, guests are invited to the shower with an invitation that shows the great outdoors. The centerpiece could be a hiking boot filled with flowers, and decorations might be travel posters of the Alps or a national park. Guests might buy gifts that would help the couple pursue their hiking hobby, such as thermal socks or a canteen. Favors could be anything that speaks to the outdoors, such as small bottles of Vermont maple syrup or decorated pinecones.

Spa Shower

A bridal shower doesn't always have to be about showering the bride with gifts. She and her attendants could plan a shower at a spa where all of them would enjoy pampering services. That's a common phenomenon at the Robert Andrew DaySpa Salon in Gambrills, Maryland, a full-service salon in the Washington, D.C., suburbs. (For more information about having a bridal shower at the Robert Andrew DaySpa Salon, call 410-721-3533.)

"We recently had a shower here where the ladies spent four hours with us," recalls Bob Zupko, spa owner. "Our spa director worked with them so that they received individual services at the same time and then joined one another in our private dining room for lunch together." Some of the treatments the bride and her attendants were treated to included a salt glow body rub and European facial. The spa provided a small cake and champagne for the ladies to enjoy, and they topped off the day by getting manicures and pedicures in the same room together. "They were laughing and gossiping and talking about the wedding," he recalls. "They had a great time."

Thank-You Notes

Ever since I was old enough to write, my mother instilled in me the importance of writing thank-you notes. At family gift-giving get-togethers, it became the ritual joke for my family to tease me about the gift list I always kept. That is, whenever opening gifts, I would keep a pad of paper and pen nearby so I could write down who gave me what. I think some of my cousins felt threatened by my organization at such a young age, but I know the gift givers always appreciated receiving my prompt thank-you notes.

Having gotten used to making gift lists came in very handy when Bill and I were getting ready to write our thank-you notes. Because I'd kept meticulous notes on who had given us what wedding presents, writing the thank-you notes was a snap.

Another trick I learned was to order thank-you notes without our names on them. Instead, we got thank-you notes that featured the same flower border as our wedding invitations and read THANK YOU on the cover. We ended up with so many left over that we used them years later to write thank-you notes to people who sent gifts when Jane was born.

I know Bill shares my belief in promptly writing thank-you notes to people who send gifts, but frankly he doesn't enjoy letter and note writing as much as I do. (Besides writing for a living, I'm an avid letter writer. As a child, I had twenty-one pen pals.) One of the things that make our marriage a success is acknowledging that I like to write thank-you notes and Bill doesn't. So, whenever a thank-you note needs to be written, I don't expect Bill to do it. Instead, I do it myself. It keeps everyone involved happy, and it guarantees that our thank-you notes go out on a timely basis.

How to Write Meaningful Thank-You Notes

Florence Isaacs is a New York–based writer and author of Just a
Note to Say . . . The Perfect Words for Every Occasion
*(Clarkson Potter, 1996), a book that helps you craft correspondence.
Naturally her book touches on the issue of thank-you notes, and
recently I spoke with her about the importance of thank-you notes
and how to write meaningful ones.*

LI: *Do you recommend taking time to individualize each thank-you note?*

FI: Absolutely. You want your message to be meaningful. You
have to realize what is going on in the mind and the heart of the
gift giver. As far as the giver is concerned, he or she has probably
spent a good amount of money on your gift and a good amount of
time thinking about the right gift to give you. I know, for example,
that when I buy a wedding gift, I usually agonize for quite a while
about what is the right choice. Therefore, the most important information to convey to the gift giver is that you received the gift and
that you really liked it. Remember: this person has bought you a
gift to please you.

LI: *How important is timeliness in sending a thank-you note?*

FI: Very. It's important for the gift giver to know that you received
the gift, and the best way to do this is to send a thank-you note
fairly quickly. To send a thank-you note six months after you
received a gift is not appropriate, and it could be conceived of as a
slap in the face by the gift giver. Technically, you're supposed to
write a thank-you note as soon as you get a gift, but that's not always
possible. If you can get the note out in a week or two, that should
be fine.

LI: *After the hundredth thank-you note, it may be difficult to come up with
something original to say. What's the best way to word a thank-you note?*

FI: You have to look at how you really feel about the gift. In some
cases you will really be thrilled with the gift, and there's no reason
you can't express those emotions exactly. For example, if someone
gave you a ceramic bowl that you really love, go ahead and use
words like "I loved the ceramic bowl" in your thank-you note. It will
sound as if you really mean what you're saying, and since you do,
that's great.

Personally, I think you should avoid using what I call "washed-
out" words, like *lovely* to describe the gift. For example, avoid say-

ing something like, "Thank you for the lovely gift. It was so thought-ful of you." That's a cookie-cutter thank-you. However, if you're going to put more details in the thank-you note, such as how you're going to use the gift, then it's probably OK to use the word *lovely*.

When I write thank-you notes, I try to vary the words that I use. You can start with saying thank you and close by saying, "I really appreciate your thoughtfulness." This way, you're using *thank you* and *I appreciate* interchangeably. If you're having trouble coming up with creative ways to say thank you, use a thesaurus.

LI: *How detailed should a thank-you note be?*

FI: The important thing is to talk about the item—whether you like it or not. Even if you don't like it and are going to return it, you can still describe the object and how you might use it. For exam-ple, if someone gives you a leather-bound album that you think is really ugly, obviously you can't tell him or her that. But what you can say is how you might use it, such as "You can be sure we'll have pictures from our honeymoon to put in the album you gave us." Describing the gift in as much detail as possible lets the gift giver know that you're talking about his or her gift and not some generic gift. However, if you're stuck and can't figure out how you might use this ugly leather-bound photo album, you can compliment the giver by saying "You always have such good taste" or "You always take so much time to think about what you're going to buy." Or if you *really* have nothing to write, you can talk about the wedding and mention how nice it was to see that person there.

LI: *How long does a thank-you note have to be?*

FI: It can be just a line or two. The best notes are often the short-est ones. You can write a very personal note in a couple of sentences. How many sentences does it take to describe the elegant crystal vase? You can say, "When the sunlight hits the elegant crystal vase you got us, it just sparkles. Thank you so much." If you can add "I love it" with an exclamation point, that's great. But don't do it if you hate it. I don't advocate lying in the thank-you note just to create great prose. But if you want to add some feeling to the note, you could say, "It was so thoughtful of you" with an exclamation point so you can give the impression that you're very happy about receiv-ing the crystal vase.

LI: *If you are going to be very busy, can you get away with preprinted thank-you cards?*

"Order note cards with your first names on them. That way, you can use them for thank-you notes in advance of the wedding day as well as after you are married. In addition, write your thank-you notes as soon as the gifts come in."
Wendy, married 11/19/95

Thank-You Notes

FI: In my book, I talk about the fact that there is nothing wrong with buying a printed greeting card. The key is to write something personal in handwriting in addition to the preprinted message. Personally, I would not have preprinted thank-you cards made. It is true that it could save time, but if you're going to add a couple of handwritten lines anyway, why not simply write something from scratch? You have to remember that you're busy today, and the person who bought you the gift was probably busy, too. Yet he or she took the time to pick out your wedding gift. We've all heard our mothers say, "If someone can take the time and trouble to buy you a gift, you can take the time and trouble to write a thank-you note." Well, you know what? Mother knows best.

LI: *Is it solely the bride's responsibility to write the thank-you notes or can you get your groom involved, too?*

FI: More and more grooms today are writing thank-you notes. Couples are finding it easier if the responsibility of writing thank-you notes is shared. By all means have the groom help out. He may write to his family and friends and you to your family and friends. But if you make a pact to split the details, make sure he does it. Or if you feel that your groom should help you out but you know deep down in your heart that he'll probably never get around to writing them, then take on the responsibility yourself. Thank-you notes are not worth fighting over.

LI: *What do you do if the gift was money?*

FI: Etiquette books say you should mention the amount you receive, but I don't feel comfortable doing that. If the gift is money, tell the gift giver, if you can, how you're going to spend it. I would say, "Thank you very much for the check" and then talk about the fact that you used it for the honeymoon or toward the down payment on the house. If you're going to use it to pay off the caterer, don't say that. Instead, say, "Your generous check will be put toward our nest egg."

LI: *Should you write thank-you notes to your parents?*

FI: Absolutely. And in fact, when writing notes to parents or family, you can even take some risks with what you say, because you want to let them know about your feelings. For example, if your parents gave you a memorable wedding, you're giving them a gift back by telling them how much this meant to you. "I've always wanted a big wedding. Everything was so perfect, and I appreciate that even if you didn't agree with me on certain choices, you allowed it to be my wedding and you went along with my wishes." Certainly, ending with, "I love you" is a wonderful touch. If you write a note to your parents that is truly from the heart, you don't even have to say thank you. If you end the note with "I love you"—what powerful words those are. I think parents would dissolve in tears of happiness. That makes for a wonderfully genuine note.

Thank-You Notes Tips

Crane's Wedding Blue Book (Fireside, 1993) is a veritable bible on all wedding-related correspondences. It includes information on the proper monogram for your thank-you notes and the etiquette of gift-acknowledgment cards. While the average bride and groom may not be concerned with monograms on note cards, they should take the following thank-you note tips (reprinted with permission) to heart.

* Don't worry about style. Write your thank-you notes in the style in which you usually speak. Use contractions; they're more personal. They'll make your notes sound more like you.

* Don't let your thank-you obligations pile up. Write your thank-you notes the day you receive your presents. Your notes will be fresher and will sound more sincere.

* Just write. Writer's block comes from thinking too much about style and substance. You know pretty much what you want to say. Just say it. And don't worry about repeating yourself. Everybody understands that it's impossible to write something original on each thank-you note. Besides, your thank-you notes are not going to be passed around and compared.

"If you're like my brother, you can use your computer address file to keep track of gifts you got for thank-you notes. My brother and his wife got married on Saturday, opened gifts on Sunday, and entered all the gift information into their address database and printed out a hard copy on Monday. On Tuesday, on the plane to Orlando, they wrote all their thank-you notes and mailed them when they got there. Folks were sure surprised to get thank-you notes while my brother was still on his honeymoon!"
Karen, married 1/10/98

Thank-You Notes

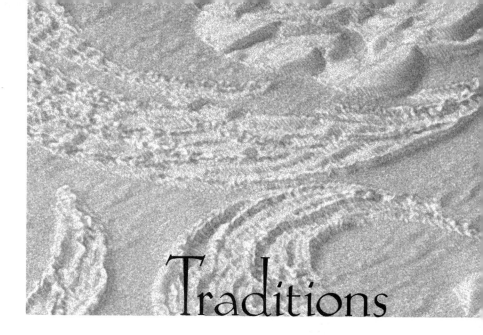

Traditions

You know the old custom of carrying things "old, new, borrowed, and blue" with you on your wedding day. But do you know where the tradition comes from? Upon researching wedding traditions, I discovered that during Biblical times blue, not white, was considered the color of purity. The idea of wearing something old and something borrowed is usually to have the good luck of the original owner passed on to you. And having something new symbolizes you and your husband's new life together.

I have to admit that as Bill and I planned what we were going to wear for our wedding reception, we didn't really take into consideration any of the typical wedding traditions—I guess because we weren't having your typical wedding to begin with. But it turned out that we were able to fit some of the traditions into our celebration without even realizing it.

For example, the something old was Bill's wedding band. It belonged to his grandfather Pasquale who, unfortunately, died the year before Bill and I became a couple. Therefore, I never got to meet him. But I feel as if I had.

Anytime you mention his grandfather to him, Bill starts to tell these wonderful stories about his sweet grandfather, a produce retailer. For example, during the Great Depression, at the end of the day he gave out leftover fruit and vegetables to poor families in the neighborhood rather than taking it home for his own family. Pasquale, who came to this country from Italy as a teenager, loved to tell Bill and his brother John stories about the "old country," and I completely understand why Bill would want to keep a part of his grandfather with him at all times—namely, by wearing his wedding ring.

We also found ways to work the other three components of "old, new, borrowed, and blue" into our wedding celebration. New were my dress, hat, shoes, and Bill's tie. Blue was Bill's button-down shirt. And borrowed was my grandfather's backyard, where we hosted the party.

The History of Wedding Traditions

When Charlene Hein decided to become a professional bridal consultant, she started to study for her newfound profession with the Association of Bridal Consultants. Part of that education included learning about common wedding traditions. Based on what she learned through the Association of Bridal Consultants and from the brides she's worked with in recent years, here is the history of some of the most common wedding traditions.

Engagement Period

In days past, before a man would get on bended knee to ask his beloved to marry him, he would seek permission from his intended's father first. This simple question often turned into a bona fide interrogation, with the bride's father asking the prospective groom about his background, upbringing, and financial ability to support his daughter. If the father did not like any of the answers, off the gentleman went. On the other hand, if the engagement was approved, then the couple could expect to pursue a courtship with a chaperone always present.

Today, of course, the decision to be married is one made by the bride and groom—not their parents. However, some traditional fellows may still feel that it is proper to ask permission of the bride's father. In addition, couples today don't use chaperones on dates or worry about being caught in a stolen kiss. Instead they may worry about how they're going to break the news to both sets of parents that they're actually living together outside of marriage.

Bride's Father Paying for the Wedding

This tradition can be traced back to the existence of the *dowry*, or the price the parents paid to encourage an eligible suitor to marry their daughter. In some foreign societies, this custom exists today. According to tradition, the dowry was the last thing the parents had to pay for their daughter. It was assumed that after the wedding the groom would take care of all the financial needs of his wife.

Even today, many husbands assume that it is their responsibility to support their wives—and any children they bear—without having the women contribute to the family finances. However, it is becoming more common for couples to split the cost of the weddings with their parents—or even pay for the entire event themselves—and it is equally common for women to continue working after being married to help support their families.

Attendants

There are varying theories on the history of attendants. Some believe that the tradition dates back to a time when a bride was abducted from her family, not purchased, and therefore the groom needed help from his attendants to pull off the task. Others once believed that evil spirits would try to invade the joining of two people. To trick the spirits, the members of the bridal party dressed alike—bridesmaids like the bride, ushers like the groom—so that the spirits couldn't tell the actual couple from their attendants. Today, of course, attendants are included in the wedding to act as witnesses (the best man and maid of honor often sign the marriage certificate) and to support the bride and groom on this, the happiest of days.

Lighting Candles

Torches symbolize life and love. However, since most modern couples wouldn't think of parading around a church with a torch in hand, the symbol of the flame has been replaced with the unity candle. Lighting the candle together represents the two persons becoming one. Unity candle lighting can also include the extended family to symbolize two families becoming one. Therefore, some couples now ask their mothers to light candles and place them on appropriate sides of the altar. Then, the bride and groom use the candle their respective mothers have lit to light their own unity candle, thus bringing together both families.

Shoes

Marriage today is viewed as the joining of two families rather than the giving of the bride from one family to another. However, in ancient times, shoes often represented the transfer of ownership of the bride. For example, upon presenting the groom with his dowry,

"Here's how I did the 'old, new, borrowed, and blue' tradition. For old, I wore my husband's grandmother's platinum/diamond wedding band. For new, I considered my engagement ring. For borrowed, I used a lace hankie offered by a friend's wife, who used it at her wedding in the late fifties. I had the florist wrap this hankie around the bottom of my bouquet. And for blue, I put Dr. Scholl's gel insoles in my pumps."

Amy, married 8/3/96

Traditions

"For the old part of the tradition, there was the diamond in my engagement ring. It is the diamond my late father gave my mother. For new, there was my dress. For borrowed, I used the veil my mother wore. And for blue, I did something kind of sneaky and painted my toenails blue."

Kymmi, married 11/30/96

a father would also present him a shoe, to symbolize the transfer of ownership. The same would be accomplished if the bride's father nailed one of his daughter's shoes to the bedpost of the marriage bed. Today, some couples continue this archaic tradition by tying shoes to the bumper of the getaway car or throwing shoes at the bride and groom as they drive away.

Flowers

Originally, brides didn't carry flowers simply because they complemented their dresses. Instead, flowers symbolized one of the first gifts the new husband and wife would give each other. The groom would pick flowers for the bride, and she in turn would take some of the flowers from her handpicked bouquet and slip them into his lapel. This is the reason many florists insist on using the same flowers in the bride's bouquet and the groom's boutonniere.

Tossing the Bouquet

It used to be that the bride would toss a separate bouquet at each of her bridesmaids. Hidden inside one of these bouquets was a ring. Whichever bridesmaid caught the bouquet with the ring inside it was the next woman to be married.

Today, bouquet tosses at weddings involve the bridesmaids along with all the single women in attendance. Even though only one bouquet is tossed, the same soon-to-be-married good luck is said to be bestowed on the lady who catches the bouquet.

Because many brides do not want to part with their wedding bouquet, they often commission their florist to make a special tossing bouquet.

Tossing the Garter

History tells us that much like today's wedding receptions, people often drank too much and ended up a bit inebriated. During this time of drunkenness, male guests would often rush the bride and try to rip the garter from her leg, which, they thought, would bring them good luck. In order to save herself from being mobbed, savvy brides started taking off their garters themselves and tossing it to the crowd before things got out of hand.

Today removing the garter has become a ritual that involves both the bride and groom. The husband usually removes the garter from his bride's leg, to much fanfare created by whooping guests and an enthusiastic deejay, and then tosses it to the unmarried men in attendance. Unlike the bouquet tossed to the single women, it is unknown whether catching the garter will bring a young man a bride.

Wedding Cake

Years ago newlyweds enjoyed a wedding cake as a symbol of their intended fertility. Today, the cake is nothing more than a photo op and dessert for the guests.

Cutting the cake has its own symbolism as well. Usually, the bride cuts the first two slices of cake to symbolize her traditional role as the food preparer. The groom then feeds his bride the first piece of cake she cut, thus showing that he is the provider for his bride. Oftentimes the groom may place his hand over his bride's when she cuts the cake. Perhaps this is to show his power over her.

The top layer of a wedding cake is never touched but rather is intended to be saved for the couple to eat on their first anniversary. A modern twist on the tradition, probably created after too many couples tried to enjoy their stale, year-old cake, is to have a baker re-create the wedding cake for a first-anniversary celebration.

Transportation

*I*n the weddings we've been to in recent times, Bill and I have seen just about every variety of wedding-day transportation possible. There was the wedding of one of Bill's college friends, which took place in a picture-postcard-perfect New England town. The wedding ceremony was in a tiny, white, spired chapel across from the village green, and the bride arrived in a horse-drawn carriage—very romantic. We've also seen people drive to and from the wedding ceremonies in an antique white Rolls-Royce and baby blue 1960s Chevy.

If Bill and I were going to have a special car to take us from our planned wedding ceremony to the reception, we probably wouldn't have splurged for a limousine or classic car. Instead, we probably would have borrowed my mother's white Jeep Cherokee, and, in fact, it was the car in which we arrived at our garden reception. It was as low key as we hoped our day would be, it was white, and, of course, it was free.

Car Talk

Susan Price is an accredited bridal consultant through the Association of Bridal Consultants and owner of I Do Weddings in San Luis Obispo, California. For more information, call 805-546-9969. One of Price's areas of expertise is wedding-day transportation. Here, she shares her wisdom on finding a limousine, classic car, or whatever mode of transportation you choose on your big day.

LI: *What transportation choices are available today?*

Nuptials News

The average cost for a limousine at a wedding is $192, according to *Bride's Magazine*.

"If you've hired more than one car, make sure each driver is clear as to what his or her responsibility is. On my wedding day, both limousines arrived at my home. When I inquired as to whether or not my fiancé and his ushers had been picked up yet, both drivers looked at each other and said, 'He did it.' Meanwhile, the groom-to-be and the ushers were having a grand old time at his parents' house while guests arriving at the church had to seat themselves."

Carreen, married 11/26/93

SP: You can choose from a variety of transportation methods. There are limousines, horse-drawn carriages, classic cars, trolleys, and more.

LI: *How do you find out what companies in your area offer?*

SP: A good place to start is by looking in the yellow pages. If you know of any people in your area who were married recently, you can ask them for recommendations as well. And, of course, if you hire a consultant, you can ask the consultant for his or her opinion on transportation companies, too.

The other thing I would do is ask vendors in the wedding industry, especially those that are impacted by transportation companies, such as churches. Find out what their experience has been with limousine companies' arriving on time, and see if they can recommend anyone. You have to realize that in the wedding industry, by Monday morning, everyone knows what happened at various weddings the previous weekend. So word does get around about good—and bad—wedding vendors.

LI: *What sort of questions should you ask the various companies you call?*

SP: One of the first things you want to determine is if they specialize in weddings. Many limousine companies do, but not all of them do. Some may call themselves a limousine company, but their cars are used primarily for airport pickups or executive travel around town. Ask how many weddings they've done in the past year.

One of the reasons you want a company that specializes in weddings is they understand the timetable of a wedding, and they may offer a discount if you rent more than one limousine. In addition, some companies have Just Married banners that they can hang on the car, or they'll decorate the car for you, if that's what you'd like done.

Find out the age of the cars they rent and whether they have additional resources available. For example, because limousines are used constantly, they need maintenance all the time. There is always the possibility of a car's breaking down, so you want to make sure that a limousine company has more than one car in its fleet to act as a backup in case of mechanical difficulties.

Ask if the company has a smoking policy. If you and your spouse smoke, you'll want to know that you'll be able to light up. However, some companies may prevent you from doing so. On the other hand, if you're sensitive to smoke, you don't want a driver who is going to puff all the way to the church. And you surely don't want to get into a car that smells of smoke. In fact, you might want to find out if the company has any nonsmoking cars. If they don't, ask if they'll steam-clean the interior of the car so it doesn't smell of smoke.

You also need to be aware of the drivers' records. Find out what the company's hiring policy for drivers is. Do they do a check on driving records through the Department of Motor Vehicles? Do they hire drivers who have speeding violations or arrests for hazardous driving?

Some companies may have hiring minimums, so you'll want to ask about that as well. For example, if a limousine company is very popular in your community, on Saturdays or during summer months they may be in great demand. Therefore, to make their time with you worthwhile, they might charge you for more time than you actually need the limousine.

Ask how much buffer time they allow between events. If they often schedule back-to-back pickups, that could be a problem. For example, if the wedding before yours runs late, then that might affect how timely the driver is in picking you up for your wedding.

Find out if the cars are air-conditioned. If you're getting married in the summer or live in a hot climate, you may assume that the cars will be air-conditioned, but some of the older models may not be.

LI: *Should you get referrals or check references on a limousine company?*

SP: Absolutely. The companies I use have excellent drivers and have been very accommodating to me, and if you called to ask me about their service, I wouldn't hesitate to tell you how wonderful they've been to work with. As usual, it's a red flag if the company refuses to give you names and numbers for referrals.

LI: *Besides providing basic transportation, what else can you expect to get from a limousine or classic car company?*

SP: Some companies offer certain amenities as part of the package deal. For example, champagne is normally included for you and your groom to drink on the way from the ceremony to the reception. However, some companies may offer you the opportunity to specify what brand of champagne you get. This request may incur additional charges, however.

Sometimes people want to have a fully stocked bar or at least a partial bar in the limousine. These are the sorts of details you need to arrange ahead of time.

I find that many of the limousine drivers are real hams and they get off on opening the bottle of champagne for the couple. Not only is this fun, but it also makes for a great picture for the photographer.

Talk about decent drivers. I had one driver this year who dropped the couple off at the wedding and we sent him on his way. He had fulfilled his obligation to the couple, and we didn't expect to see him again. But two hours later, he walked in the door. He said, "I forgot to give the bride and groom their luggage for their honeymoon." He remembered that it was in his trunk, and he knew the right thing to do was to return it. That was quite nice of him.

LI: *You mention good-spirited drivers. How can you ensure that you get one?*

SP: Honestly, it's not always possible to interview the driver. However, if you have friends who have used a certain limousine company, you can ask for the name of a particular driver they liked. You can do the same with the couples you call for references.

In addition, you can ask the company how long the drivers have been with them. It will give you a decent idea that they are a good company if they have drivers who have been with them for awhile.

LI: *When you book the limousine for your wedding day, should you expect the company to throw in a free ride to the hotel after the reception or to the airport the next day?*

SP: With most of the companies I've worked with, trips like that would cost extra. Sometimes a driver will do it for free if he or she likes you, but you can't plan on that. If you need the ride to the airport the next day or home from the reception, then you're probably going to have to book that in advance.

LI: *How does payment and tipping the driver work?*

SP: You need to ask ahead of time what the company's policy is. Some companies will include the tip in the bill, and some won't. Sometimes the driver is better off waiting for the tip, because he or she can get more money that way. Find this out ahead of time so you'll know whether or not to have cash ready to tip the driver. Personally, I think having to tip the driver on your wedding day can be a real downer. I think the less financial garbage that you have to deal with on the wedding day, the better.

Most companies will have you arrange for payment beforehand. Or they might take an imprint or the number of your credit card ahead of time but then not run the charge through until the day of the wedding.

LI: *Do you need a contract with a transportation company? If so, what should that contract say?*

SP: Yes; make sure you have a contract. One of the most important items to include in a contract with a company that rents limousines is that if they are going to switch a limousine on you, you want to know ahead of time. For example, when you visit a company, they'll probably show you the cars they reserve specifically for weddings. However, if all those cars are booked or the one you specified breaks down, you may end up with some awful car that doesn't look anything like the limousines you originally saw. Therefore, you need to be notified in advance if another car is going to show up on your wedding day.

You also want your contract to specify what the driver's attire should be. For some companies, a suit is acceptable attire for a driver to wear, but you'll want to know that ahead of time. If they promise that the driver will be wearing a cap and gloves, put it in the contract. You want there to be a certain level of dignity to the driver. I once saw a limousine driver arrive to pick up a wedding couple, and he was wearing tennis shoes, a sweatshirt, and jeans. That was completely unacceptable.

Your contract should also spell out the places and times of pickup and any additional stops you might need to make along the way.

LI: *If you decide to use a vintage car or another means of transportation on your wedding day, what do you need to keep in mind?*

SP: One of the neat things about hiring a classic car is the reaction you get from the crowd. If you arrive in a 1958 Jaguar, people will say, "Oh, it's cool."

As you would with any other transportation company you hire, you want to be sure that the company renting you the classic car has insurance. If you get in an accident and they're not insured, you might not be covered. You may end up in the hospital and have to pay your own bills.

Maintenance usually isn't as big a deal with classic cars as it is with limousines, because renting out the car for weddings is how some people afford their hobby. They usually have a one-car fleet. Because it's a really specialized vehicle, it will be very well maintained. In our experience with classic cars, they're usually in better running shape than an everyday car. However, if you're afraid of what might happen should the car break down, you might want to go with a company that has more than one car in stock. Then, of course, find out about the maintenance records for all the cars.

Transportation

217

If the car is especially great-looking, make sure the owner will have the car available to you for picture taking, if you so choose.

Another means of transportation to and from the ceremony and reception is a horse-drawn carriage. I've even had brides and grooms arrive on horseback. Just as a classic car will be more expensive than a limousine, a horse-drawn carriage will probably be more expensive than both. For example, there's a company in my area that charges about $250 just to pick the bride and groom up and take them to the ceremony.

You're going to have some special concerns that you'll need to address if you decide to hire a horse. For example, animals can get sick, so find out if there are backups available. In addition, horses are not able to handle standing still for any length of time, so you may find yourself in a time crunch on your wedding day if the horse arrives early. The horse's driver will probably encourage you to speed things along so the animal doesn't become anxious waiting around.

However, it works the other way, too. I've been panicked many times by one company that has horse-drawn carriages. They usually arrive exactly when the bride and groom are scheduled to leave the church for the reception, but it makes for a touchy time when the people may be wondering where the couple's transportation is. But when the horse does arrive, it is a spectacular sight.

LI: *What other important points are there to keep in mind when hiring a transportation company?*

SP: You should always put a deposit down with any vendor you're going to book for your wedding day. That is your insurance that the vendor will come through for you. In addition, you need to reconfirm everything the week before your wedding. This is especially true if you have a Sunday wedding or a wedding on a nontraditional day. It's sad but true that vendors could forget about you if your wedding is on any day other than Saturday. Most wedding vendors are used to working on Saturday, but not necessarily on Sunday, for example.

Transportation Tips

John G. Bays is owner of Regal Limousine Service in Springfield, Virginia. Bays is the proud owner of a white 1978 Rolls-Royce Silver Shadow II. If you are interested in renting his car for your wedding, call 703-440-3651. Here are his tips for hiring a transportation company.

* Don't be afraid to compare prices. Renting a car for your wedding day could cost as little at $39 an hour or as much as almost quadruple that.

* In my opinion, full service on the wedding day includes picking up you and your father at home and transporting you to the church; taking you and your groom and whomever else to the reception; and then taking you and your groom to a hotel or airport afterwards.

* Some transportation companies offer a number of different cars, some of different make and model. For example, a specialty car company may have a range of Rolls-Royces, Mercedes Benzes, and Jaguars. However, if it doesn't, don't be afraid to mix and match cars from a variety of companies.

* Be clear about the time and date of the wedding and don't forget to give the driver directions.

* You should expect a 100 percent refund in case of mechanical failure.

A Trolley Good Time

For bridal parties that are bursting at the seams, sometimes a limousine or classic car just won't do. While some couples are turning to white vans to transport themselves and their attendants from the ceremony to the reception, others are choosing a more whimsical mode of transportation—the trolley.

One company that specializes in wedding-day trolleys is the Great American Trolley Company in Cold Spring, New Jersey. This company offers a range of trackless trolleys that hold a varying number of passengers—from eighteen to twenty-seven. Each wedding trolley is white and has been given a name based on a term of endearment, such as Cutie, Lovey, and Sweetie.

To help you celebrate, the trolleys are often bedecked with bells, streamers, and Just Married signs. In addition, music, such as the song "Going to the Chapel," is played during the ride to the church or synagogue, and if you choose, the trolley driver can take a detour through you or your groom's neighborhood so you can wave to well-wishers.

Besides renting trolleys, the Great American Trolley Company also offers minicoaches that you can offer to guests after the wedding. "The big concern now is how guests are going to get home from the reception, especially if they've been drinking," says Susan

Adelizzi-Schmidt, the company's marketing director. "If guests know they have a ride waiting to take them home from the wedding, they can stay longer and have a good time."

The Great American Trolley Company serves weddings in New Jersey, southeastern Pennsylvania, and northern Delaware. There is also a satellite division in Myrtle Beach, South Carolina, to serve the needs of brides and grooms in South Carolina. For more information, call 800-4-TROLLY.

Tuxedos

When Bill was best man in a wedding recently, the groom decided it would be a good idea for all his ushers to rent tuxedos. Not only would all the guys be wearing the same suits and shoes, but also they wouldn't have to worry about schlepping their tuxedos on the plane.

We arrived for the Saturday night wedding on Thursday afternoon. The next morning the guys were off to get their tuxedos, and by noon they were done. They'd been fitted for the tuxedos, tried on shoes, paid for the ensemble, and brought it back with them to the hotel room. If only getting bridesmaid dresses were so easy.

Renting a Tuxedo

Jack Springer is the executive director of the International Formalwear Association (IFA), a trade association for the tuxedo industry. IFA represents those who rent, sell, and manufacturer tuxedos. IFA has a brochure that outlines the basics of formalwear. To receive one, send a self-addressed, stamped envelope to them at 401 N. Michigan Avenue, Chicago, IL 60611. In addition, IFA can refer you to a tuxedo retailer near you. Call 312-321-6806. Here Springer answers some of the most commonly asked questions about renting tuxedos.

LI: *Why would a groom choose to rent a tuxedo, especially if he owns one already?*

JS: Usually a groom chooses to rent a tuxedo for his wedding because he wants everyone to be wearing the same type of formalwear. This is especially true when there's a large bridal party that

Nuptials News

According to the International Formalwear Association, 65 percent of all tuxedos that are rented are done so for weddings.

needs to look coordinated. Or he could be having a daytime wedding, when technically it's not proper to wear a tuxedo. However,
instead of simply wearing a suit, he wants to have himself and his
bridal party dressed in formalwear. For example, when my son was
married at a daytime wedding, I wore a stroller, with long tails, and
an ascot. That's the appropriate formalwear for a wedding occurring before six o'clock.

Besides time of day, the formality of your wedding will affect
what attire the groom and his ushers wear. If you're having a very
formal evening wedding, then the men will dress in full tails, white
tie, and white vest. If the invitation says "white-tie," it's tails. If it
says "black-tie," it's a tuxedo. And truth be told, most men who are
participating in a very formal evening wedding do not have dress
tails hanging in their closet, so it makes sense for them to rent.

LI: *What about the color tuxedo the groom chooses?*

JS: For an occasion that calls for a traditional tuxedo, the groom
can choose black or navy. Either color is perfectly proper. Actually,
most tuxedos used to be midnight blue but looked black. Now most
of them are black, but you can still get a dark blue tuxedo if you
want. Believe it or not, one of the most popular tuxedo colors is gray.
It shows up at weddings more often than any other color tuxedo.

LI: *Does the groom need to take a swatch of fabric from the bridesmaid
dresses with him when he selects the tuxedos he and his ushers are going to
rent?*

JS: No. Men's formalwear doesn't have to coordinate with the
bridesmaid dresses. However, you and your groom might decide that
it would be nice if the men's accessories match, so you might find
a tie, vest, or cummerbund with the same colors in it as the bridesmaid dresses.

LI: *What does the groom need to know before he heads out to a rental store
to look at tuxedos?*

JS: In today's market, there are so many types of tuxedos available, including those with designer labels, such as Christian Dior.
These designers offer more than tuxedos, however. They also have
accessories, such as cuff links and bow ties, to go with their tuxedos. The groom should keep in mind that he and his ushers will pay
more to rent a designer tuxedo. And while so-called regular tuxedos come with basic accessories, they'll pay more to have designer
accessories. Therefore, he should know his budget—and that of his
ushers—ahead of time. A groom wouldn't want to choose a high-

priced tuxedo that will make everyone bankrupt. He should find a tuxedo that is complementary to and affordable for everyone.

LI: *Can a groom go to any old rental place to get his tuxedo?*

JS: I wouldn't suggest it. Instead, I would go to a location that has inventory, not just two or three tuxedos that you try on. You want a full-service specialist who has the samples and inventory on hand. The problem with stores that carry only one or two tuxedos is they have to order each tuxedo from a wholesaler. While there's usually no problem with the wholesaler's delivering the tuxedos on time, the problems arise when there is a mistake in the measurements. For example, if a guy measures as a 46 long but for some reason the order was filled with a 36 long, well, then, there's going to be a problem. If the shop owner doesn't have inventory on hand, what is the misfitted usher to do? However, if they've rented from a store with a large stock, the store owner will probably be able to go in the back and find a tuxedo that fits.

The best way to find a reputable rental store is to talk to anyone who has been married recently. Find out what their experience was like. Personally, I would go to a specialist who is a member of my association—the groom will see the logo on the door. What it means to be a member of the IFA is that the proprietor is probably in the mainstream of the industry, and he or she is trying to stay abreast of trends and current operating procedures.

LI: *Besides the formalwear, what else can a rental shop provide for the groom and his ushers?*

JS: It is particularly important that everyone has the same formal shoes. That's because when pictures are taken, street shoes just don't make it with tuxedos. If a guy happens to be wearing patent leather street shoes, it would make it. But how many men own patent leather shoes? When you think about it, a true formalwear specialist can offer a man everything he'll need—from accessories to shoes.

LI: *How soon before the wedding should the groom-to-be start looking for a store from which to rent tuxedos?*

JS: If the wedding party is coming in from all over the country, the groom needs to decide what his party will wear as soon as possible. Once he has decided on the formalwear they're going to rent and the shop from which they will rent, then he should send his groomsmen a form on which they can write their sizes. (Most tuxedo stores can supply the form.) When his attendants return their measurements, the groom will give those to the tuxedo specialist

Tuxedos

223

who is handling the wedding. This way the tuxedo specialist can have the outfits ready for the out-of-towners to come in and try on the day before the wedding.

LI: *Does it make sense for the groom to find a tuxedo shop with many locations so his ushers can go for fittings before they get to the wedding?*

JS: Not always. It's probably simpler for the ushers not to have to carry their formalwear to the wedding—especially if they're flying—and then have to carry it home as well. I suppose if the groom knew the designer and exact style number of the tuxedos he wanted to rent, he could suggest that the ushers get them themselves. But in most cases, for out-of-town people, it makes life much easier if they just do the formalwear fittings the day before the wedding. Then, their only concern is taking the tuxedo with them to the hotel.

LI: *I know bridesmaids are supposed to pay for their dresses. Is it the same when ushers rent tuxedos?*

JS: Yes. It is the groomsmen's responsibility to pick up the tab for their tuxedo rental. That's why it's important for the groom to select an affordable tuxedo.

LI: *You mention finding an affordable tuxedo. Does the groom have any negotiating power with the rental shop?*

JS: Absolutely. The groom should always shop around and see what kind of incentives different shops have to offer. Very often the store will say that if he rents a certain number of tuxedos for his ushers, his tuxedo is free. Or they might throw in certain designer accessories for free if the groom and his groomsmen rent a certain number of designer tuxedos. Each shop differs, so a groom shouldn't be afraid to shop around.

Another thing the groom should agree on beforehand is when the tuxedos need to be returned. Usually it is the Monday or Tuesday after the wedding, and it is the best man's responsibility to return the formalwear. However, because people may be leaving before or after the usual return time, the groom should find out how flexible the shop is about when the formalwear can be returned.

LI: *How much should a guy expect to pay to rent formalwear?*

JS: Average prices range from $50 to $125 per tux, including accessories and possibly shoes. It's just like renting a car. I can rent a Yugo or a Mercedes. In the end, you get what you pay for.

I believe that most grooms end up renting up, not renting down. That is, if it's a special occasion like a wedding, he reasons that for an extra $20, he can get a smashing tuxedo and look fantastic.

Buying a Tuxedo

If you've decided to dress formally for your wedding and your fiancé doesn't own a tuxedo, now might be a good time to begin shopping for one. According to Jack Springer (executive director of the International Formalwear Association, a trade association for the tuxedo industry), any man who works in an office environment or lives in an area such as a city where black-tie events occur often should own a tuxedo. "If a man wears a tuxedo twice in a year, he's made back his investment. That's because he can buy a tuxedo for the same amount of money that it would cost to rent one twice," he says. "In addition, it's a lot more convenient for him to go to the closet to get the tuxedo then it is to drive to the store down the street."

Here are some basics for your fiancé to keep in mind when he hits the stores.

* You'll probably end up spending for a good tuxedo what you would for a good suit.

* You may find you have better luck going to a store that rents and sells tuxedos exclusively. As opposed to a department store, where the main focus isn't on selling tuxedos, a specialty store will know more about tuxedos and offer you a greater selection.

* Invest in a good-quality tuxedo that you can wear for the next ten years. Try to stay away from any tuxedos that seem to be in style currently, such as the five-button or Nehru jacket tuxedos that all the stars in Hollywood are wearing. While this kind of tuxedo seems cool now, it may look foolish next year. A more classic-looking tuxedo will be made from wool and will be either a peaked single-breasted, a notched single-breasted, or a shawl double-breasted.

* If you decide to go for a double-breasted tuxedo, you don't have to worry about accessories such as a cummerbund or a vest. Because of the way the jacket will close on you, nothing you're wearing underneath will be visible, except for your shirt and tie.

* A single-breasted tuxedo will give you more versatility with accessories, which can change the look of your tuxedo in a

second. Right now, the hot accessory is the vest, and you can switch vests to match the mood and formality of the party you wear the tux to. For example, you might buy a reversible vest that is black on one side and has your favorite football team's logo on the other. Then, for the more formal occasions you attend, you can wear the black side of the vest out. However, when the company you're in would appreciate the whimsy of the football theme, you can wear the other side of the vest showing out. Remember: if you wear a vest, you don't wear a cummerbund.

* You can't just wear any white shirt with a tuxedo, so be sure to buy one that matches the tuxedo you get. The most proper shirt you can wear has French cuffs. Then you'll need to invest in shirt studs and cuff links.

* While your cuffs should be French, you have a few more options with the collar. The most common collar is the wing tip. The tips can be either long or short. If they're long, you wear them under your tie. If they're short, they should stick up over the tie. The hot collar now (but perhaps not next year) is the collarless shirt, called a Nehru shirt. Obviously, you can't wear a tie with a collarless shirt, but you can wear a jeweled button cover over the button nearest your throat. The third collar type is the turndown collar. It's a standard shirt collar.

* The proper tie to wear with a tuxedo (if you're wearing a collared shirt, of course) is the bow tie. Most men wear a pretied bow tie, because either they aren't dexterous enough to tie it themselves or they simply don't know how to do it. The tie will look better if it is tied before each wearing, and the specialist from whom you buy your tuxedo can show you how to tie it properly.

* Tuxedos are never worn with belts. Instead, suspenders are used to hold up the pants.

* You need special shoes to go with your tuxedo. Patent leather shoes are the formalwear shoe of choice. They aren't designed like a regular dress shoe that laces up. Instead, they're more loaferlike and look like a ballet slipper.

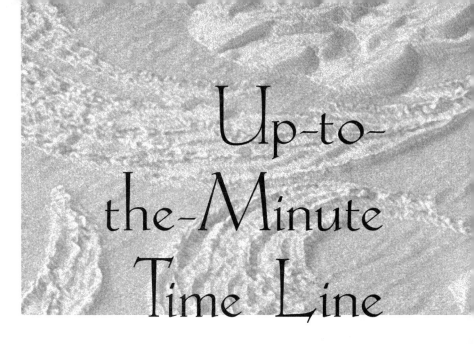

Up-to-the-Minute Time Line

*S*taying organized throughout the wedding-planning process is the key to getting everything done in time for the big day. So that I wouldn't miss any meetings with or payments to our caterer, I marked such dates on my calendar. One bride I know bought a separate engagement book so she would have a place to record wedding meetings and information only.

While conventional wisdom says that most brides begin planning their weddings a year in advance, that isn't always the case. Most of the experts I interviewed for this book had numerous anecdotes to share of brides and grooms trying to throw together last-minute weddings.

With that in mind, following is a general time line that you can use to stay up-to-date on all your wedding plans.

At Least Six Months Before the Wedding

Decide on the type of wedding and reception you'll have, including the size and degree of formality.

Determine a wedding budget.

Find a church/synagogue/ceremony site, and set a date and time for the wedding.

If you're having a religious wedding, meet with your clergyman and, if necessary, make an appointment for premarital counseling.

Choose and ask attendants.

Make a guest list and, if you're involving your parents in creating a guest list, ask them for their input as soon as possible.

Once the guest list is set, find a reception site and hire a caterer.

Order invitations and announcements.

Order the bridal gown and any attire for attendants.

Find a florist.

Hire a photographer. If you plan to have a formal portrait taken, arrange for that now.

Secure musicians for your ceremony and reception.

Hire a limousine or specialty transportation company to take you, your groom, and your bridal party and ushers to and from the wedding.

Order thank-you notes.

Select china, silver, and crystal patterns and register your preferences at your store(s) of choice.

Begin planning honeymoon.

Secure a location for your rehearsal dinner, if you're having one.

Two Months Before the Wedding

Notify bridesmaids about fittings and accessories. If possible, have shoes dyed in one lot.

Select gifts for bridesmaids and ushers.

As soon as your final gown fitting is done, have your formal portrait taken.

Go over finalized menu selections with caterer.

Make any necessary medical and dental appointments.

Make an appointment with your hairdresser.

If you're buying a house, start house hunting.

Address and stuff invitations or take envelopes to calligrapher.

Make housing arrangements for out-of-town guests.

Pay balance due on honeymoon, if you haven't already done so.

One Month Before the Wedding

Mail invitations.

Go for blood tests, if necessary.

Apply for marriage license.

Select rings.

As gifts arrive, write thank-you notes.

If possible, pack honeymoon clothing.

Check on the accessories for your wedding gown and for
bridesmaid dresses.

Make final arrangements with florist, photographer, and
caterer.

Arrange for a place for bridesmaids to dress.

Send wedding announcement with photograph to newspaper.

Two Weeks Before the Wedding

Call any guests who haven't yet responded.

When guest list is finalized, create seating charts and make
place cards.

One Week Before the Wedding

Reconfirm with all vendors, including hairdresser,
photographer, caterer, florist, and band or deejay.

Call travel agent to reconfirm departure times, hotel
reservations, and any other reservations related to the
honeymoon.

*Source: Association of Bridal Consultants, New Milford,
Connecticut.*

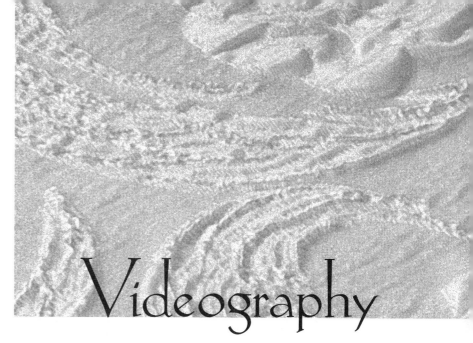

Videography

Nothing is more annoying than being at a wedding where the videographer with a really bright light on top of a camera follows guests around the dance floor, pestering them for an interview. I was at such a wedding. I finally relented and talked to the guy, but the finished product includes a very fed-up me saying something snippy into the camera. This is hardly what you want to remember about your wedding—guests saying something insincere so that the videographer will finally leave them alone.

Thankfully, video technology and videographers have come a long way since then. No longer must bright lights be used to capture images, and many of the videographers today are more sensitive about not intruding into the lives of guests as they enjoy the wedding.

The videos themselves have changed a lot, too. When my dad remarried in 1982, he hired a video crew to shoot his wedding and reception. His video was a choppily cut documentation of the day's events—interesting if you knew the parties involved but hardly anything worth watching. Compare that with the wedding video of my friends Stephanie and David, who were married just a few years ago.

Their video opens with a montage of their baby pictures and includes voice-over of them recalling their college courtship. The scenes from their traditional Jewish ceremony are tastefully shot, and the reception is captured, through clever editing, as the good time it truly was. Obviously, Stephanie and David did their homework when hiring a wedding videographer. They have a great wedding video to show for a great wedding day.

Finding a Videographer

Anne Kearns Fers is the owner of Gold Star Video in Trumbull, Connecticut, at 203-377-5665. She believes there are certain tried-and-true ways to find a videographer who can give you a wedding video that you'll love watching for years to come. Recently, she shared some of her secrets with me.

LI: *What is the best way to find a wedding videographer?*

AKF: The first and best way is through referrals. Ask any friends who had videographers at their weddings what they think of the work that person did for them. If they recommend the videographer highly, call him or her. If you can't get a referral from a friend, you can go to an association. Each state should have a videographers' association. For example, I'm a member of the Connecticut Association of Videographers. You can also call the Association of Bridal Consultants for a referral. Their membership includes videographers. What's great about turning to an association for referrals is you know that the videographer has to have submitted his or her work to the association in order to have been admitted. That's a comforting thought.

LI: *Once you have the names of a few videographers to consider, what should you do?*

AKF: You definitely want to meet with each so you can get a sense of who the person is and whether you think you'll like working with him or her. During your meeting be sure to look at several pieces of the videographer's work. Don't let the videographer show you just one demo tape, because that could be a compilation of the best work he or she has ever done.

Another thing to keep in mind is that there are a lot of unobtrusive videographers out there—and obtrusive ones as well. You should ask the videographer how he or she works and where the videographer places himself or herself during the ceremony and reception. If you don't want a camera in your face, you should tell the videographer. There are still a lot of people who want to get in there and direct the whole show and if you want that, that's OK. But if you don't, you have to talk about that beforehand.

LI: *How do you know what to look for in a wedding video?*

AKF: You definitely want to look for work that is conducive to your kind of wedding. For example, if you're going to have an outdoor wedding, don't look at tapes of church weddings only. Likewise, if you are having an early-morning wedding, what good will it do you to look at videos shot at nighttime receptions?

Another thing to keep in mind is that videography is subjective. Different videographers have different styles of shooting and different ways of working, so the finished product is going to vary from one to another.

Because editing is key to a great wedding video, find out who will edit your tape. If that is going to be someone other than the person who will shoot the video, then make sure you see examples of the editor's work, too.

LI: *What if a videographer tries to sell you a package with something like special effects in it?*

AKF: It's important to talk about the variety of packages the videographer has to offer and not just go with the first one he or she suggests. Make sure the videographer shows you examples of videos from different packages. Very often, the price of a package is based on the number of cameras that are used to shoot the video, how many hours the videographer spends shooting video, and the type of editing used. And if the videographer offers a package with special-effects editing and you like what you see, then maybe that's the package for you.

LI: *How can you avoid hiring a videographer who is going to blind the wedding guests with a camera light?*

AKF: You want to ask what kind of light source the videographer uses. I would suggest under 100 watts, which is a very soft light. Find out if the videographer plans to bounce a light off the ceiling so that the light isn't directed at everyone on the dance floor. Bounced light gives the picture a nice soft look. If the videographer has to use a light at all, find out how much time during the wedding he or she estimates having to use it.

LI: *What should you put in a contract with a videographer?*

AKF: A lot of people are concerned about when they will get their tape, so you might want to put an estimated delivery date in the contract. If you met and clicked with a certain videographer at a studio, put his or her name in the contract. This guarantees that that videographer—and not someone else—will show up on your wedding day.

In my contract I have all the services that will be included for the price. That's standard operating procedure as far as I'm con-

Videography

Nuptials News

According to *Bride's Magazine*, the average budget for photography and videography is $1,208.

cerned, and you should expect the same in your contract. Of course the total cost of services rendered should be in the contract along with any extra costs you may incur, such as from overnight deliveries or ordering additional tapes in the future.

LI: *When is a good time to hire a videographer?*

AKF: You should hire a videographer six months to a year beforehand. Many people hire their videographer with their photographer.

Questions to Ask a Videographer

Wedding and Event Videographers Association (WEVA) International represents professional wedding videographers nationally and internationally and sponsors educational and informational programs for professional development in the field. WEVA, with nearly four thousand members worldwide, also provides free referrals to brides and grooms at 800-501-WEVA. Here, WEVA chairman Roy Chapman poses important questions that you should ask any videographer you interview.

Are you a member of a professional association like WEVA? Whether or not the videographer is a member of a professional organization will give you an indication as to how serious he or she is about the industry and his or her commitment to being a wedding videography professional. For example, the WEVA convention is the only gathering in the industry where wedding videographers can get together to learn about new technology and trends in the field.

Have you shot any weddings similar to the one I'm having? If you are having a wedding in a huge cathedral, it's important to look at the work of a videographer who knows how to shoot in an environment like that. Oftentimes, you may discover that the videographer you're hiring has actually done weddings in the very locations where you're going to be married and have your reception. In instances like that, you'll definitely want to see video from both places. This will give you the clearest sense of what your final wedding video is going to look like and how the videographer works in those settings.

May I see a complete wedding from start to finish? By doing this, you'll get a better feel for the videographer's ability to cover all the day's events. A highlights tape of the same wedding won't give you the same effect. Remember, you're not buying a demo tape—you're buying a videotape of your complete wedding. So ask to see a tape that shows all the aspects of the same wedding.

May I look at three different weddings? Viewing complete tapes of different weddings will give you a sense of how transitions are handled, how the sound was recorded during the ceremony, and whether the video itself is shot clearly throughout.

Did you shoot the video I'm watching? If not, who did? Make sure you view the work of the videographer you want to hire. To guarantee that the chosen videographer is the one who shows up for the job, add his or her name to your contract.

How would you describe your style of videography? A videographer's style should match your preference. For example, if you're not thrilled with the idea of special effects and all the videographer can show you is tape after tape filled with special effects, then maybe this videographer isn't right for you. You should like what you're seeing on the small screen. That's why it's so important to interview two or three videographers. As you're watching various tapes, see if there are any styles in particular you like. Some videographers may describe their work as being like a PBS documentary or more slick in nature, like a music video. Seeing different styles will help you rule out the styles you don't like—and hone in on the ones you do.

What kind of lighting do you use? The answer to this question can be a good indicator of the videographer's knowledge of emerging trends. The new state-of-the-art video cameras are extremely light-sensitive—even more so than the cameras from two years ago. What this means for the bride is the videographer can record most images in available light. During daytime weddings and in most normally lit rooms, there is no need for additional lights. Some videographers may still need a small lamp on top of the camera to shoot in lower-light situations, but the lamp shouldn't be more than 30 watts or so—in other words, not blindingly bright. You should find out if the videographer has shot weddings in available light and then ask to see samples of that work.

How many cameras do you use? A few years ago, because of the cost of camera equipment, most weddings were shot with one camera. Today's bride should insist on at least two cameras— for example, one that can be set up in the balcony of the church and the other up front near the altar.

How much does it cost to have more than one camera? The price most videographers charge for a multicamera event depends on whether both cameras are manually operated or not. For example, some videographers set up a camera that is activated by remote control, which cuts down on the cost of labor.

What kinds of packages do you offer and how do they differ? It's very important to see the difference between the packages and between ceremony coverage of one or more cameras. As you're viewing videos, ask the videographer to point out the difference visually between the coverage and the packages. For example, if you're unsure how many cameras you're going to want or need, look at multicamera coverage with two, three, and four cameras. If you're unsure of the difference between the multicamera videos, ask the videographer to point out the subtleties.

How much editing are you going to do after the wedding, and who will be doing it? If the videographer isn't going to be the person doing the editing, make sure that when the videographer and his or her crew are shooting the video at your wedding, they make a log of the important shots and the important people in the shots. That way special friends or family members won't be edited out of the final video by mistake.

How much will different packages cost? You could spend as little as $500 or as much as $10,000 on your wedding video. Make sure you get clear examples of the price differentials between wedding videographers and what you get for your money.

If necessary, will you attend my rehearsal? This is an excellent opportunity for the videographer to meet the key players in advance and to make any final changes on how he or she plans to videotape the ceremony.

Will you be using wireless microphones, and how many? Years ago, many videographers clipped a mike to the groom's lapel and called it a day. That made for great sound when the vows were being recited, but it didn't pick up anything else that was going on during the ceremony. Today, expect that both the bride and groom will be miked, along with the pastor, the musicians, and anyone else who might be speaking during the ceremony.

Can we go over your contract? You want to review the videographer's contract while you're still in the studio so he or she can explain all the different clauses. If you're getting ready to sign on the dotted line, make sure the names of the videographer and the editor, if you decided on one, are on the contract as well. The contract should also include any special requests for the videographer's attire, such as a tuxedo or a dark suit.

Videography Vocabulary

There have been a number of high-tech advancements in videography technology recently. Following are the definitions WEVA uses to describe some of the more common terms in today's videography.

Chip The image-capturing device of a camera is a chip. Cameras can have from one to three chips. The higher-quality cameras have three chips.

Digital editing After it is shot, the video is downloaded to a disk and then uploaded to a computer. All of the editing occurs on the computer.

Live switching This technique is a lot like those used on a newscast. Instead of all cameras rolling at once, the director switches between cameras to give a variety of points of view. This can cut down on postwedding editing costs, because all the editing is done on the spot.

Lux ratings The light sensitivity of a camera is designated by its lux rating. Years ago, 30 lux was typical for video cameras. Today, however, a camera can have a lux rating of 7 or less. A camera with a low lux rating needs less available light to capture a clear image.

Recording formats The best traditional recording format is called Betacam, but other good formats that are popular among wedding videographers are Hi-8 and S-VHS. The very latest format is called DV—digital video.

Remote-control cameras The person who is directing the camera(s) may stand in the back of the church and watch the camera output on video monitors. The videographer literally directs how the cameras move or zoom in and out by using a remote control to send commands to the cameras.

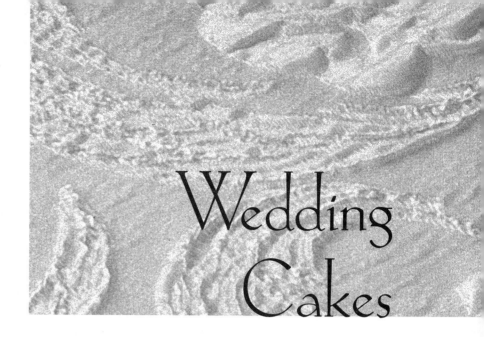

Wedding Cakes

Besides the walk down the aisle, perhaps the most memorable moment at a wedding is when the bride and groom cut their cake—and maybe smash it in each other's face. No doubt, you'll want your cake to be delicious and beautiful. Finding a caterer or baker to give you your consummate confectionery can be as challenging as looking glamorous for the photographer when you've got icing in your hair. But knowing what to expect of a baker and what questions to ask is the key to having a great cake—and eating it, too.

One of the factors affecting our decision to hire the caterer we did was her ability to make magnificent baked goods. Our initial meeting with her took place on her Victorian home's wraparound porch. Bill and I settled into a wicker couch and enjoyed lemonade and freshly baked brownies and zucchini bread while looking through the caterer's personal photo album of wedding cakes she'd made. As our taste buds went wild for the treats we were eating, our eyes feasted on some of the most gorgeous cakes we'd ever seen. We knew right then and there that this would be the person to make our cake.

Not a pair to follow tradition, Bill and I decided to have two cakes. As admitted chocoholics, we decided that our tiered wedding cake would be chocolate. Then, since Bill is of Italian descent, we chose an Italian blueberry cheesecake for our groom's cake. As expected, both cakes were delicious, and there wasn't a slice of either cake left over by the time our party ended. We knew our guests had enjoyed themselves and eaten well.

wedding wisdom

"Select the flavor cake that you and your husband like best. My husband loves chocolate cake with vanilla frosting, which is what we had as our wedding cake."
Wendy, married 11/19/95

"Since our neighborhood baker specializes in cheesecakes, we decided to have a wedding cheesecake. We had three different flavored cakes, each on pedestals of varying heights."

Nancy, married 11/16/96

Wonderful Wedding Cakes

Teresa Yodice, president of and chef at Hearts of Palm Catering, in Brightwaters, New York, specializes in baking wedding cakes. Here she offers advice on how to find someone to make a wonderful wedding cake for your big day. For more information on Hearts of Palm's catering services and the wedding cakes they make, call 516-968-4047.

LI: *Should you rely on your caterer to provide your wedding cake or do you need to hire someone else to bake the cake?*

TY: The first thing you should ask your caterer is if he or she specializes in wedding cakes. It will depend on the caterer's kitchen and whether it includes a baker. Some caterers who don't have a baker on staff will step away from wedding cakes. Others aren't so honest.

LI: *How would you know if your caterer can deliver a magnificent wedding cake?*

TY: Someone who truly loves to bake, like me, will show you what he or she can do. I have photo albums filled with pictures of the cakes I've made, and I show them to any prospective clients. Our cakes have ranged from a five-tier cheesecake garnished in a traditional wedding fashion, to a cake that was decorated to look like a fruit basket and was topped with fresh fruit.

LI: *How much should you expect to spend for a wedding cake?*

TY: Not surprisingly, the price of a wedding cake depends on who makes it and where you live. That is, a caterer or specialty baker will charge more than a neighborhood bakeshop, and a cake in New York City will cost more than one in Cincinnati. For example, a specialty baker in Manhattan may charge $2,000 for a cake alone. Compare that with a neighborhood bake shop, which can whip up a beautiful cake for about $300. I would say that a traditional five-tier cake would go for about $800 or $900, but that's New York prices.

LI: *Why do some caterers charge cake-cutting fees?*

TY: Whether or not there's a cake-cutting fee is one of the first questions you should ask your caterer. If you've hired an independent, off-premises caterer and he or she charges you a cutting fee because you're not using his or her cake, well, that's dishonest. You're paying your caterer for service time, and, in my opinion, cutting and serving cake is part of that service. However, it's different with an on-premises caterer (that is, one that is part of the package deal that you get at a reception site). If cake is part of the package and you're taking out a portion of that package by bringing in your own cake, for example, then you have to pay some sort of compensatory money, such as a cake-cutting fee. You should ask about this up front, and if necessary, use it as a negotiating point.

LI: *Is it true that some on-premises caterers use a fake wedding cake?*

TY: Yes. These fake cakes are touted as a money-saving method. On-premises caterers tell you that they'll bring out this fabulous cake so you can do a beautiful cake-cutting ceremony. But what they'll really serve guests is a pound cake with vanilla icing. Oftentimes, the cake you're cutting for your pictures is made from Styrofoam and whipped cream. Once the cake cutting is over, that beautiful cake is repaired, put back in storage, and brought out again for a cake cutting at the next wedding. It's a way to do things in bulk without spending a lot of money on wedding cakes.

LI: *What if you want to have two cakes, a bride's cake and a groom's cake?*

TY: This is a Southern tradition, which is really appropriate in any region of the country. It gives guests two cakes to choose from. For one wedding I did, the bride's cake was chocolate with buttercream filling, which was great for any guests who love chocolate. The groom's cake, on the other hand, was an Italian cheesecake topped with fresh blueberries. It was a real hit.

Besides serving both cakes, couples have the option of cutting up the bride's cake and serving it for dessert and then packaging the groom's cake in little boxes and giving it to guests as a favor to take home.

LI: *If you want to save the top tier of your wedding cake so you can eat it on your first anniversary, how do you make sure the cake is still delicious a year later?*

TY: First of all, the cake should be stored in the freezer. It would never last a year in the refrigerator. Also, make sure the package you put the cake in is airtight. If it means putting it in a Tupperware container and then in a Ziploc bag, do it. Otherwise, the cake will end up not tasting like the delicious wedding cake you shared on your big day but like a mixture of the cardboard cake container and the freezer.

"One way I saved money was by having a dummy wedding cake. Only the top tier was real, and guests were served sheet cake for dessert. No one had any idea. The cake looked so beautiful that even I couldn't tell it wasn't real!"
Stephanie, married 6/15/96

Wedding Cakes

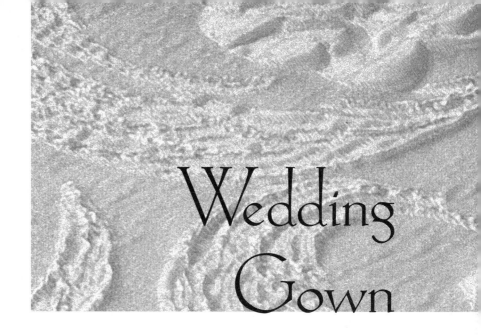

Wedding Gown

I consider myself very lucky. I found my wedding dress by chance one day. I was walking through the dress department at Lord & Taylor when I saw this ivory gown that looked as if it had been transported from the 1920s right to the present. It had buttons down the front, delicate details interwoven in the fabric, a scoop neck, and a dropped waist. It was perfect. I tried it on, and I knew right then and there that it would be the dress I would wear for my wedding. Funny thing is, I wasn't even engaged at the time, but I knew Bill would be popping the question soon. So I bought the dress. When I brought it home, Bill was shocked that I'd actually bought what looked like a wedding dress. Being the good-natured guy that he is, he started to laugh at me. He wasn't threatened by what I'd done—he was amused by it.

Turns out I didn't get the chance to wear the dress on our actual wedding day, because the dress I bought was more for summer attire. Since we were married on a cold day in November, I wore a crisp white shirt and a black-and-white polka-dot skirt. However, I knew we were planning on having a garden brunch the following June, on our previously set wedding date, so I would have the chance to wear the dress. I did, and everyone loved it. I'm so glad I bought that dress, even if it was a gutsy thing to do at the time.

Buying Your Gown

One of the most exciting days in the wedding-planning process is the day you start to shop for your wedding dress. What you'll wear

wedding wisdom

"When I tried on this one wedding gown, I knew it was *the* dress. I ended up ordering it the next day."
Jacinda, married 7/1/95

the day you and your fiancé become husband and wife is probably something you've dreamed about since you were a little girl.

A great way to get a sense of what dress styles will be available for your wedding is to buy bridal magazines and look at both the advertising of and editorials about wedding dresses. Many times advertisements and fashion spreads will include information about where you can buy the featured dresses. If you find a dress you like and a store listed near you, rip the page out. It will be amazingly helpful for the salespeople at the bridal salons you visit to be able to see photographic examples of the dresses you like.

Don't despair, however, if you find a dress you like but no information about a store near you that might sell it. Most bridal salons can order a dress directly from a manufacturer even if they don't sell it in the store. Or they can show you dresses they do carry that are similar to the ones you show them from the tear sheets you take along.

While you may have some luck bargaining with your retailer on the price of your bridesmaid dresses, don't expect a retailer to discount the cost of your wedding gown. These once-in-a-lifetime dresses have a high profit margin. In addition, if the retailer is special-ordering your dress from the manufacturer, it isn't worth it for them to offer you a discount. However, if you're buying your dress off the rack and it is dirty or torn somewhere, don't hesitate to ask for some money off. You may not get the answer you want to hear, but it doesn't hurt to ask.

Whether or not you decide to buy your gown from an independent bridal shop or a bridal salon in a department store is entirely up to you. Following, experts from a bridal shop and a department store bridal department explain the process for buying a dress from each kind of store.

Bridal Boutique

Grace Porritt, owner, A Formal Affair in Boulder, Colorado.

If you want the pick of the litter, you should be prepared to buy your wedding gown from a bridal boutique at least six months before your wedding. You have to realize that most manufacturers run on a sixteen-week delivery time. In order to work with this schedule, you need to shop for your dress at least twenty weeks before you'll need it. This advance planning will help prevent headaches should there be any problems with the dress. For example, a couple of weeks ago we had a dress that arrived marked as a size 18, just as the bride had ordered. However, once she tried to put it on, we realized it had been mislabeled and was probably closer to a size 8. Fortunately, the manufacturer was very understanding and accommodating, and they shipped a new dress to us the next day.

Another issue that adds to the long lead time for buying a wedding gown is alterations. At least 90 percent of dresses need to be altered. Most dresses are cut for a woman who is five foot nine. But since most women are not five foot nine, you're going to need at least one alteration to do a hem. In addition, any dress that comes with a train will need a bustle added to it. All in all, you can count on having about three alterations, which should span over one month.

When you're budgeting for your wedding gown, keep in mind that most stores do not include the cost of alterations in the price of the dress. Ideally, I believe you should find a store that has an alterations person on-site. That way if, when first trying on the dress, you have questions about what the dress will look like on you when it's all said and done, the alterations person can come out to the sales floor and answer your questions. When you're trying on the dress, he or she can pull it this way or pinch it that way to give you an idea of how alterations will affect how the dress looks on you.

Understand that wedding gown alterations can be expensive, but there's a reason they cost so much. It's a complicated process to alter a wedding gown, especially if it has bead work. Therefore, don't be tempted to take your dress to someone who you think can do the job for less than the alterations expert the bridal shop suggests. Sure, this person may charge less, but does he or she know how to work with wedding gowns? You have to understand that once the dress leaves the store, it's not our responsibility anymore. However, if the alterations expert we use does something wrong, then we'll stand behind the dress we've sold you.

If you don't have a lot of time before your wedding, you might have a better chance of buying a dress off the rack at a bridal boutique than you would at a department store. For example, if you're a size 8, 10, or 12, you can probably find something in store inventory to fit you. (Most manufacturers send dress samples out that fit bodies in the size-8 to size-12 range.) The reason you may have better luck finding an off-the-rack dress at a bridal boutique is that a smaller shop is more likely to keep some kind of inventory of dresses. A great way to find this out is to call ahead, especially if you know you won't have time to order a dress.

You should also find out ahead of time the reputation of the stores you plan to visit. You've probably heard horror stories about bridal shops not delivering wedding dresses on time. While I've never done that, unfortunately unscrupulous business owners do exist. Therefore, it's a good idea to talk to any recent brides you know about their experience at a local bridal shop. If you feel it's necessary, you can call your local Better Business Bureau to see if any complaints have been lodged against certain shops.

One thing that you need to keep in mind is that a shop owner can give you only an estimated delivery date for your gown. The shop owner is the intermediary and has limited control over when the dress will arrive. But it isn't unreasonable to expect that your wedding dress will be in the store in time for your wedding. A good way to stay on top of the dress's estimated date of delivery is to check in with the store on a regular basis. By staying top of mind, you are less likely to have your dress slip through the cracks.

You should expect to pay half for your dress when you place the order and then the balance due within 30 days of the dress's arriving. Most shop owners, like me, won't refund your money if you change your mind about the dress or have to cancel your wedding. However, that doesn't mean that I'm a heartless creep. Recently a woman had to cancel her wedding because her fiancé died. It was very sad, and I felt really sorry for her. Obviously, she didn't need her wedding dress anymore, but I didn't want to lose out either. So I decided to take the dress back and see if I could sell it off the rack. I made a deal with her that if I sold it, I would give her a portion of her money back. I did end up selling the dress, and everyone ended up satisfied.

Once your dress is in the store and the alterations are finished, please don't be tempted to take it home sooner than you have to. When we deliver a dress to the bride's home on the morning of her wedding, the dress has been pressed and stuffed and it's ready to wear. If you take the dress home beforehand and start trying it on again and again, you could ruin it. Or you could spill something on it by mistake. Or something even more awful could happen.

Recently a bride took her dress home early because she wanted to show it off to her family. Unfortunately, she left it lying on her bed, and her dog soiled it. We ended up having to order all new fabric for the bottom of the dress; luckily we were able to fix it in time for her wedding. But it's a chance you really shouldn't take. Let the bridal shop hold onto your dress until just before your wedding. That way you know it's safe and will look gorgeous when you go to put it on.

Department Store Bridal Salon

Margaret Redmond, bridal buyer, Neiman Marcus Department Store, Dallas, Texas.

I find it very helpful when women have looked through bridal magazines before visiting our salon. It helps give the consultant or salesperson a good place to start in selecting dresses for them to try on. Of course, when suggesting dresses, the consultant will also take into consideration the woman's size and coloring and when and where the wedding will be held.

Some of our more popular wedding gown designers are Christos, Vera Wang, Helen Morley, Richard Glasgow, and Amsale. While our gowns range in price from $1,500 to $13,000, the average bride pays about $2,500 for her dress.

We're very fortunate that wedding dresses aren't discontinued on a regular basis and that they don't go in and out of season. Therefore, any picture you see in a magazine will tell you that the dress is currently available. However, that doesn't mean that we will necessarily carry that designer. But we can show you something comparable.

At a department store like Neiman Marcus, we have samples only in the bridal salon, and they're usually cut in a size 8 or size 10. If you're a size 14, obviously you can't try the dress completely on. But we can hold the dress up to you so you can get an idea of what it will look like on you. Everyone in the business works this way, and brides are usually willing to deal with the fact that they may not actually try on their wedding dress until they've paid for it, we've ordered it, and it's arrived in the store.

We find that our manufacturers can deliver a dress between three and four months after we've ordered it. Therefore, it's wise to start looking for a dress six to eight months before your wedding. However, I've worked with many women who have begun shopping for and found their dream dress a year or more ahead of time. Many brides-to-be want to find and order their dress so they can get on with the rest of their plans. For such a bride, what she plans for her wedding will often center on what kind of dress she finds.

When a dress comes in, we normally do three fittings. We do the first fitting to get the dress to fit the bride properly. A few weeks later we'll do a second fitting to check on how those alterations look. Usually, at this time our brides are getting ready to have their formal portraits taken. So after the second fitting, we press and stuff the dress and deliver it to and then pick it up from the photographer's studio. This is all at no extra cost. Finally, a week before the wedding we do the last fitting. Then we press and stuff the dress again and deliver it to the church or hotel in time for the wedding.

As with most bridal salons, alterations are not included in our price. Alterations, on average, cost between $250 and $350. A bride has the right to take her dress to be altered somewhere else, especially if she wants to save some money. However, once the dress leaves the store, we can't be responsible for any work that is done on it. It's important to pay for quality alterations, and our prices are based on the time it takes to alter the dress. For example, if the dress is intricately beaded, the alterations person has to remove each bead before fixing it and then put it back on afterwards. This is detailed work, and it can take a few days.

The great thing about buying your dress from a store like Neiman Marcus is not only do we provide you with a gorgeous dress and quality alterations, but also you can take advantage of any services available throughout the department store when buying your dress. For example, it's not unheard-of for an associate from our jewelry department to visit the bridal salon while the bride is trying on dresses. At that time, the jewelry department associate can offer suggestions on jewelry to wear with various dresses. In addition, the bride can buy her shoes, stockings, and lingerie here.

Designing Your Own Dress

There are some women for whom the idea of wearing a wedding gown that looks as if it just walked off the pages of a bridal magazine is just not appealing. For these women, it's important that their wedding dress be different and more reflective of their personality. For them, having a custom-made dress is the best option.

Deborah Leininger is the sort of person these women should call. She's owner of Paper Dolls Bridal in Minneapolis, a company that specializes in custom-made dresses. "Women who hire me to make their wedding gowns tend to be creative or artistic, and they want to have fun with their wedding gowns," she says. "They want people to remember the dress they wear." For example, she recently made a dress that looked a lot like a Monet painting. The bodice was handpainted with Impressionist-looking flowers, and the headpiece was a bow of silk roses dipped in glitter.

Many of Leininger's brides are having theme weddings and want their dresses to reflect the theme. One time Leininger worked with a woman who was a "Star Trek" fan and was planning a futuristic wedding. "Her dress was modeled after something you might have seen during the first season of 'Star Trek'," she recalls. "The dress was silver with high lapels, and she wore boots with it."

Another bride was having a Scottish wedding and wanted a gown that looked like something a bride in sixteenth-century Scotland might have worn. "I did as much research as I could on Scottish costumes so the dress would look as authentic as possible," says Leininger, who often taps into her art history background or spends time at libraries looking at history volumes for design ideas. The finished dress had a brocaded bodice with a Basque neckline and a long flowing skirt. It looked fantastic with the kilts the groom and his ushers wore.

Many of the brides who hire Leininger don't even live in the Minneapolis area. "I get calls from all over the country," she says. She charges $25 an hour for a consultation, and then between $1,200 and $2,000 for the finished dress. "For the same price you could go to a store and buy a wedding gown," she says. "But why not spend the same amount of money on a handmade gown that no one else in the world has?"

To contact Deborah Leininger about having a dress custom-made, call 612-922-6079.

Tips for Cleaning and Storing Your Gown

When you've invested a lot of time, effort, and money in choosing a wedding gown, you don't just want to take it to any old dry cleaner to be cleaned and stored. In fact, a wedding gown should never be cleaned like a regular article of clothing. Instead there's a certain cleaning and preservation process that should be used with wedding gowns, called Web-re-stor.

I recently spoke with Sally Lorensen Conant, Ph.D., a spokesperson for Web-re-stor Association, the wedding gown restoration specialists association, about tips for cleaning and storing a wedding gown.

LI: *How do you know if a dry cleaner in your area specializes in wedding gowns?*

SLC: You can call our organization to find the wedding gown specialist nearest you. Otherwise, you need to ask the dry cleaner some specific questions. Just because you walk in to a dry cleaning store and see wedding gowns hanging all over the place—as some

Wedding Gown

proprietors are known to have—doesn't mean that the establishment specializes in gowns. In fact, if you see gowns hanging in plastic bags, then you can be sure that the dry cleaner doesn't specialize in it. That's because any reputable cleaner knows that the worst thing you can do with a wedding gown is put it inside a plastic bag.

LI: *So what are some of the questions you want to ask during your initial meeting with a dry cleaner?*

SLC: First thing you need to ask is Do you clean gowns on-site as opposed to sending them out? Many cleaners will send wedding gowns out to another company to clean, but that lessens the dry cleaner's accountability should something go wrong. If you don't have access to the person who does the actual cleaning, then you're at a disadvantage.

Ask what precautions the dry cleaner takes to protect the delicate fabric and the beading on the gown. There are certain things that a good dry cleaner will do to minimize damage. A good answer to such a question would be that he or she tests the materials first to make sure they are dry-cleanable. Another thing you want to hear is that he or she will turn your dress inside out and put it in a bag when it's cleaned. If it's a really old gown, you may want it cleaned by hand, so you should ask about the dry cleaner's ability to do that.

You also need to ask about how he or she guards against latent stains—that is, stains that are invisible now but will show up years from now. For example, if there's a sugar stain on your dress, it will be transparent today. But ten years from now, you may discover a brown caramelized sugar stain on your dress. To prevent this from happening, you want to hear the dry cleaner talk about the specific chemicals he or she uses to prevent stains.

LI: *What about a dress that says "dry clean petroleum only." What does that mean for you and the dry cleaner you use?*

SLC: Dry cleaners used to use petroleum solvents, but they're flammable. So now many use something that is made of 98 percent perchloroethylene. However, petroleum is a little less harsh on a wedding gown, which is why some manufacturers recommend that you clean the gown using petroleum solvents. Any experienced dry cleaner will know how to use either one, but because petroleum isn't the cleaning solvent of choice anymore, you may have to hunt around to find someone who uses it.

LI: *What's important to know about storing your wedding gown after it's been cleaned?*

SLC: Find a cleaner who uses a container and wrappings that are acid-free. If not, the acid in the paper he or she uses to stuff or wrap the dress will eventually seep into the gown's fabric and cause brown scorches, as if you'd burned it with an iron. Those marks will not come out. You don't want to hear that the dry cleaner stores a dress in plastic. Plastic is a bad idea because it emits fumes that yellow dresses. In addition, plastic traps moisture. If there is moisture in the gown, it will cause it to mildew.

LI: *I've heard of horror stories of brides who took their dresses to be cleaned and had them stored, and then when they opened the boxes years later, either they were empty or they didn't contain their dresses. How can you prevent this from happening?*

SLC: You should ask ahead of time if you can inspect the gown before it's packaged. Then you'll know that it's been cleaned properly, and it is indeed your dress. Sometimes dry cleaners will use a box with a window on it so you can see the dress inside. Make sure the window is made from an acid-free material and not plastic.

LI: *How can you find a qualified dry cleaner in your area?*

SLC: You can call the Web-re-stor national office at 800-501-5005. We have members in 450 cities, and we'll put you in touch with a gown specialist nearest where you live.

Appendix

*M*any of the experts I interviewed for *The Portable Wedding Consultant* own or run businesses or offer services that might interest you beyond the pages of this book. With that in mind, following is an alphabetical list of all the service-oriented experts mentioned in the book, including their mailing addresses, E-mail addresses (if appropriate), and telephone numbers. I've also included a brief description of each person's expertise. Good luck with your wedding planning!

Susan Adelizzi-Schmidt
Great American Trolley Co., Inc.
821 Shunpike Road
Cold Spring, NJ 08204
800-4-TROLLY
Susan Adelizzi-Schmidt is the marketing director for the wedding trolley division of the Great American Trolley Company. Besides renting trackless, San Francisco–style trolleys to transport the wedding party, this company also offers minicoaches.

Franca Alphin
Duke University Diet and Fitness Center
804 W. Trinity Avenue
Durham, NC 27701
800-362-8446
Franca Alphin is a registered dietitian. The Duke University Diet and Fitness Center offers a Jump Start program that provides pre-

planned meal cards for sensible eating. The complete program, including cookbook, nutrition manual, and shopping lists, costs $75. Call the toll-free number listed to order.

American Rental Association
1900 Nineteenth Street
Moline, IL 61265
800-334-2177
The American Rental Association is an international trade association of more than 6,800 independent rental dealers and equipment manufacturers. If you are in need of an affiliated rental company near you, call the toll-free number listed for a referral.

Brenda Anna
Riversdale Chamber Ensemble
4904 Somerset Road
Riverdale, MD 20737
301-699-5079
Brenda Anna is a violinist and manager of the Riversdale Chamber Ensemble, which provides ceremony and reception music for weddings in the greater Baltimore and Washington, D.C., areas.

Maryetta Bartlett
Bartlett Florist
814 Grove Street
Clifton, NJ 07013
201-471-6480
Maryetta Bartlett is the third-generation owner of Bartlett Florist, which has been in business since 1921.

Staci Barton
Loews Ventana Canyon Resort
7000 North Resort Drive
Tucson, AZ 85750
520-299-2020
Staci Barton is the catering manager who is responsible for planning weddings from start to finish at Loews Ventana Canyon Resort.

Mark Bass, CFP
Pennington, Bass & Associates
3223 South Loop 289
Suite 230
Lubbock, TX 79423
806-797-8349
Mark Bass is a certified financial planner.

John Bays
Regal Limousine Service
7828 Mulberry Bottom Lane
Springfield, VA 22153-2313
703-440-3651
John Bays is the proud owner of a classic white 1978 Rolls-Royce Silver Shadow II, which is available for weddings in the greater Washington, D.C., area.

Joyce Scardina Becker
Events of Distinction
41 Heather Avenue
San Francisco, CA 94118
415-751-0211
Joyce Scardina Becker is a certified bridal consultant. Her company specializes in corporate events and meetings, private parties, and weddings.

David Bentley
Bentley Studio, Ltd.
Le Chateau Village
10403 Clayton Road
Frontenac, MO 63131
314-991-2502
David Bentley is a traditional wedding photographer.

Rita Bigel-Casher, CSW, Ph.D.
274 Madison Avenue
New York, NY 10016
212-532-0032
http://www.dbsinyc.com/bigel/bridesguide/
Rita Bigel-Casher is author of *Bride's Guide to Emotional Survival* and an individual, couples, and family therapist.

Karen Brown
Memories in Bloom
1570 South Dairy Ashford
Suite 122
Houston, TX 77077
713-556-5200
Karen Brown is a professional bridal consultant and owner of
Memories in Bloom, a florist that specializes in wedding flowers.

Roy Chapman
Wedding and Event Videographers Association
  (WEVA) International
8499 South Tamiami Trail #208
Sarasota, FL 34238
800-501-WEVA
Roy Chapman is chairman of WEVA International, which represents professional wedding videographers worldwide. To find a WEVA
member near you, call the toll-free number listed.

Sally Lorensen Conant
Web-re-stor Association
454 Old Cellar Road
Orange, CT 06477
800-501-5005
Sally Lorensen Conant is a spokesperson for Web-re-stor Association, an association of dry cleaners in 450 cities that are experts
in cleaning and preserving wedding gowns.

Crane & Company
30 South Street
Dalton, MA 01226
800-5-CRANE-6
Crane & Company is a purveyor of fine papers for wedding invitations, wedding stationery, and wedding thank-you notes. For the
location of the store nearest you that sells Crane & Company products, call the toll-free number listed.

Wendy Cromwell
Robert Andrew DaySpa Salon
1153 Route 3
Gambrills, MD 21054
410-721-3533
Wendy Cromwell is a professional esthetician and makeup artist.

Noreen deGale
The Calabash Hotel
Box 382
St. Georges, Grenada
West Indies
800-528-5835
Noreen deGale is the wedding coordinator at The Calabash Hotel. She helps couples plan island weddings and honeymoons.

Bev Dembo
Dembo Productions
345 Brookside Lane
Glencoe, IL 60022
847-835-5000
Bev Dembo is a professional bridal consultant and state coordinator for the Association of Bridal Consultants. Her company offers full-service consulting for weddings in the greater Chicago area.

Diamond Information Center
466 Lexington Avenue
New York, NY 10017
To receive a copy of the Diamond Information Center's brochure "How to Buy Diamonds You'll Be Proud to Give," send a self-addressed, stamped envelope to the address listed.

Laurence Elliott
National Association of Mobile Entertainers (NAME)
Box 727
Huntington Valley, PA 19006
215-676-4544
Laurence Elliott is vice president of NAME, a trade association representing deejays. The association can provide a referral to a disc jockey in your area.

Anne Kearns Fers
Gold Star Video
257 Pinewood Trail
Trumbull, CT 06611
203-377-5665
Anne Kearns Fers is owner of Gold Star Video. Her specialties include shooting wedding video in an unobtrusive manner.

MaryAnne London Gears
Chapel of Love
Mall of America
240 North Garden
Bloomington, MN 55425
800-299-LOVE

MaryAnne London Gears is owner of the Chapel of Love, a wedding chapel that accommodates up to seventy-five guests. She can plan weddings with as little as twenty-four hours' advance notice. An adjacent store sells bridal accessories.

Gary Gordon
Samuel Gordon Jewelers
5521 North Penn
Oklahoma City, OK 73112
405-842-3663

Samuel Gordon Jewelers is a fourth-generation retail business that specializes in high-end jewelry.

Nancy Gorski
Gorski Financial Services
240 144th Avenue
Madeira Beach, FL 33708
941-643-6800

Nancy Gorski is a certified financial planner and author of *My Own Money Planner*, a personal diary of financial and legal affairs. It is available for $20.

Gina Hart
Cappelli Hair Face Body
1939 South Telegraph
Bloomfield Hills, MI 48302
810-332-3434

Gina Hart is a makeup artist who specializes in wedding-day makeup.

Joan Hawxhurst
Dovetail Publishing
P.O. Box 19945
Kalamazoo, MI 49019
616-342-2900
dovetail@mich.com
Joan Hawxhurst is editor of "Dovetail," a newsletter by and for Jewish/Christian families. A one-year subscription costs $24.99. She is also the author of *Interfaith Wedding Ceremonies* (Dovetail, 1996).

Charlene Hein
Everlasting Memories by Char
1474 South Ward Street
Lakewood, CO 80228
303-988-3049
Charlene Hein is a professional bridal consultant serving brides in the greater Denver area.

Barbara Hoffman
Hoffman & Hoffman
P.O. Box 7411
Louisville, KY 40207
502-458-2300
Barbara Hoffman is a certified etiquette expert. She offers "Wedding Party" pamphlets, which outline the responsibilities of the maid of honor, bridesmaids, best man, and ushers. A minimum of ten pamphlets must be ordered.

Myrna Ingram and Beatrice York-Blitzer
Empress Travel
444 West Jericho Turnpike
West Hills–Huntington, NY 11743
800-291-3313
Myrna Ingram and Beatrice York-Blitzer are co-owners of this travel agency, which specializes in honeymoon travel. A honeymoon registry is available.

Appendix

Sardi Klein
137 West Broadway
New York, NY 10013
212-608-2777
Sardi Klein is a photojournalist-style wedding photographer who shoots Manhattan weddings only. She also specializes in corporate head shots.

Deborah Leininger
Paper Dolls Bridal
3116 Idaho Avenue South
St. Louis Park, MN 55423
612-922-6079
Deborah Leininger creates custom-made wedding gowns.

Teddy Lenderman
Bearable Weddings by Teddy
6650 Long Road
West Terre Haute, IN 47885
812-535-3067
Teddy Lenderman is a master bridal consultant and author of *The Complete Idiot's Guide to the Perfect Wedding* (Macmillan, 1995).

Bob Lindquist
Mobile Beat Magazine
P.O. Box 309
East Rochester, NY 14445
716-385-9920
Bob Lindquist is editor-in-chief of *Mobile Beat Magazine*, a magazine geared toward professional disc jockeys. Each year the magazine publishes a Top 200 list of most-played songs, including first-dance songs at wedding receptions. For subscription information, write to the address listed.

Larry Maloney
Forbes Travel Service Inc.
Squirrel Hill
5835 Forbes Avenue
Pittsburgh, PA 15217
800-345-2984
Larry Maloney is president of Forbes Travel, which offers a honeymoon registry.

Rick Mikula
Hole-in-Hand
147 West Carleton Avenue
Hazleton, PA 18201
717-459-1327
Rick Mikula's Hole-in-Hand breeds and sells butterflies that can be released at a wedding ceremony. Butterflies cost $100 per dozen and are shipped overnight.

Gerard Monahan
Association of Bridal Consultants (ABC)
200 Chestnutland Road
New Milford, CT 06776
860-355-0464
BridalAssn@aol.com
Gerard Monahan is president of the ABC, the only organization dedicated exclusively to serving wedding professionals worldwide. ABC can provide referrals to association members in your area, including bridal consultants, caterers, and photographers.

Kathy Moore
Ambiance Party Services
913 Park Avenue
Garner, NC 27529
919-779-9303
Kathy Moore is a professional bridal consultant. Her company offers full-service wedding and special-event planning.

PaperDirect
100 Plaza Drive
Secaucus, NJ 07094
800-A-PAPERS
PaperDirect is a cataloger that provides various papers and envelopes for couples who choose to print their own invitations. Supplies for creating place cards, ceremony programs, and thank-you notes are also available.

Appendix

Lois Pearce
Beautiful Occasions
60 Connolly Parkway #11-107
Hamden, CT 06514
203-248-2661
Lois Pearce is an accredited bridal consultant and state coordinator for the Association of Bridal Consultants.

Grace Porritt
A Formal Affair
1441 Arapahoe Avenue
Boulder, CO 80302
303-444-8294
Grace Porritt is owner of A Formal Affair, a shop that sells bridal gowns, bridesmaid dresses, and various bridal accessories.

Susan Price
I Do Weddings
2368 Leona Avenue
San Luis Obispo, CA 93401
805-546-9969
Susan Price is an accredited bridal consultant who specializes in planning weddings.

Professional Photographers of America
57 Forsyth Street N.W.
Suite 1600
Atlanta, GA 30303
800-786-6277
Professional Photographers of America is a professional organization of more than fourteen thousand photographers. The organization can provide a free referral to wedding photographers in your area.

Margaret Redmond
Neiman Marcus
1618 Main Street
Dallas, TX 75201
214-741-6911
Margaret Redmond is the bridal buyer for Neiman Marcus. Only three Neiman Marcus store locations have bridal salons. They are in Dallas, St. Louis, and Houston.

Cheri Rice
The Personal Touch Bridal Agency
15210 Waco Street N.W.
Anoka, MN 55303
612-421-4525
Cheri Rice is a master bridal consultant and a state coordinator for the Association of Bridal Consultants. She works with brides in the greater Minneapolis area.

Donna Schonhoff
La Donna Wedding Expressions
49966 Van Dyke Avenue
Shelby Township, MI 48317
810-731-8400
Donna Schonhoff is a bridal consultant whose company can plan a wedding in its entirety or offer day-of event coordination only.

Jack Springer
International Formalwear Association (IFA)
401 North Michigan Avenue
Chicago, IL 60611
312-321-6806
Jack Springer is executive director of the International Formalwear Association, a trade association representing manufacturers and retailers of men's formalwear. The IFA can provide a referral to member formalwear retailers in your area. Plus, by sending a self-addressed, stamped envelope, you can receive a brochure called "Your Formalwear Guide."

Corinne Soikin Strauss
The Artist's Wedding Studio
237 West Mount Airy Road
Croton-on-Hudson, NY 10520
914-271-8807
Corinne Soikin Strauss specializes in making hand-painted silk *huppahs* for Jewish wedding ceremonies.

Michael Taylor
Hank Lane Music and Productions
65 West Fifty-fifth Street
New York, NY 10019
212-767-0600
Michael Taylor is director of operations for Hank Lane Music, a co-op of ten bands that specialize in playing at wedding receptions.

Michelle Vincent
Jacobson's Styling Salon
300 Briarwood Circle
Ann Arbor, MI 48108
313-665-6111
Michelle Vincent has been creating wedding-day hairstyles for the past twenty-one years.

Sue Winner
Discount Bridal Service
Sincerely, Sue Winner
333 Sandy Springs Circle
Suite 130
Atlanta, GA 30328
404-255-3804
Sue Winner is an accredited bridal consultant and state coordinator for the Association of Bridal Consultants. She owns two businesses. Her Discount Bridal Service helps brides find gowns and bridesmaid dresses for 20 percent to 40 percent below retail; and Sincerely, Sue Winner specializes in invitations.

Jon Wool
The Chicago Caterers
716 West Fifth Avenue
Naperville, IL 60563
630-355-1208
The Chicago Caterers is one of four full-service catering divisions of Culinary Enterprises, a food and beverage provider for wedding and special events in Chicago as well as the entire state of Illinois, southern Wisconsin, and parts of Indiana and western Michigan.

Teresa Yodice
Hearts of Palm Catering, Inc.
100 Concourse East
Brightwaters, NY 11718
516-968-4047
Teresa Yodice is a full-service caterer and specialty wedding cake baker. She serves weddings and special events in the New York tri-state area.

Bob Zupko
Robert Andrew DaySpa Salon
1153 Route 3
Gambrills, MD 21054
410-721-3533
Bob Zupko is owner of the Robert Andrew DaySpa Salon, a full-service salon that is available for bridal showers or general treatment services.

Index